For the Record

For the Record
LANGE AND THE FOURTH LABOUR GOVERNMENT

Edited by
Margaret Clark

© 2005 Margaret Clark

Published in 2005
by
Dunmore Publishing Ltd
P.O. Box 25080
Wellington
books@dunmore.co.nz

National Library of New Zealand Cataloguing-in-Publication Data

For the record : Lange and the fourth Labour Government /
edited by Margaret Clark.
Includes bibliographical references and index.
ISBN 1-87739-910-8
1. Lange, David, 1942- 2. New Zealand Labour Party. 3. Prime
ministers—New Zealand. 4. New Zealand—Politics and
government—1972- I. Clark, Margaret, 1941-
320.993—dc 22

Text: Adobe Garamond Pro 11/12.8
Printer: Keeling & Mundy, Palmerston North
Design and typesetting: Matthew Bartlett
Cover: Central Media Ltd, Wellington

Copyright: No part of this book may be reproduced without written permission, except in the case of brief quotations embodied in critical articles and reviews.

Contents

MARGARET CLARK
Foreword — 7

MICHAEL CULLEN
Opening remarks — 9

PETER LANGE
A life with David — 13

COLIN JAMES
What made the revolution? — 18

MARGARET WILSON
Oh what a party — 25

JIM BOLGER
Lange and Parliament — 31

RICHARD PREBBLE
Cabinet government — 36

MICHAEL BASSETT
Cabinet making: Cabinet breaking — 39

KERRY BURKE
The youthful, united Cabinet — 45

GEOFFREY PALMER
Working with David Lange: a personal recollection — 50

ROGER DOUGLAS
How we did it — 56

GRAHAM SCOTT
One adviser's view of the economics and politics of economic policy — 60

DAVID CAYGILL
Industry policy — 66

KEN DOUGLAS
What were the real issues? — 79

GARY HAWKE
Bliss at dawn – social policy in the first term of the Lange Government   85

HILARY STACE
Labour owes us – the 1984 women's forums   119

GERALD HENSLEY
The bureaucracy and advisors   129

JOHN HENDERSON
The warrior peacenik: setting the record straight on ANZUS and the Fiji coup   136

DENIS MCLEAN
A serious non-meeting of minds   144

MERWYN NORRISH
The Lange Government's foreign policy   150

BRUCE BROWN
The great debate at the Oxford Union   158

TED WOODFIELD
International trade relations   168

ROSS VINTINER
Dark ink   173

IAN GRANT
Lange takes the high ground while Douglas burrows deep into the economy   190

JON JOHANSSON
The Falstaffian wit of David Lange: rhetorical brilliance in the Beehive   199

STEPHEN LEVINE AND NIGEL S. ROBERTS
Not quite Camelot   208

Appendix I: Transcript of an interview by Linda Clark with Margaret Pope on Radio New Zealand   218

Appendix II: Transcript of an interview by Linda Clark with Roger Douglas on Radio New Zealand   230

Notes   243

Notes on Contributors   255

Index   257

Foreword

Lange and the First Term of the Fourth Labour Government was the title of a two-day conference held in May 2004, in the Legislative Council Chamber and Grand Hall of Parliament.

This was the sixth in a series organised jointly by Victoria University's Stout Research Centre and the Association of Former Members of Parliament. The five earlier conferences also resulted in books published by Dunmore Press and edited by me. These were *Sir Keith Holyoake: Towards a Political Biography* (1997); *Peter Fraser: Master Politician* (1998); *Three Labour Leaders: Nordmeyer, Kirk and Rowling* (2001); *Holyoake's Lieutenants* (2003), *and Muldoon Revisited* (2004).

The year 2004 marked the twentieth anniversary of the fourth Labour Government's coming to power, so it seemed appropriate to invite people who had served or been part of that exciting government, or witnessed it at close hand, to commit memories to paper before they faded. You will see how extraordinarily vivid they remain for the participants, and how some disputes remain unresolved and wounds unhealed.

It was in recognition of this possibility that we decided to confine the papers of this conference to the first term of the fourth Labour Government when so much by way of reform was accomplished, and before the post 1987 election acrimony broke out. There are foreshadowings herein, but the 1987–90 dramas remain to be dealt with elsewhere.

At the time of the conference David Lange complained to the *Herald* that he had not been invited. Lydia Wevers, Director of the Stout Research Centre, and I wrote an apologetic letter explaining that we had been reliably informed that he was too ill to come, and that we had felt that an invitation would be upsetting. He wrote cheerfully accepting our apology "unreservedly" and wishing us well. I am sure he would have been delighted with the range and quality of the contributions to this volume, and deeply satisfied that there is still a widespread fascination with the achievements of the government that he led. It is of great importance that those who make our history should also be encouraged to help write it.

The committee that helped me organise the conference consisted of Lydia Wevers, Hugh Templeton and Bruce Brown. Adrienne Nolan prepared the manuscript for submission to the publisher. We are grateful to Jonathan Hunt for permission to use Parliament's facilities for so memorable an occasion, and to Radio New Zealand for permission to include the two appendices.

Margaret Clark
Professor of Political Science,
Victoria University of Wellington

MICHAEL CULLEN
Opening remarks

Former Prime Ministers, Ministers, Members and ladies and gentlemen. It is an honour for me, on behalf of the Prime Minister, to open this conference on the first term of the fourth Labour Government. This is not to be confused with the fourth term of the first Labour Government, since two leaders more unlike each other than Peter Fraser and David Lange could scarcely be imagined.

We are, of course, now some twenty years on from the election of the fourth Labour Government in what has been called the "schnapps" election of 14 July 1984. As you will recall, Sir Robert Muldoon had, in what politicians refer to as a tired and emotional state, called an early election. The pretext was that he could not rely on the vote of Marilyn Waring. More probably, he realised he could not write anything like a convincing Budget to take to Parliament and the country before the next General Election.

After a final macabre piece of post-election melodrama in which Sir Robert not so much refused to fall on his sword as refused to accept it was sticking through him, David Lange became Prime Minister.

This was to prove, arguably, the most radical government in New Zealand's history; more radical in some ways than Savage's. It was perhaps also the best educated and most talented seen to that point. It was, especially for a Labour Government, peculiarly dominated by lawyers: Lange, Palmer, Caygill, Prebble, Hercus and O'Flynn were all lawyers in the senior group and others were in the legal fold outside that group.

There was also a motley assortment of historians—three in Cabinet and myself as senior whip. Most of the rest of Caucus came from some kind of professional or academic background.

It was, on average, a very young Cabinet and Caucus—I suspect the youngest at least since the formation of political parties, and much younger than those of recent years. A number of ministers were still in their thirties, the leadership in its early forties. This was incontrovertibly New Zealand's first truly post-Second World War Cabinet in that only a few of its members had been formed by the experiences of the war. Most had grown up in the golden years of post-war prosperity and consensus, though the youngest had also been affected by the student radicalism of the Vietnam War era. Phil Goff, it is rumoured, is still trying to destroy photos of himself as a long-haired radical. Stan Rodger, of course, wishes he could find one.

If there is one conclusion to be drawn about the first term of the fourth Labour Government, it is that it quickly laid the seeds of both its victory in 1987 and its catastrophic defeat in 1990. For three years a façade of disciplined unity was maintained at the expense of an honest internal debate about basic principles and direction.

At the same time, the Government appeared to have become so convinced of its own intelligence, courage and competence in the pursuit of change that change became the end not the means. In so doing the Government lost sight of the innate conservatism of most New Zealanders, who were now faced with simultaneous change on almost every front.

This was reinforced by the lavish praise heaped upon the Government by its new fair-weather friends in the Business Roundtable and elsewhere. In the same way that business people are often easily seduced by flattery from academics (usually in pursuit of their money and influence), so was the Government seduced and flattered by big-business support.

The final element that laid the ground for both subsequent success and failure was the course of the economy. The fundamental political assumption made about the consequences of radical economic reform was that pain would be followed by gain with roughly the right timing from an electoral perspective.

In other words, it was expected that in the immediate term the rapidity and scale of the reforms would lead to a slowing in the economy as the adjustment process unfolded. Then the economy would begin to grow on a stronger sustainable basis as the reforms produced the expected efficiency gains. This would lead to re-election on a rising economy, with the delivery of social gains in the second term, and hence relection for a third term.

In fact, of course, this did not happen. Certainly much of the real economy declined fairly spectacularly under the burden of structural reform in the first term. But buoyed by the ideological enthusiam of many business and, especially, financial leaders, a speculative bubble masked this to a considerable extent. New Zealand went into the 1987 election and the subsequent sharemarket crash with a weakened economic base and with probably the most overvalued sharemarket in the developed world. The economy was not to recover for another five years. It is during this period of radical reform from 1984 to 1992 that the largest part of the present gap between ourselves and Australia emerged.

The remarkable thing in retrospect is that while much of the change was necessary, it was, after an initial promising start, mishandled, so that the reforms produced smaller benefits and higher costs than could reasonably have been anticipated. But the Labour Government was not alone in being responsible for that. In many respects the prime culprit remains the preceding Muldoon administration, particularly the final bizarre year. By 1984 Sir Robert had turned New Zealand into an economic version of the Mad Hatter's Tea party. Deficits and debt were rapidly expanding. Twenty percent of all tax revenues went to service the debt. We were well into the second year of a wages-prices-interest freeze with no exit route in sight. All sectors of the economy seemed to be subsidising each other. We were trying to maintain a fixed exchange rate with practically no reserves. And so on and so on. Some have called this socialism but that is to praise the level of intellectual coherence underpinning it far too highly.

Somehow from all this fiscal prudence we had to salvage rational market and price signals, the ability to succeed or fail on our merits, efficiency in the government and private sector and much else which ought to be, but seldom is, common ground in a well-ordered democracy. And, unlike in Australia, this could not be done with a high level of tripartite deal-making, for there was no real willingness to do so in the absence of any common purpose, shared goals or perceived mutual benefits.

What happened instead was that the Labour Party's old trade union base was largely ignored but kept modestly quiescent by the Government avoiding any radical industrial relations reform. In the meantime Treasury, the Treasury Ministers and big business colluded to restructure much of the economy on the basis of a thoroughgoing neo-classical ideology misleadingly called Rogernomics. I say misleadingly because for all his drive, energy, clarity and purpose Roger Douglas was in no way the author of it and not even its clearest articulator within the caucus or in the public at large.

During this first term, despite the internal dissent expressed by Jim Anderton and others, the economic reforms proceeded apace. But underlying them was a broader theory of society and the economy which was so far at odds with Labour's traditional philosophy that sooner or later the mother of all conflicts was going to break out. As we now know, it nearly did so before the 1987 election but in the event was postponed until shortly after.

The fact that the economic restructuring of the first term had such high costs, the fact that it was carried through in such a single-handed and non-consultative way, and the fact that, unlike in Australia, little or no transitional assistance was given to business to adjust so that the costs in human and other terms were much higher than they needed to be, should not detract from their necessity in general.

But the means did, as I said, become the ends. Cliches such as 'crash through or crash', 'there is no alternative', 'we must not become a sitting target' became not just the *modus operandi* but almost the *raison d'être* of the government. Any other approach was seen as wimpish and wet. And above all of it sat the Prime Minister, fearsomely intelligent and quick-witted but economically illiterate, politically clumsy in some respects, without an independent base in the caucus and the party, but increasingly concerned at the general drift of events.

An extraordinary amount was done. The fundamentals of financial and economic reform; local government reform; the nuclear-free policy; fiscal reform (largely, I have to point out to my Act ex-colleagues, by substantially lifting tax revenue); tariff reform; the corporatisation of state trading entities and much else. However, much that the fourth Labour Government is credited with doing actually occurred in the second term, including the controversial state asset sales, ports reform, the Public Finance Act.

The electorate in 1987 gave its initial verdict. It was basically a continued thumbs up from the new fair-weather friends and thumbs down from the traditional Labour base. While Labour picked up seats on a net basis, the voting gap narrowed as National dramatically recovered from 35 percent to 44 percent of the vote. The majorities of many Cabinet ministers were slashed, and in seats such as my own, St Kilda, the majority stayed the same, but the vote was well up in the wealthier suburbs and well down in the old heartland.

Much of the rest of the heartland had breathed deeply and given us the chance to deliver on the promised social gains and hoped that the experience of broken promises of 1984 [such as the surcharge] would not be repeated. This laid the ground for the conflicts of the second term. And they led in turn to the nemesis that descended upon us in 1990 and after: the creation of both the Alliance and Act parties, the emergence of MMP and the long period in the wilderness.

In some ways then it was, for an historian, an odd government to judge in its first term, for its epitaph had been written nigh on 150 years before in the opening lines of Charles Dickens' *A Tale of Two Cities—the best of times and the worst, the age of wisdom and the age of foolishness, the epoch of belief and of incredulity*, and so on. The good news is that, despite the occasional hysterics from the *National Business Review*, there has been no Bourbon restoration.

That New Zealand is a more dynamic, varied, exciting, colourful place in 2004 than in 1984 can in good part be attributed to the fourth Labour Government. But so can the fact that the country is more socially divided, with greater extremes of wealth and poverty, an inadequate consensus around social goals, an electoral system which arguably does not assist in good government, and we have a propensity to spend too much of our time reliving old arguments rather than addressing new problems.

But one thing is sure—future historians will make a living from our labours for a long time to come. And for that my former colleagues in academia should be profoundly grateful.

PETER LANGE
A life with David

Sitting in the audience with Mum at the Victoria League's annual speechmaking competition for high school students, about 1957, in a grand hall somewhere "in town" was not pleasant for several reasons: having the face wiped with the spit of the parent, listening to boring speeches about the Empire, as well as being inside while my mates were back at Otahuhu building a causeway across the Tamaki river with only their bare hands and bits of stick. We'd made huge progress the day before in our efforts to get to the promised land of the Middlemore Golf Course without getting our feet wet so that we could nick golf balls, but hadn't allowed for the forces of the tide and so a large part of the mudworks needed to be redesigned and rebuilt. The only Empire my gang was interested in was the Empire Sweet factory that the most fortunate boy in our class had out the back of his house, which today, 50 years on, still churns out the same excellent frosted caramel bars. But David was up for some sort of speechmaking cup, and Mum and a token kid—me—were his support team. I haven't a clue what he spoke about but everything seemed to go well, and while I don't recall his winning a cup or anything, Mum was satisfied enough to buy us an Adams Bruce icecream on the way home. That bit I remember, along with getting home to take off the dreaded lace-ups and head barefoot to the river to find my gang bored with taming the tide and now starting on the tallest tree-hut in the Southern Hemisphere—including South Africa—using bare hands and bits of stick. I apologise for not remembering more details of David's performance but my heart was not in it. I do remember him waving his hands quite a lot in a slightly unnerving way; unnerving only because none of the other boys I knew from Otahuhu would ever wave their hands like that and I suspect it was almost certainly on Mum's instructions. And in contrast to the next time I heard him speak in public his voice was rather high-pitched.

That next time was some years later in the Auckland Town Hall during one of those "Great Debates" that crop up from time to time. Once more I don't recall what it was about or even why I was there, except that I had not heard David speak in public since his voice had broken and perhaps I was curious to see or hear for myself the performance of someone who seemed to be making an impression as a young lawyer and public speaker around Auckland. His performance was quite astounding, not so much for the content, which I recall as being perceptive and amusing, but for the fact that here was a person whom I had grown up with and got into arguments with—dreaming of one day winning one—and done the dishes with, and gone to Boys Brigade with, suddenly now manifested as a performer, a stranger almost, whom I was enjoying being entertained by. At the same time I wanted to tell the guy next to me that he was my brother, you know, so that he would envy my good fortune and perhaps even think that I could speak like that too. But I'm afraid there's not room in one household for more than one who speaks like that; my father would happily have told you this as he came off second-best yet again in a "discussion" about making one's bed; able to counter David's legal arguments against making one's bed only with a short but effective reply that would not have been allowed in court unless it had been cleared first.

We led different lives as schoolkids—David's life fairly solitary, and mine gregarious—but our paths crossed at the meal table, where we fought with our two sisters, family events, where we again fought with our two sisters, and Sunday rituals. We both listened to the radio constantly; me to the Lever Hit Parade, Life With Dexter and the Goon Show, and David to any station that had talking on it—politics, current affairs. It wasn't really until our late teens and early twenties that our interests coincided. That came about because the Boys' Brigade company we attended out of family duty became wide open for a takeover and we turned it into a kind of travel club. Along with a group of boys uninterested in the paramilitary thrust of the traditional Boys' Brigade, we organised canoe trips down the Wanganui, went camping in the Hokianga, to the Ureweras and, finally, the Grand Tour of New Zealand—36 boys in our own bus for three weeks, dossing down in church halls and walking the Routeburn, stopping at beautiful places so that all 36 boys could throw stones at each other. David remarked that we should have just camped in a gravel quarry for three weeks. We celebrated the last night of our tour at Opotiki in a church hall, where David cooked a three-course meal for all 36, using the modest equipment in the church kitchen and a ramshackle church stove.

Later we both hitch-hiked separately and with other mates around New Zealand and parts of Australia and, while hitching is not so common these days, I see it as one of the most helpful formative experiences of my youth (starting at 14 with a trip to Taihape) in that I, a shy sort, was forced to relate to a range of up to 10 people a day, create discussion, winkle out information and keep the driver awake with interesting chitchat. I would imagine that David found it much easier with his conversational skills and he was probably as good as I was at creating a series of fictional autobiographies so that one's life story became much more interesting for the driver, though there was always the danger of discovering that he too was an aerobatics ace. The other benefit that hitch-hiking produced was that we could explore, cheaply and at the drop of a hat, places that looked interesting on the map and so a sense of curiosity developed and was satisfied, and that affected a lot of our subsequent view of life. David was the sort of person who would go into a driveway that said "No Entry" just to find out why someone would put up a sign that said that. And if these episodes may not have been high adventure on the scale of Hillary and Shackleton, they hinted at a curiosity in the unexplored that we both developed in later years, mine more hands-on as I built oxymoronic objects such as a chocolate teapot, a kiln built out of ice and a brick boat, while David went on to more influential adventures as the fourth Labour Government reshaped the country, and of course later took on formidable international political missions at places like the UN, Oxford University and Baghdad.

I don't know why people turn out the way they do—sometimes decent parents turn out ratbags and ratbag parents turn out decent citizens—but none of us four kids raised by my parents has much of a stomach for style, fashion, putting on a front. That might have resulted from watching Mum trying to put on a front but failing dismally, because her Australian working-class upbringing always won out. Mum always lowered the tone or, more accurately, brought things down to earth, whether it was a social occasion, a church service or interior decorating, but not in a coarse way, more from exuberance and quirkiness. Pop had no pretensions, only common sense, good humour and concern for those he came in contact with. Neither was sophisticated, and neither expressed strong political beliefs, though it was clear that Mum would have preferred at some time to graduate to Mission Bay, send her kids to private schools and bury her working-class background, while Pop preferred to stay in South Auckland, send his kids to Otahuhu College and overlook his middle-class upbringing. His own mother was very proper and basically not a lot of fun to us because of that—certainly she never expressed much warmth to her grandchildren, preferring to make sure we had a good grasp of etiquette so that she might not be ashamed of us. It didn't work; although these things are never a complete waste of time and when you, formerly a boy from Otahuhu, are asked to dine with the Queen then your grandmother's tuition in the correct way to eat (tip the soup plate away; if you transfer the fork to the right hand, you may never pick up the knife again during that course; never use a pencil grip on your knife and so on) could easily be the most useful thing you ever learned, and could make dining with Her Majesty less of an ordeal. The threat of having the Queen wipe your face with spit on her hanky must have been there all the same.

Our favourite grandparent of the three we knew was definitely Mum's father, Sam Reid, who was a bit of a "hard case", a Tasmanian who managed to regularly blot his copybook and who eventually reversed the trend of social misfits who were exiled to Tasmania by being exiled from Tasmania—to Temuka. His philandering and drinking habits in Launceston were never completely forgiven by his wife and kids, but he fell into line in later years and became an entertaining and generous grandparent, best remembered for his hearty laugh that on one occasion had him falling backwards in his chair to end up on the floor with his feet in the air—a moment that I can still see, when he seemed to balance for an age tipped halfway over, with the hearty laugh now gone and a look of terror and dread on his face, before finally losing the battle and landing on his back, but within seconds of finding he was still alive, roaring with laughter again. Those were times when you laughed until you thought you might be sick. I don't remember his wife ever laughing; I'm sure it's not a lot of fun being the wife of a popular and gregarious spendthrift. She and my mother became rabid WCTU temperance advocates. Sam later gave up the drink but he'd left a lot of trouble in his wake, including another daughter Dawn who has been a surprise addition to our family only in the last few years, sadly appearing only after all of her five siblings had died. I'm sure the surprise is mutual as she tries to absorb this whole new extended family. Grandpa saw out his days in very modest and quiet circumstances, like a naughty boy made to sit quietly until the bell went.

My father loved New Zealand and we drove all over it in his 1948 Dodge, always camping or staying with friends or church contacts, never at hotels. He earned an income that would have been less than most GPs but more than our working-class neighbours (although when he heard what David and I earned at the Westfield freezing works where we both worked for several seasons, he seemed slightly put out), but Mum managed to siphon a lot of it off to church missions and the less fortunate (another "discussion" at this point by David about who exactly was less fortunate—them, living on a beautiful Pacific island, or us next to three freezing works), so we never lived extravagantly. All the same there was probably a perception of us as the local gentry, but if living in a house full of kitsch, and getting long trousers well after the last boy in class had got his, and going to school with a Biblical text ("honour thy father and thy mother" is one I remember) painstakingly engraved on your hardboiled egg is privilege, then forget the revolution. Some of those eggs would be a hit on the Antiques Roadshow now …. "Tell me sir, where did you come by this fine piece of mid-twentieth-century eggshell calligraphy?" "My Mum put it in my lunch when we went to the 1950 Empire Games but I hid it under my bed and found it just last week still in good shape and as relevant today as it was then."

We had a comfortable but slightly odd upbringing. Anyone who organises a prayer meeting (kneeling not sitting) for the family on an almost daily basis, and dragoons your mates who happen to be calling in to get you to help dig up the Tamaki river so that they suddenly find themselves praying instead of digging, has to be unusual. Perhaps they prayed that the tide would stop and our causeway would get to the other side, or more likely that they would soon get out of this strange place. Somehow Pop seemed to slide out of these embarrassments but his form of Christian service was slightly more hands-on and useful.

However, it must be said that Mum's hospitality was huge, and included people from foreign-sounding places coming to stay, often for months. They seemed to cope with the quirky stuff and many kept in contact for years after. We had one of the first Austin Minis in Otahuhu and I had to take a preserving pan full of curry to a social lunch at the church for a group of surprised native Fijian freezing workers staying nearby. Mum had got the curry powder from a couple of nurses from Ceylon who had stayed with us and left it behind, and figuring that anyone with a dark skin would be fond of curry, had made a huge batch and got me to put it in the boot and drive it to the lunch. I must have taken off too quickly because it slopped over the side, and when I got around to cleaning up the mess an hour or so later I found that it had stripped the paint off the car and there was only shiny metal where there should have been red paint. I recall the Fijians struggling with the meal, eyes watering and noses running, and can imagine their discomfort working on the killing chain the next morning.

Growing up as the kids of two such different people, both of whom cared enormously for us and everyone around us, but showed it in such different ways, meant that we were exposed to a culture of concern for others, and also to a variety of options about how to get through the day. You needed to develop common sense, humanity, rationality, scepticism, intellectual enquiry and contrariness just to survive a day in Mum's life. We were all cared for, and while that caring might have taken weird turns from time to time, we all ended up with an extremely fine sense of the absurd, a level of awareness of the needs of others and a sense of justice and fairness.

COLIN JAMES
What made the revolution?

Lange was, of course, leader in the formal sense of holding the position of Leader of the Labour Party. But he was in fact more a salesman (at least in the first term) for those who drove the policy change that characterised his government. They were in effect the leaders, though they didn't have the title.

Lange himself declared, in answer to a question by me in 1983 as to what he stood for: "I surge for the thing that I feel." He was, as Prime Minister, definitely a surger. And he felt a great deal, painfully at times. He became by the end of the first term a lonely figure, tossed by forces far greater than he could ride, let alone tame, detached from his own government in the second term and, in the end, detached from "the things he could feel". He tried to find his way back to the good society expounded by his doctor father—the Good Samaritan society, you might call it, which I suppose sums up his political instinct; he was not a political philosopher, still less an ideologue and especially not an apostle for the free-market economy his prime-ministership facilitated. So there were some marvellous pieces of political theatre: the flat tax died in early 1988 and in late 1988 Richard Prebble and Sir Roger Douglas departed in high drama. But by then there was no way back: Lange was stranded in the hard glare of market economics and efficiency and his titular leadership died there in 1989.

Lange was caught up in a revolution. Being a "surger", the revolutionary nature of his government exhilarated him: he exulted in the meeting with Rod Deane, then deputy governor of the Reserve Bank, in London to approve the Cabinet's wish to float the currency in March 1985. His *tour-de-force* in the Oxford Union debate in March 1985—"I can smell the uranium on your breath from here," he told an interjector—scandalised foreign service mandarins but delighted and warmed much of the nation and large numbers of non-New Zealanders round the world. His weekly press conferences were the best show in town—one-liners at a rapid-fire rate. He was at home in the theatre of politics and could project the headiness with verve and humour: in that sense he was at one with the revolutionary mood of the times.

I want to stay on that word "revolution" for a moment. Brian Easton has declared it a counter-revolution, but I think that focuses too tightly on the economic reforms and the overturning of Keynesian policies. The fourth Labour Government was about far more than economics; it ploughed up every policy field, in some cases very innovatively. Moreover, it did this amid rapid and deep social change that was independent of, and infected the tone of, Lange's Government—and made its time in office not just a period but an era. It is in that wider context that I want to situate Lange's Government and the Parliament of 1984–87.

I argued the case in *New Territory* for calling the period from 1984–92 a revolution on the grounds that it represented a change in the value system—not a violent overthrow of the existing order but nonetheless a "cultural" revolution, causing social, cultural and economic upheaval and insecurity to large numbers of people, sweeping away one élite and its ideas and replacing it with a different élite and ideas. Of course, there was much continuity of institutions and customs, but there was enough discontinuity, I think, to call it a revolution.

I indicated in *New Territory* and have argued more vigorously since that that revolution was this nation's independence revolution. I don't mean by that the ban on nuclear ships and opposition to apartheid sport and other foreign policy or constitutional initiatives. I mean something much deeper, in the nature of social and cultural change: the sentimental detachment from Britain, the development of a vibrant local cultural expression.

I think this began in the 1970s and took the form of an unselfconscious New Zealandness in writing, plays, music, dance and art and craft, whose creators no longer looked over their shoulders to the mother culture for comparison or differentiation. Of course, it didn't happen in a flash and a case could be made that in art and craft it began earlier. But it did suddenly in the late 1970s become much more noticeable and voluminous and, to coin a current vogue word, brash.

This was the generation that came to adulthood in the 1960s, stretching its creative wings.

The pivotal year for me was 1978, with *Plumb* and *Foreskin's Lament*. By 1980 first-run New Zealand plays at Circa were unremarkable. Then revisionist interpretations of the country's history appeared in the 1980s. *The Piano* and *Heavenly Creatures* were just around the corner.

Of course, there had long existed a popular culture that was distinct from Britain's—outdoorsy, sporting, egalitarian, male and in some way "better". But until my generation, born at the end of or after the Second World War and reaching adulthood from the 1960s onward, that popular culture also included the notion that Britain was "home"—maybe in the sense of having escaped from home but nonetheless representing the place they knew they had come from. "Home" was my parents' generation's word for Britain. Recently arrived British migrants were "homeys".

The 1960s generation, which made its impact on higher culture from the 1970s and in politics from the 1980s, did not call Britain "home". Yes, Britain was, and still is, the automatic port of call for those on OE, but it has become a foreign country. "Home" now is New Zealand, with a distinct landscape, a distinct approach to daily life, distinct ways of thinking and distinct ways of expressing itself—a distinct popular culture and, from the late 1970s, a distinct high culture.

I contend that the independence revolution amounted to the "indigenisation" of the ethnic-Europeans (overwhelmingly Anglo-Celts and more Anglo than Celt). After the 1980s there could be no re-attachment of the umbilical cord, much as Richard Worth might still want to reclaim the right of appeals to the Privy Council.

This indigenisation was both an exhilarating and a difficult time—rather like adolescence. And New Zealand policymakers behaved rather like adolescents in the 1980s—recklessness mixed with experimentation. It was, for a journalist, a very heady time. For ordinary folk it was rough. Large numbers lost jobs or income or both. Old certainties disappeared. In my view, it was this indigenisation which accentuated and largely accounted for the speed, breadth and depth of the policy change in the 1980s.

Of course, there were other factors driving policy change. Large movements were sweeping the world and fetched up here: market economics; the women's movement; the environmentalist movement; and the indigenous rights movement.

Market-based economic theory had made a powerful comeback and, coupled with new theories—agency theory, transaction theory, utilitarian libertarianism and moral hazard, the theory of public choice and so on—washed up here in the Treasury and elsewhere among younger economists. These ideas arrived at a time when policymakers had run out of regulatory options and the economy was in serious imbalance: more, or even different, regulation was not an option. A new type of globalisation—of information, people, capital and money, in part facilitated by technological changes in transport and information storage, processing and exchange—had started to seep through trade and regulatory barriers. Something had to give in economic policy and, because of that, to some extent in social policy as well—indeed, there had already been precursors of change in the pre-1984 government.

And the values revolution which had swept through our sorts of countries in the 1960s had generated an openness to policy change among many of the generation which grew to adulthood in that decade. The incoming Cabinet in 1984, the main players of which were largely of that generation, and a younger generation of bureaucrats were ready to roll.

Add to that potent brew the fact that New Zealand is a village-like polity. A few well-organised and well-connected people, with an agreed plan, can drive through big change quickly. In 1984–87 an inner group of five ministers, and Lange, could command the Cabinet, using shock tactics; the Cabinet commanded the Labour Caucus; the Labour Caucus commanded the Parliament. We had, from 1984–87, effectively a one-party state, controlled from the top and incorporating top officials in the key ministries.

I will come back to that later. For the moment I want to stay in the wider context of the ethnic-Europeans' indigenisation here. My argument is that it was that indigenisation that was a crucial, perhaps the crucial, factor determining the rapidity, breadth and depth of policy change. Social change drives political change and in the 1980s New Zealand was amidst a social sea-change. The 1980s upheaval amounted to our independence revolution.

So, while there were powerful factors driving change and that change was therefore bound to be extensive, New Zealand's change was faster, broader and deeper than in other countries. What made the difference, I think, was the independence revolution.

But that's not all. There were two complications to the indigenisation of the ethnic-Europeans. One was the reindigenisation of the Maori. From the late 1960s on, and particularly through and after the land occupations in the late 1970s, Maori reclaimed their culture and language, claimed the right to seek redress for past injustices and then claimed a right to a place in the power structure. All of this was either operating in the mid-1980s or in genesis.

This reindigenisation of the Maori did not occur in isolation. As I indicated above, worldwide, indigenous peoples were asserting claims to recognition and status. But there were special circumstances in New Zealand, not least the relatively high percentage of Maori compared with, say, the Americas, Australia or Japan. And there was the Treaty of Waitangi as a mechanism for addressing and responding to claims. Arguably the most momentous legislation of the 1984–87 Parliament, a Parliament noted for momentous legislation, was the Treaty of Waitangi Tribunal Amendment Act 1985, which extended the jurisdiction of the Waitangi Tribunal back to the date of the signing of the Treaty. What would in 1984 have seemed an amazing array of developments has flowed from that and the subsequent court decisions and administrative initiatives have consituted a virtual mini-revolution.

This mini-revolution—the reindigenisation of the Maori—both complemented and complicated the ethnic-Europeans' indigenisation. It added piquancy, momentum and sidestreams to the independence revolution. Moreover, it was more strongly rooted than the indigenisation of the ethnic-Europeans, since it was attached to the land and underpinned in that attachment by an animist culture that sees everything interrelated through whakapapa. Many liberal non-Maori in the 1980s felt culturally inferior to Maori.

That leads to the second complication of the ethnic-Europeans' indigenisation, which is best demonstrated by Te Papa's arbitrary 1840 cut-off point for non-Maori history. That cut-off suggests there is no cultural history, indeed no history for non-Maori beyond 1840—though, of course, there is a rich history, one from which has come the well-fed, technologically advanced country we live in, the great democratic freedoms and great traditions of music, writing, art and architecture. The newly indigenised ethnic-European culture will not be complete until it reclaims those European historical and cultural roots as an integral element. We are what we have been as much as what we are.

There is a third complication: miscegenation. This has meant until now that many Maori—my guess is at least three-quarters—are in effect members of the ethnic-European indigenised culture and not of the reindigenised Maori culture, and only a quarter (though this element is growing) are both Maori and European; that is, bicultural. Very few non-Maori are bicultural.

But this is changing: among those under 30 there is a much greater knowledge of, contact with and practice of elements of Maori culture. I think over the next generation or two the ethnic-European culture will incorporate more and more Maori culture. I also think that Maori will be more relaxed as Maori believe it secure again and become more open to modernisation than the past generation has allowed. I think more Maori will be both ancient and modern as a growing number of the emerging under-40s leaders are. This has been evident for a couple of decades in the graphic arts and music. Again, culture leads politics.

In short, over the next couple of decades or generations I believe we will see a meshing of the two cultures. This is not a merger; nor is it a one-way street which only Maori travel. It is the establishment of a national identity which draws on both cultures in different ways. The unselfconscious reference to Maori terms and practices by younger New Zealanders is a pointer. Almost without noticing it and with little fuss, non-Maori are acquiring some Maori habits and language. No indigenised ethnic-European in this country can avoid being part-Maori in culture even if not in ancestry. The two indigenisations may often appear in conflict but they are also entwined.

But that was all far in the future in 1987. My point in traversing all this is to underline the massive social and cultural change that was under way as the 1984–87 Parliament smashed the icons of the 1950s consensus.

Just look at the record. A selection:

- the extension of the Waitangi Tribunal's jurisdiction;
- the State-owned Enterprises Act, which reversed a century of state initiatives and put much of the state-owned part of the economy on a commercial footing;
- massive tax changes and the GST;
- the floating of the currency, freeing of interest rates, deregulation of the financial sector and freeing of foreign investment;
- a bold start made to dismantle the hermetical protection of the economy from imports (I first heard the heretical words "free trade with the United States" at a retreat run by Mike Moore in late 1984);
- the removal of subsidies;
- the targeting of social services but greatly increased spending on them, especially to assist Maori;
- the anti-nuclear law and the end of ANZUS;
- the decriminalisation of homosexuality;
- a Ministry of Women's Affairs and more funding for services useful to women;
- the removal of the Economic Stabilisation Act;
- a new Constitution Act.

How did the record stack up against the 1984 manifesto? That promised, in order of priority, "full employment, economic growth, fairness and social justice, maximum possible stability in prices, a more democratic approach to economic management, greater control by New Zealanders over their own economy". In 1987 in *The Election Book*, I concluded about those priorities: "On every count the Labour government has failed." I saw the record as mixed on another set of promises:

> … a fair prices and incomes policy; an investment strategy to help restore full employment and reduce the external deficit; reform of industry assistance; a fair tax system; monetary policy that underpins a balanced growth strategy; fiscal policy that tackles the problems caused by the internal deficit; and the retargeting of public resources to ensure a more effective delivery of those services to those in greater need.

Ministers insisted in 1987 they had not abandoned the objectives, just changed the choice and priority of the means. With hindsight, we can say, as some argued at the time, that the means far overshadowed the ends and the ends are now necessarily different as a result.

By the 1987 election, Labour was bleeding from its core vote. Though its share of the vote went up four percent in that election, it was swelled by recruits from the National side of politics. That was unsustainable and portended serious damage to Labour. Lange in 1986 encapsulated this, though failed to act on his insight: "You are seeing a certain amount of redistribution now but it is perverse. It is a negative redistribution .... Those in the least-assured position are still eroding in terms of the quantity and quality of their living. It's amazing we haven't been slugged for not doing more on that before now." The slugging had begun but it was not until the next term he felt its full force.

In fact, as noted above, Labour in 1984–87 actually increased social spending on education, health, housing, lower-income assistance and welfare. In that sense it was a true social democratic government. But salary rises ate up much of the new spending in health and education. And Labour committed a cardinal sin against New Zealand-style social democracy: it abolished the guaranteed job, the cornerstone of the welfare state for 50 years. For that there had to be utu. And in 1990 there was.

How could the Government carry out its revolution in a parliamentary democracy which is supposed to have checks and balances and to subject governments to the popular will? In the 1920s and again in the 2000s such radical action would have stalled in the mixed Parliaments of those divided eras. But in 1984 checks and balances were minimal; New Zealanders had come to trust governments too much. The 1984–87 Parliament was in effect a pawn of a determined and radical executive. That Parliament was the high point and last gasp—of the post-1935 parliamentary dictatorship, the winner-takes-all political culture.

In fact, even in 1984–87 there was the whiff of change in the offing—from 1978 Social Credit had had a small presence in Parliament, though not enough for most of that time to have any effect on the executive's will. After 1987, though the two parties regained their duopoly for a time, they then began to fragment. By 1995 we had entered the current period of minority and/or coalition government.

The catalyst was Sir Geoffrey Palmer's Royal Commission in 1986 which recommended a change in the voting system. This looked at the time an exercise in futility and in the 1987–90 Parliament an FPP select committee reached for the pigeon-hole. But in 1990 National insouciantly promised a binding referendum and an angry public took the opportunity to leg-rope future governments to vexing small parties.

Sir Geoffrey, whose contribution to the 1984–87 Government and Parliament was immense, made several important changes to parliamentary procedure: he set up a new committee, chaired by an Opposition MP, to scrutinise regulations; he instituted the important rule that all bar exceptional legislation automatically went to select committees for scrutiny (previously there had been government discretion to withhold bills) and enabled select committees to initiate inquiries on their own motion; and he removed the financial control of Parliament and its staff from the control of the Leader of the House and thus from the direct control of the Government. These changes did not seriously impede governments he was in, but have become a crucial feature of MMP Parliaments.

So what of the 1984–87 Parliament? It was a momentous and revolutionary Parliament. But it was so only because it was under the thumb of a bunch of determined revolutionaries and operated under rules which left it highly manipulable. And it met amid social change on the scale of an independence revolution. Small wonder we can't go back to those days and that we shall look back on them with wonder.

MARGARET WILSON

Oh what a party

When I came to prepare this paper I discovered that I had little personal memory of this period and that those who have written about it tend not to mention the Labour Party, only the parliamentary party. I was therefore forced to refer to my own essay "Labour in Government 1984–1987", which was an attempt to try and explain the role of the Party during that period and its relationship to its government from my perspective as the then Party President.

A quick read of that essay reminded me why humans are so resilient—we have a capacity to forget. It reminded me also, however, how the Party is frequently discounted in any analysis of government. In some ways also it is not surprising that little attention is paid to the role of the Party. The role of political parties is little researched or understood within the context of our political system. They are private organisations with a public purpose. They are the vehicle under which individuals gather to work together to achieve a commonly accepted set of goals or objectives. The Labour Party is the longest established political party—over 90 years old—and as such has a considerable history and tradition influencing its policies and mode of operation.

Within the New Zealand political context, the Labour Party's historic role has been to produce what is now fashionably called 'conviction' politics and politicians. It is the party the people elect in times of crisis. It is the party of ideas, the party of reform, and the party that does not shirk the hard decisions. As such the Labour Party attracts people of strong will, with definite ideas, and a determination to make a difference.

The Labour Party has always represented those in society who do not have great personal wealth or access to power. Its policies reflect this position. There is, however, a pragmatic understanding that wealth must be created before it is distributed. The rights and freedom of individuals are understood to be best achieved through protecting and promoting equality and equal opportunities for all. And it has always seen the development of New Zealand as an independent, culturally inclusive society.

The reason I start with this analysis of how the Labour Party sees itself in the political spectrum is because I think it is necessary to appreciate the role played by the Party during the period of the fourth Labour Government, and in particular the first three years. It may also explain why the economic policies of the fourth Labour Government were seen by many members as being at odds with its traditional approach to economic matters and why many felt betrayed by the Government's embracing of neo-liberal economic policies.

I am aware that many commentators of that time characterised the Party as either being obstructive to the Government's goal of restructuring New Zealand, or not obstructive enough in hampering the Government's ability to govern and bringing about its demise earlier. As the party president at the time I bore much of the criticism from the Left and the Right, and from their perspective I am sure it was justified. Roger Douglas voiced his criticism of the Party, as did Jim Anderton. Both eventually resigned from the Labour Party to form new parties. This left the Labour Party free to rebuild from its core base and within a decade be re-elected to form a government.

I think it is fair to say that when the Labour Government was elected in 1984 the Party was locked in an ideological struggle over how to move beyond the excesses of the Muldoon era. The Party membership was not opposed to change; it knew change was required. It was the nature of the change that was the subject of endless policy debates and political positioning to effect power. And the essence of the difference was how best to protect the interests of those people in our society who had little personal wealth or power. Would a free-market approach really do this? What was to be the role of the State? Would greater inequality result and damage the life chances of those we represented? These were just some of the questions that lay at the root of the differences.

The election of David Lange as the parliamentary party leader clearly signalled the economic policies of the right would prevail in the Party's manifesto for the 1984 election. Those of us in the opposing faction renewed our efforts to ensure that the policies reflected the positions of those we represented. As it turned out, the early election pre-empted that debate and ensured that the policies of structural adjustment prevailed. The financial crisis created by Muldoon provided the opportunity and the necessity to move quickly to set a totally new course in economic policy.

The fact that the Party was to be marginalised from any future contribution to economic policy was apparent from the outset. The exclusion of party officials from the Economic Summit was a public declaration by government that there was no role for the Party in policy formation. Of course the attempts to exclude the Party only served to intensify the opposition, and eventually ensured the splits to the Left and the Right of the Party. The lack of a parliamentary opposition had also made the Party the only effective opposition. This was not a role the Party sought but it was best positioned to articulate the concerns of those most affected by the changes.

It is important to note, however, that during those first three years every effort was made to maintain engagement between the party organisation and the parliamentary party. Apart from party conferences and council meetings, the Joint Council of Labour was revived as a forum for the Government to explain its policies and the trade unions to put forward their views. The leadership of Jimmy Knox did not make this easy. He was not given to sustained rational discussion, and Roger Douglas had little tolerance for long tirades.

It was also apparent that members of Cabinet, in particular the Minister of Labour and Richard Prebble, were determined to create a labour market in which there was no effective collective representation. The Labour Relations Act 1987 was the result of long negotiation between the Party, ministers, and officials, and was an attempt to provide a way to introduce greater flexibility, while preserving the right of individuals to collective representation. The story of the relationship between industrial and political labour during this period has yet to be told.

The economic debate within the Party was an attempt at a more successful engagement between party members and their government. The travelling roadshow at which arguments for and against the economic policies were presented and debated at least raised the general level of discussion within the Party. This exercise did lead to greater understanding of the Government's reasons for promoting the policies it did. And if the Government had not attempted to apply the same approach to social policy and to remove the public service infrastructure and conduct wholesale privatisation of assets accumulated by generations of New Zealanders, there would have been greater support from within the Party.

It is sometimes forgotten that there was a range of views within the Party on the question of the appropriate economic policy. For example, the GST proposal was only passed at the annual conference with the support of the Service Workers Union. This was after the Party had gained agreement that the GST policy must ensure low-income earners were not disadvantaged. Family assistance packages emerged soon thereafter. It would be a false picture, therefore, to assume that there was not engagement and that this engagement did not produce results for all the Party and the Government.

It was clear, however, that engagement with the Party was time consuming and frustrating for many ministers. It was a constraint on the operation of government and was not appreciated by some ministers or their officials. From the officials' perspective, once a government was elected, the Party ceased to exist and their ministers were assumed to have become apolitical. While that may be a correct constitutional position, in reality it created considerable tension. For party members the Government was their government in a way that was different from the rest of the country. The Party had supported government members to their present position and there were therefore obligations in terms of access and performance.

One issue where the interests of the party members were to prevail was the non-nuclear policy. This issue, whose story has been told, unlike the economic policy, united the Party and had considerable support from Caucus as well. I recall that it was the one issue over which I was required to indicate to the Cabinet that the Party would be prepared to have a major split from the parliamentary party. After considerable debate, the Party executive informed Geoffrey Palmer, who was Acting Prime Minister at the time, that the Party would not support nuclear-powered and/or -weaponed ships entering New Zealand.

There was debate over whether or not we should support nuclear-powered ships if they did not carry nuclear weapons. The decision eventually went against support because the damage to the environment would still be considerable if there was an accident, and also there was no guarantee that such ships would not have nuclear weapons because the United States maintained a 'neither confirm nor deny' policy.

The fact that the Government decided to pursue a policy consistent with that of the Party's resolution was due to the fact that the executive did not want a major confrontation over an issue which, at the end of the day, was not as important to them as the rest of the economic reform programme. There was also a serious question as to whether the Cabinet had the votes in Caucus. It was also understood that this policy had the support of the majority of New Zealanders and not only Labour Party members.

Of course, governments must govern in the interests of all New Zealanders, but there is a tension between whose interests prevail in a particular case. It was the management of that relationship between government and party which was a major factor in the success of the Government at the 1987 election. While the differences had not disappeared, there was an understanding that election success was a priority for both the Party and the Government. Throughout the campaign the tensions continued and were seen in the nature of the campaign itself and in the selection of candidates. Much of the negative media attention received by the Party at the time was over candidate selection.

I came to the conclusion by the end of election that the divisions within the Party were too deep to heal or to manage. The struggle was simply who would control the Labour Party in the future. For the Party, election success was therefore important to ensure the maintenance of a viable organisational structure. Equally important was to ensure a strong party leadership that maintained connection with the parliamentary party. The fact that the Labour Party did survive to form a government within a decade is a tribute to those who worked so hard during this period.

It was also due to the fact that after the election Roger Douglas unveiled the next phase of his plan. Although this is often associated with the flat tax proposal, the programme was basically an attempt to apply laissez-faire economic principles to social policy. This was the step too far for those remaining faithful to the Labour Party, and, importantly, it led to David Lange publicly criticising the programme and eventually Roger Douglas and others leaving the Party to form ACT.

Although David Lange never had an easy relationship with the Party, I had determined from the time I was elected president that I should engage with him to see if we could find ways to work together. It was this engagement that led to the estrangement between myself and Jim Anderton who considered the Party should have taken a position of outright opposition to both David Lange and the executive. While I considered such a position appropriate when in opposition, history had taught us it is important to minimise conflict when in government. I therefore determined to try and negotiate policy changes from within and not through public criticism unless absolutely necessary.

I was aware that my engagement with the Government provoked criticism from the left of the Party. I understood their frustration and anger that a Labour Government was not producing the policies they supported. I also knew politically that the Government's programme did not have majority support in the Party or the country. While New Zealanders are innovative and open to change, we are also a conservative people who value stability. Our history tells us that the Left contributes to our political life through initiating and supporting political movements, and on occasions aligning itself with the centre of the Labour Party. It has considerable influence from time to time, but has never achieved mainstream electoral support.

Although I had been positioned as being on the left, I saw my role as trying to achieve as much as possible for the people Labour represented. A Labour Government gave you access, and it seemed irresponsible not to take advantage of it. I therefore met with David Lange for an hour every week of the three years I was President. We met before Caucus, which gave us both the opportunity to talk through how to manage the conflict, and differences played out every week in that forum. My successors continued to have a good relationship with him and thus maintained an essential connection between the Government and the Party. This connection became even more important during the next three years as the Government started to unravel.

Although the fourth Labour Government has been, and will continue to be, remembered for the programme of structural economic adjustment, it is important not to forget that many people in the Party kept the political agenda for social and cultural justice alive and even advanced it. Much of my time was spent trying to ensure that women were treated equally and given equal opportunities. The foundations for the advancement of women today were laid in the 1970s and 1980s. It was also during the first term of the fourth Labour Government that the Party worked with Geoffrey Palmer and Koro Wetere to gain the support necessary to legislate for redress of historical grievances under the Treaty of Waitangi back to 1840. We recognised we could not progress as a nation until we confronted the injustices of our past.

The first three years of the fourth Labour Government were highly productive years. This was not surprising after a decade of Muldoon playing King Canute and trying to stop the influences of the world intruding on New Zealand. The fourth Labour Government threw open our doors to the world and the winds of change nearly blew us away. The Party did not doubt change was required; the argument was always over the nature of the changes. An assessment of the Party's role will depend on the interests that individuals and groups were pursuing at the time. For me the task was to ensure the survival of the Party at a time when both the Left and the Right wanted to claim exclusive ownership. In such a struggle it was important to remain grounded. The Labour Party was formed to represent the interests of people without wealth or power in the political system. My touchstone was always whether the policies furthered the interests of these people.

The way in which those interests are expressed and represented varies from time to time. What cannot change, however, is the engagement between the represented and those who represent them. It is a constant conversation. Whenever one party dominates the conversation the balance is broken, and the party and the government become dysfunctional. From my perspective, that conversation did continue during the first three years and while at times it was heated, abusive and very direct, it was alive and people were engaged. People took their politics seriously and were prepared to commit time and energy to it.

I conclude with two points. The first is an apology to those who seek character analysis of the chief players at the time. While I came to learn that individuals do make a difference in politics, I also learnt that individuals are driven by complex motives and that simplistic judgements on others reflect more on those making the judgement. Secondly, I make the observation that the role of the political party in the future deserves analysis. I would suggest that MMP, technology and globalisation are having a major impact on the role of political parties in our system.

JIM BOLGER
Lange and Parliament

The invitation, extended more than a year ago, to contribute to this retrospective look at David Lange and the first term of the fourth Labour Government all seemed straightforward back then so I said yes. I accepted the need for a view from the "other side"—although 20 years on I still get no joy recalling the scale of the National Government's defeat, I also recall the enthusiasm that greeted Labour's victory and especially the warm and enthusiastic welcome that was extended to David Lange as Prime Minister by the commentators and public alike.

It has been interesting to look back over David Lange's first term as Prime Minister and of the Labour Government he led. It was a time of rich debate around issues across the political spectrum. There is far too much to cover, so I will focus on two of the big issues of the 1984–87 government: economic reform and the anti-nuclear policy.

Let it be said at the beginning and without equivocation that David Lange was a master of parliamentary debate and an outstanding orator; few could match him in my years in Parliament. His mastery of the English language and his gift of almost instant rebuttal with penetrating one-liners on all subjects made him a formidable parliamentarian. He used his exceptional communication skills to full effect in his first term as a Prime Minister and deserves much credit for holding his at times very nervous MPs and Labour Party members on side despite the introduction of many policies that offended the core of Labour's traditional constituency. For a party that had its roots deep in the belief of state ownership and that the Government was the only vehicle to deliver to the poor and underprivileged, it was a striking achievement that David Lange was able to hold his team together during the first three years.

Here I want to add that although it is correctly accepted that it was Roger Douglas, as Minister of Finance, who introduced, promoted and was responsible for the right-leaning economic policies of the 1984–87 Labour Government, it was David Lange's unlikely support for these policies, in the eyes of his supporters and commentators alike, that held the ship of state, on what could fairly be described as a steady course despite many cross currents.

It was not all excitement and plain sailing. The then *Evening Post* repeated in its 28 November 1984 edition only four months after the election that already angry superannuitants meeting in Kapiti were calling for the Government to resign because of the surtax on Super. In the same edition George Gair stated that there was now a widespread sense of injustice at having been deceived by sweet words and callous actions. Rex Austin from the deep south spoke out about domestic and industrial electricity prices which were to rise 22 percent and 32 percent respectively. From the beginning it was a challenge.

The importance of the 1984–87 Government can be measured not in what it put in place over those three years, but, more importantly, what endured in principle if not in all the detail. Given that New Zealand's Parliament is the fastest law-maker in the west, virtually nothing survives for very long in its original form.

In two hugely important areas—economic policy and the anti-nuclear component of foreign policy—the general thrust of 1984–87 continued, 20 years later. That is a big achievement. These policies have been broadly accepted, not without debate, by both the National and Labour-led governments that followed.

In parliamentary terms nothing starts in a vacuum and while it was clear that Roger Douglas's thinking on economic policy had moved on a long way from some of his earlier writings, it seems to me that the particular circumstances he inherited as Minister of Finance in July 1984 gave him the opportunity to move the economy further and faster to the right than he would have dared to imagine even weeks earlier.

A still disputed political/economic issue is whether the suggestion, however muted, by the campaigning Labour Party that it favoured a devaluation of the NZ dollar, in itself not a radical idea, exacerbated the situation, when it became very clear that Labour was going to win comfortably in 1984. I don't intend to try and resolve that issue today, but it was debated at length in 1984. Whatever the correct position was, it remains true that Roger Douglas, with important cover from his leader, turned traditional Labour Party economic theory on its head in the three years 1984–87. In Parliament we had the somewhat bizarre experience of the centre-right National Party being accused by the centre left of not being radical enough or right wing enough in our economic thinking. Labour speakers constantly taunted National MPs about how Labour had stolen their clothing. Certainly there was no shortage of economic and political commentators who strongly endorsed that viewpoint. The new approach all held together, even if it required a lot of tape to cover up the cracks, while the sharemarket boomed, and most seemed to think, or at least hope, that they would soon also enjoy the new-found wealth that seemed to be just about everywhere. All many wanted to talk about was their share portfolio.

It was indeed a heady period for David Lange, Roger Douglas and Labour, but it also was a precursor to the divisions that saw the Labour Party seriously at war with itself after the world and New Zealand stock markets crashed shortly after the 1987 election.

While the economic policies were driven by the need to deal with particular aspects of the New Zealand economy, David Lange's move on anti-nuclear policy in his first term had a much longer history within the Labour Party.

In 1973 the third Labour Government, under the leadership of Norman Kirk, in a spectacular move sent a frigate, with Cabinet Minister Fraser Coleman on board, to the test zone around Mururoa to protest against French atmospheric testing. That certainly created attention, but New Zealanders, while interested, were generally not yet seriously engaged in the debate.

In my view, the protests surrounding the 1981 Springbok Tour eight years later were a turning point, mobilising New Zealand society, and in many ways marking a distinct movement away from the more conservative approach of being interested but not involved. Importantly, the Tour protest eventually made it acceptable to cross party and family lines to express strongly held beliefs.

The same came to be true three years later with the anti-nuclear issue. Again we witnessed a move from across a broad spectrum of society to oppose nuclear weapons. In political terms this all came together on 12 June 1984 when Richard Prebble rose in his seat in Parliament to propose the introduction of his private member's Nuclear Free New Zealand bill. New Zealand has never been quite the same since.

The bill led then National Leader Sir Robert Muldoon to the conclusion that he couldn't hold a majority in Parliament so he called an early election for 14 July 1984. Of continuing interest is that Richard Prebble's bill was drafted to prohibit the entry of nuclear-powered ships and nuclear weapons into New Zealand as well as prohibiting the building of nuclear reactors.

Why that blanket prohibition is of great interest is that David Lange in the book he wrote in 1990 *Nuclear Free – The New Zealand Way* states that he was never opposed to nuclear propulsion; on page 33 of his book he makes the point: "I could not see how the arguments I mustered against nuclear weapons could properly be used to justify a ban on nuclear propulsion!" He went on: "Shutting out their nuclear-propelled ships for the same reasons we shut out their nuclear weapons seemed to be offering an unnecessary affront to the Americans". He then relates that very soon after he became leader in early 1983 he announced he wanted the Labour Party to review its policy on nuclear propulsion. Then, as he put it, there followed a hard lesson in practical politics "in which I scarcely opened my mouth before the argument was lost". As David Lange explained it, he did not have command of the Labour Party outside Parliament and the rest, as they say, is history.

There are two significant markers in that experience that were completely overlooked when the nuclear debate exploded after David Lange became Prime Minister. The first is that Lange didn't wish to unduly dismay or anger the Americans, and the second was that he clearly saw a big distinction between nuclear weapons, which he totally opposed, and nuclear propulsion, which he believed was a different issue.

Hansard has recorded that in the first reading debate on the Prebble bill the then Prime Minister Muldoon said that ANZUS would not survive if the bill passed, and our current Prime Minister, Helen Clark took the opposite view: "that of course New Zealand could be nuclear free without infringing the ANZUS Treaty."

Rob Muldoon went further and said in concluding his speech that the Government would not support the bill and further that it could not remain the Government if the bill became law. Former Labour Leader Sir Wallace Rowling quickly picked that up, wittily remarking that it was another good reason to pass the bill.

The debate on the introduction of the bill was not concluded until the following day, and despite Marilyn Waring crossing the floor and voting for the introduction, the motion to introduce the bill was defeated by one vote. I should add that while all this excitement was going on in Wellington I, as Minister of Labour, was leading the New Zealand delegation to the ILO Conference in Geneva.

After the July election Parliament reopened on 15 August. The Governor General's speech did not lead with proposals for anti-nuclear legislation, the issue that had brought about the early election, but with the other big issue of the first term of the Lange Government, eloquently referred to in the speech as "severe structural imbalances" in New Zealand.

The importance of the Economic Summit Conference to be held the following month was highlighted with the commitment to invite a number of significant groups to attend. There was a commitment to "involve all sections of the community in decision making". The alleged lack of such involvement in the 1984–87 government was to become a major issue inside and outside the Labour Party.

There was little in the speech to scare the political horses in the Labour Party membership much less the general public. All the familiar positions were included: the aim to increase employment, new wage-fixing mechanisms, and new superannuation conditions for public servants. The role of railways as a primary freight carrier over long distances would be restored, public urban transport would be provided and of course there would be examination of the primary health services. Even the administrative services to Parliament were to be recognised.

The big nuclear issue was only mentioned at the end in the form of non-controversial commitment to continue to promote a comprehensive test-ban treaty, urge massive reductions in existing nuclear arsenals and, in concert with our neighbours, promote the establishment of a South Pacific nuclear-weapon-free zone. This was a rather conventional speech from a new government. Nevertheless when the Impress Supply Debate commenced the following day the first National Party speaker, Deputy Leader Jim McLay moved immediately to debate the nuclear issue and that to some extent set a pattern that was followed in many debates.

The nuclear debate moved to Oxford in early 1985 when David Lange pitted himself against the conservative American evangelist the Rev Jerry Falwell on the topic that "Nuclear weapons are morally indefensible".

The debate was carried live on TVNZ early on a Saturday morning and the audience was huge. I am sure no matter which side of the debate they favoured in New Zealand, most were proud of the Prime Minister's quite outstanding performance. It was David Lange at his best—eloquent, penetrating and, when required, very witty. For the record, the motion was carried 298 to 250. Of much more enduring interest though, was that the profile of the anti-nuclear argument had been given a very big international audience.

David Lange's success clearly worried the French Government, with the subsequent shameful attack by French agents against the Greenpeace vessel moored in Auckland and the unwillingness of that government to help bring the agents to justice. The episode was a sorry reminder of raw power in international politics.

Lange's contribution to the nuclear debate both inside and outside Parliament was his unique ability to convey the sense of outrage felt by many supporters. Such was his enthusiasm and passion that it undermined the belief held by many that David Lange's anti-nuclear policy was but a sop to old Labour supporters to distract them from the economic policies that Roger Douglas and others were implementing—policies which were clearly contrary to long-held Labour beliefs.

The years 1984–87 were difficult for the National Opposition. First we had our own internal problems, as evidenced by two leadership changes. David Lange and his colleagues were riding the wave of reform that many of our supporters thought National should have followed years earlier. Labour's anti-nuclear policies were clearly popular with a large cross-section of the public. Yet, as time proved, the apparent strength and cohesion of Labour failed when the sharemarket crashed and blame was being enthusiastically handed around.

For David Lange his first three years were the best. He was a great player on the parliamentary stage and he and his Government's policies made a difference in many ways. It is said that the collapse of the Berlin Wall in 1989 robbed the political world of much of its ideological content. The collapse of ideology has also robbed Western politicians of some of the glue that held their political parties together.

In New Zealand the first-term Lange Government robbed or, more correctly put, changed forever the old Left–Right economic debate. The Labour Government's open embrace of market principles rather than some version of central planning is an important and enduring feature of the 1984–87 Lange-led Government.

From the other side of the political fence I nevertheless welcomed that change as necessary. In my view, the shift has strengthened the New Zealand economy. The great irony is that if David Lange's personal view on the anti-nuclear issue had been accepted by his party, then we would not have a ban on nuclear propulsion today and we might have a free-trade agreement with the world's largest economy.

Politics is a fascinating business that does determine our future, and David Lange was very good at it.

RICHARD PREBBLE
Cabinet government

The Lange Labour Government was not government by Prime Minister, Finance Minister, Troika, Treasury or the Roundtable. There is a desire by the media and by commentators to personalise, and so they miss the reality: that it was government by Cabinet.

The Kirk-Rowling Government had, in very important respects, been government by Caucus. Kirk had taken a number of important issues to the Caucus. The result was Cabinet ministers debating with each other, inconsistency, and a reduction in the quality of decision-making. Bill Rowling as Finance Minister had found it impossible to implement a coherent response to the oil shock.

The Labour Caucus held many discussions to identify the reasons for the failure of the third Labour Government. We also had the benefit of the Australian Labor Party's view—that the Whitlam Government's erratic performance was in part due to its reliance on government by Caucus. Long before David Lange became leader the Labour MPs had agreed that the next Labour Government would be government by Cabinet. All ministers would be required to support Cabinet decisions—not just publicly—but also in the Labour Party's forums. From 1984 to 1987 all ministers observed this. It was only broken in 1988 when David Lange famously overturned, by press statement, the decision by Cabinet to adopt a flat tax.

The Labour Cabinet, even though it did not have a majority in the Caucus, was never defeated on any proposal. Within the Labour Party, the Cabinet was never defeated—except by one vote by the Wellington regional conference that rejected GST. In every regional and annual party conference, the economic programme of the Labour Government was never rejected by the Party.

There were just two important exceptions to government by Cabinet. The first was the nuclear policy. There was never a Cabinet paper on the nuclear policy and Cabinet ministers had never heard of the *Buchanan*. Geoffrey Palmer had also been kept in the dark and as acting Prime Minister declined to visit the *Buchanan*. I now know that Foreign Affairs had prepared a Cabinet paper but that Lange declined to bring it to Cabinet. As there was no possibility of the *Buchanan* carrying nuclear weapons, it is very unlikely that the Cabinet would have declined the visit. The Americans and senior US officials made the mistake of believing that New Zealand had presidential government.

The second exception was in relationship to the National Executive of the Labour Party. David Lange as the leader of the parliamentary party was the Cabinet's sole representative on the National Executive. David, who did not come up through the Labour Party, hated the executive meetings, which were massive two-day affairs. He attended for only a few minutes. There was no provision for him to send a proxy and he declined my suggestion that he do so. This meant that in an important forum the Cabinet's case was just not made.

Would it have made a difference? I was summoned by the national council to explain my policies as Minister of SOEs. I accepted and vigorously set out the case for reorganising the government trading departments. I pointed out that the huge losses represented taxpayer's money that could not be spent on schools and hospitals. I also defended my policy of choosing able businessmen to be on the boards of SOE's. I heard subsequently that one of my strongest critics said, "we must never invite Richard again, he had me persuaded and we all know he is wrong".

In the interim, between the Muldoon Government resigning and the Lange Government coming into office, the Cabinet secretary had briefed Geoffrey Palmer and me on the structure of the Cabinet and its Cabinet committees. Before the Freedom of Information Act we knew nothing about the structure of Cabinet committees. The Cabinet secretary suggested we adopt, for the first six months, the existing structure, which, he pointed out, had survived successive governments.

Geoffrey and I took away his briefing document and studied it independently. We both reached virtually identical conclusions—that the present structure made no sense and we should start with a new system of Cabinet committees.

This was our new structure—the whole Cabinet met on Monday, Tuesday the front bench met to look at major policy issues, and then, throughout the week Cabinet subject-matter committees such as social policy, transport and legislation met.

It was in the Cabinet committees that the debates and discussions of the Lange Government occurred. Sometimes it took weeks and occasionally months for the Cabinet committee to be satisfied it had reached a quality solution to an issue. The Cabinet committee proposals then went to Cabinet. The Cabinet itself was not a decision-making body. Twenty Cabinet ministers is simply too large a number. Cabinet meetings rarely took more than two hours.

David Lange was a brilliant chairman. He could direct the course of the debate by the order in which he called ministers. If it was clear that a Cabinet committee proposal was either opposed by a significant number of ministers or there were real concerns, the issue would not be debated but would be either sent back to the Cabinet committee or, more likely, to another Cabinet committee.

The Cabinet itself would start each Monday with a monologue by David Lange. These were invariably very funny and very observant. I can recall Cabinet ministers having to hold onto the Cabinet table in order to prevent themselves from falling off their chairs with laughter. Having put the Cabinet into a good mood David Lange would then race through the proposals on the Cabinet agenda, which he judged no minister would have any objection to. When he reached a more substantive matter he would then select a minister to set out the case. Despite the short time that the Cabinet itself spent on issues, ministers generally felt that matters had been properly discussed. At each stage, of course, people had to be persuaded. We worked very hard to persuade our fellow Cabinet ministers, and then Caucus, of the necessity of the measures we were taking.

Caucus was a challenge, meeting for two hours a week. With 60 or so MPs that is two minutes each. We set up Wednesday night sessions for Caucus and ministers were encouraged to brief in-depth the Caucus committee with which they worked. In my case I had an SOE committee which consisted of the MPs on the Parliamentary select committee through which my legislation had to pass. We would have a meal together most Thursday nights. The MPs would explain the issues that they were facing at the Select Committee and I, in turn, would brief them on the issues that I was working on. We became very firm friends. There was a very high degree of trust and a friendship between us. We knew we were working in momentous times and that we had to rely on each other. There was also strong affection and support for David Lange. We knew how valuable he was to the Government. He had an ability to make us all proud of being New Zealanders.

David Lange gave his ministers great autonomy. He never interfered in my handling of my departments and was always publicly very supportive. That loyalty bred loyalty.

We knew that Sir Robert Muldoon had to micromanage his ministers. I know of no Prime Minister who delegated authority to ministers and then backed them to the extent that David did to his ministers from 1984–87. For example, to go around me to the Prime Minister was strongly rebuffed. It was this authority that enabled ministers to carry out sweeping reforms. It was that authority plus collective decision-making that made 1984–87 a great era of Cabinet government.

MICHAEL BASSETT
Cabinet making: Cabinet breaking

There are two essential bits of backdrop that we need to appreciate if we are to understand the selection of the new Cabinet that took place on Tuesday 17 July 1984.

First, there was a crisis. The Reserve Bank closed the foreign exchange market on the evening of Sunday 15 July pending a decision on devaluing the New Zealand dollar. There had been a run on our exchange rate since the beginning of the election campaign, starting 14 June. In all, the Reserve Bank borrowed $1.7 billion over the four weeks of the campaign to prop up the dollar. The Bank had been advising Prime Minister Muldoon to devalue for several years, and it repeated the advice several times during the campaign. He refused. Therefore, a decision had to be made immediately after the election. Since there would be an interlude of at least ten days before a new Cabinet was sworn in, the incoming government needed to be selected early so that a decision could be made which Muldoon's Cabinet would then be asked to implement.

Second, awareness of a crisis grew during Monday 16 July when Muldoon eluded Reserve Bank and Treasury officials, and then played games in the hope that David Lange could be persuaded to agree not to devalue. Muldoon hoped a bipartisan statement against devaluation would close the issue. This was no answer to the underlying problem of the grossly over-valued New Zealand dollar. Lange bluntly told Muldoon and the nation that this was so in an acrimonious television encounter on the evening of Monday 16 July.

A decision on whether there was to be a devaluation, and if so by how much, had to be made as soon as possible so that the foreign markets could re-open and what made a Tuesday Caucus doubly urgent, was that Jim Anderton, President of the Labour Party and newly elected to the House of Representatives, was circling Parliament Buildings on the Monday. He hoped to delay selection for as long as possible in the hope that he could muster a majority against devaluation amongst the new Labour members in a Caucus swollen by the election of 56 members. He was keen to reassert some of the authority he'd lost since the snap election had been called in mid June.

David Lange and his supporters knew that delay would magnify the possibility of public confusion and play into Anderton's hands. In any event, devaluation was a matter for the executive, and the sooner the incoming Caucus chose the new one, the faster that key decision could be made.

That sense of urgency won out principally because a leader was always going to be in a better position to decide a date for Caucus than a party president, who by this time was no more than a less-than-humble backbencher.

Another more general factor that is vital to understanding those first few days after the election on 14 July is the extraordinarily tense relationships that existed between the parliamentary leadership of the Labour Party (Lange) and a majority of the Caucus on the one hand, and the party president (Anderton) and two or three of his acolytes whose power base was the party executive. Anderton's two devotees were Margaret Wilson and Helen Clark. There was an intermediary between the factions in the form of Stuart McCaffley, senior vice president of the party executive, but he was not strong enough to keep the party executive in line.

Over Monday and Tuesday morning both camps worked hard on lists of candidates they wanted in the Cabinet. Those camps, and the tension behind the process, harked back to 12 December 1980 and to the trouble with Bill Rowling whose leadership kept slipping in public esteem during 1980. Anderton's plan had been to keep Rowling in the leadership until he could get into Parliament to replace him. Anderton helped sustain Rowling that day and Rowling hung on by 19 votes to 18. But he lost ground to Lange over the next two years and a fined-down Lange with a new wardrobe sauntered into the leadership of the Labour Party on 3 February 1983.[1] There were some policy differences between the camps, but, in my view, raw ambition was the principal issue motivating both groups. One of them, the Caucus, was elected by the public at large. The other, the National Executive, was the product of a thoroughly corrupt Labour Party constitution that gave very considerable power to a handful of unelected union secretaries. Within the Party at large, especially after his successful campaign, Lange now possessed the numbers against the executive, albeit by a narrow margin. Lange's mana grew between 1984 and 1987 as new MPs came up to speed with the changes that were recommended by the Cabinet. Anderton's faction collapsed quite suddenly. After the Timaru by-election in June 1985 there was little remaining co-operation between Wilson and Clark and their earlier messiah, Anderton. He became a rather lonely figure with virtually no Caucus support or even people to talk or dine with.

But while the Caucus came up to speed between 1984 and 1987, and warmed to the arguments advanced by the Cabinet, Margaret Wilson and her small clique at Head Office didn't. As she told us in her book, and explained to us at the beginning of this book, she is an ideologue whose concept of "the party" is quite close to Lenin's.[2] The system by which she had been elected first to the junior vice-presidency, and then in September 1984 to the presidency, was not much more democratic. For this reason it would be fair to say that a majority of the Caucus always thought they possessed greater moral authority than that enjoyed by the National Executive. Reasoning with Wilson about the economic crisis sometimes seemed akin to addressing a brick wall. She remained president from September 1984 until after the election in 1987. Her inability to move with the developing thought processes of the overwhelming majority of the Caucus worked against harmonious relationships between the ministry and the party executive and was a constant irritant to the Cabinet. Only Geoffrey Palmer seemed able to reason with her.

CABINET SELECTION

The new Labour Caucus assembled at 11 am on Tuesday 17 July 1984. After preliminaries, and a humorous report from Lange about his encounters with Muldoon over devaluation, balloting for the Cabinet began at about 11.30 am. Lange told us he wanted at least two women in the new Cabinet, and two Maori. In a slice at Anderton he declared that no newly elected MP should be considered for a Cabinet slot.[3]

There were 56 Labour MPs, 17 of them new to the Caucus. Most of them had not been caught up in the previous four years of intrigue, although Anderton had hoped to use any extra time after election day to persuade them to his way of thinking about who should be elected to Cabinet. A total of half the Caucus plus one was necessary for a person to get elected—i.e. 29 votes.

Lange and Palmer were declared to be automatically in the Cabinet. Ballots were held to fill the other 18 positions. John Wybrow, party secretary, and retiring MPs Mick Connelly and Bill Rowling were appointed to be scrutineers. An alphabetical list of all the Caucus names was circulated. People were given the opportunity to have their names deleted if they didn't want to be considered. Most of the newly elected did so. Anderton didn't. All MPs were then invited to delete all but 18 names from the paper.

At 12.42 pm the scrutineers announced that 14 out of the 18 positions had been filled, and those who had secured five votes or fewer on the first ballot had been removed from the next ballot.

The 14 selected on the first ballot were Bassett, Caygill, Coleman, Douglas, Hercus, Hunt, Marshall, Moore, Moyle, O'Flynn, Prebble, Rodger, Tizard and Wetere.

Balloting for the final four places took several more hours, with the names of the bottom-polling MPs falling off each time. Before long the ballot paper had many more names deleted than those still in the hunt. There were several invalid ballot forms, causing Lange to observe caustically that a prime requirement of being an MP was an ability to count! The messy ballot paper was eventually disposed of. Blank bits of paper were handed around on to which the names of those remaining in the ballot were then written. He/she was then invited to delete those for whom they didn't wish to vote. Twelve names remained viable at this point: Clark, Isbey, Jeffries, Goff, Shields, Tapsell, Wilde, Woollaston, Anderton, Burke, Butcher and Cullen. Of these, Woollaston, Cullen, Butcher and Isbey fell off over the next couple of ballots. Kerry Burke was then elected as the fifteenth Cabinet member. Anderton and Wilde fell off the ballot paper over the next couple of rounds of voting, and Goff and Tapsell together won selection as sixteenth and seventeenth members of Cabinet. Jeffries dropped off at this point.

Four hours after the process had started, the ballot for the last place was held at 3.36 pm. Two names remained: Shields and Clark. That vote saw nearly all of those who had been supporting Jeffries swing behind Shields, principally because she wasn't Helen Clark. Margaret Shields became the last minister to join the new team.

On reflection, Lange had won the Cabinet he wanted with a few exceptions. He had wanted Bill Jeffries. In the team were two women, and two Maori. On the eve of the first meeting of the new Parliament, the Prime Minister announced six under-secretaries: Butcher, de Cleene, Isbey, Jeffries, Neilson and Woollaston. They rounded out an executive numbering 26.

It was clear that Lange's party opponents had been routed. Anderton and Clark were sour and complained publicly about the under-secretaries. However, the falling out between these two after the Timaru by-election defeat divided the small opposition within Caucus and made Lange's life considerably easier.

The new Cabinet was a rather neatly balanced group. Roughly half of them were close allies of Lange's, and had been since the early 1980s. The rest had come around to accepting that he was the only leader we possessed in the Caucus. Moreover, he'd now won an election and he deserved their support.

LANGE'S STYLE
Lange's style with his Cabinet was much looser than his Labour and National predecessors'. Patrick Millen, the Cabinet Secretary, who sat in on all meetings, often complained to me of "loose ends" to decisions. It was Geoffrey Palmer who usually tidied them up. There was a general air of disorganisation in Lange's office. He did not ride his Cabinet in the way that Kirk, Muldoon, and subsequently Bolger and Clark did. For the most part, ministers were left to interpret policy and do their own thing, although Cabinet Policy Committee and the Cabinet Social Equity Committee had strong input when it came to major administrative or legislative changes.

Most ministers liked Lange's style. In that first term there was unfailing good humour around the Cabinet table. Monday mornings usually began with the Prime Minister giving a humorous account of his weekend that often had us in fits of laughter. Lange developed his own issues such as the anti-nuclear policy and the fall-out from the *Rainbow Warrior* and handled both of them well. He seemed in control of himself, and loved holding press conferences, where he'd outwit the journalists present. Attending them was one of the week's highlights for ministers' press officers, and most parliamentary journalists as well as some from outside the building were there for the fun. Few of us knew of the chaos that preceded the severance of defence ties with the US in February 1985—a subject I have dealt with elsewhere.[4] Nor did we know of his growing attachment to his speech-writer.

Whenever Lange felt good in himself it transferred to the rest of us by a process of osmosis. He supported his ministers—to their faces anyway—and stuck like glue to his Minister of Finance, Roger Douglas, during the first term. On one celebrated occasion in 1986 he declared that you couldn't put a cigarette paper between the two of them. This showed to best effect in August 1986 when, inadvertently, Douglas's office dispatched details about the Budget before it had been delivered. Lange flew home from Fiji and refused to accept Douglas's proffered resignation.

Generally, ministers felt they had sufficient time in Cabinet to discuss strategy. New or difficult issues would often be pushed across to CPC on a Tuesday morning when anything up to a full complement of ministers would attend and talk through issues with officials.

Before Cabinet on a Monday, meetings had usually taken place between the Finance troika of Roger Douglas, David Caygill and Richard Prebble, and sometimes with Lange and Palmer present as well. In Cabinet itself the minister whose proposal was under discussion would usually speak briefly to the paper. Jonathan Hunt often felt compelled to comment immediately. Someone would correct him, Geoffrey Palmer would speak, and then Douglas, Caygill or Stan Rodger would add a comment. One or two others—Phil Goff or I—would chime in. Prebble, or Moore if he was present, often lay waiting and would either push the train along or pick it up and shunt it onto another track. Jim McLay has told me that votes were quite common in Muldoon's Cabinets; I can't recall one in Lange's. This might well have been because Lange seldom had firm views on any policy issues. He was quick, however, to sense where the majority on any issue lay. During that first term he was very happy to go along with the will of Cabinet on tactical as well as policy decisions, and there was an air of co-operation, friendliness, trust and support from the top.

This camaraderie was cemented over Monday's lunch in the Cabinet dining room on the second floor of the Beehive. Since his earliest days growing up in Otahuhu, Lange had enjoyed discussions over meals, and he was usually in rollicking good form at 1 pm each Monday, especially if he'd just held a good press conference. As one approached the room, laughter rang out above the sound of knives and forks. Ours was a happy Cabinet for most of its first three years.

REFLECTIONS ON 1984–1987

Vital to that Cabinet was the ability of its players. It was the best-educated—in a formal sense—of any in New Zealand's history. There were few passengers, although the work-loads were very uneven. Geoffrey Palmer carried a huge burden that had added to it the requirement to tidy up the loose ends that remained after many Cabinet meetings. He was also Leader of the House. As Minister of Health I had neither an under-secretary nor any associate minister. Instead, I had an under-secretary for Local Government, but that constituted barely 15 percent of my workload. Russell Marshall was in a similar situation. Ann Hercus carried a large load too. Conversely, several had little to do. The initial portfolio allocations indicated how little governmental experience most of us had had.

Assisting with the bonding between us was the seriousness of the plight we were in, and the daring—some called it the audacity—of the policy decisions taken. Instinctively we realised that any splits between us would swiftly sink the lot of us. That meant that the Government was a tight ship. There were almost no leaks. For example, we sat on Paul Reeves' name as the next Governor General for nearly six months without a whisper getting out.

Linked to all this was a growing determination to break the one-term jinx that had affected the two previous Labour Governments. At first re-election seemed an unlikely prospect. Jonathan Hunt and I sat together at the initial informal Cabinet to approve a 20 percent devaluation on the morning of 18 July 1984, a proposal recommended to us by Lange and Douglas with the backing of the Reserve Bank team of Spencer Russell and Roderick Deane, and Bernard Galvin from Treasury. Hunt and I shared the view that the decisions we'd made seemed so controversial that we were bound to lose the next election. At least we could be proud that we had done "the right thing".

Doing "the right thing", as opposed to the politically easy thing, became that Government's leitmotiv—its recurring theme. So unusual was this phenomenon in New Zealand politics that it caught on with the public. The economy was clearly in a parlous state, and here was a Cabinet prepared to risk everything in an effort to fix things. A government that shrugged off political considerations was unheard of, and many members of the public came around to the feeling that we deserved support in a time of crisis.

Luck played its role too. First was the unlikely and unintended support we derived from the division amongst our opponents, both within the Labour and National parties. After he took over the leadership of the National Opposition in November 1984 Jim McLay struggled with his caucus, some of whom supported what Labour was doing, others of whom allowed themselves to be fodder in a poisonous campaign of retribution against McLay by Muldoon.

There were also several accidental occurrences that afforded the Government the rare chance of a fresh beginning. Early in July 1985, only a few days after we'd lost the Timaru by-election, the Greenpeace vessel *Rainbow Warrior* was blown up in Auckland's harbour. Lange played the issue like a trout for months to come, diverting attention from a number of painful reforms that Roger Douglas persuaded us to undertake. By February 1987 the Government was again haemorrhaging because of incompetent handling both by Koro Wetere's and Lange's offices of the Maori loans scam. Just when we thought things couldn't get worse, an earthquake occurred in the Bay of Plenty. It wiped the Maori loans scam from the front pages of the newspapers for some time and gave Cabinet time to regroup.

It's a pretty bold person now who says that that Government got it all wrong. Sure, there were mistakes. Plenty of them. But the leading lights of that ministry—Lange, Douglas, Palmer, Caygill, Prebble and Stan Rodger, with the rest of us both supporting them and doing our own things, succeeded in doing "the right thing".

As the good economic years now stretch out beyond a decade we can see that New Zealand—thanks in large measure to the floating of the dollar in early March 1985 and the deregulation that accompanied it—has been enjoying an average level of growth that is more than twice that of the preceding 20 years. That first term of the fourth Labour Government, coupled with a few equally courageous moves during the first three years of National from 1990–1993, cemented into place a world of low inflation, less regulation, and a freer climate in which to do business. The wasted opportunities of the 1987–90 government will have to await discussion on another day.

KERRY BURKE

The youthful, united Cabinet

I should start by saying that I don't agree with Michael Bassett's comments about Margaret Wilson. In my view her role was very important. It was crucial in ensuring that the Labour Party and the Government remained on speaking terms and better. The potential for a major public falling-out over policy direction was enormous, but it didn't happen in that first term. Indeed at the final Caucus before we hit the campaign trail in 1987 I proposed, and the Caucus passed, a motion of thanks to Margaret. It was mostly her work that enabled us to go into the 1987 election in such a confident frame of mind with our party organisations in support.

To the Cabinet. Perhaps the first thing that should be said is that it was a remarkably young Cabinet. Five of us—Lange, Palmer, Hercus, Shields and I—were 42 years old. Several colleagues, such as Moore, Caygill and Prebble, were in their 30s. This group included Phil Goff, who became the youngest Cabinet minister in the country's recent history. There were some older members, such as Tizard, Coleman and O'Flynn, but they were exceptions whose years served to highlight the dominating influence and energy of the younger brigade.

The second remarkable aspect of this Cabinet, and perhaps even more important than its youth given the revolutionary journey it embarked upon in office, was its unity. There were no votes by divisions taken in the Cabinet during those three years. Not once did the Cabinet divide. Not once did David Lange call for those in favour to say "aye", and not once was a show of hands called for. How did this come about?

First, Geoffrey Palmer had constructed a set of Cabinet committees that ensured that all Ministers likely to be affected by any proposal from a colleague were members of the relevant committee or joined it for the occasion. The system worked brilliantly. By the time any matter reached the Cabinet table all issues had been worked through and agreement reached. Very little time was therefore taken at Cabinet resolving differences.

What was more remarkable about this unity, however, was that it followed so soon after a period of bitter divisions within the Labour Caucus. From 1980 till 1983 the Caucus was divided into 'A' and 'B' teams comprising those who supported Bill Rowling and David Lange respectively. In simple terms the groups could be classified, again respectively, as 'wets' and 'dries' over economic policy and direction, though inevitably ambitions and personal loyalties and friendship also played their part in the formation of the factions.

I was a Rowling supporter, although he seemed drier on economic policy than David Lange, as David's later actions were to reveal. Some (much?) of Lange's support came in spite of his instinctive social and economic views, because he was seen by many MPs as being the more likely to lead us to office—to defeat Muldoon.

Rowling vacated the leadership at the beginning of 1983 and Lange was elected Leader by a comfortable margin. The real contest occurred over the position of Deputy, with Palmer defeating Moore in a very close contest. What this now meant was that every member of the Caucus had voted for at least one of the new leadership team. The foundation was laid, therefore, to establish a much more united team than had existed hitherto.

After some months of David Lange's leadership, however, I still felt that he was unsure about those of us who had been opposed to him earlier and that this was affecting his security going into the 1984 election. I decided to go to see him to say that I really wanted him to win. En route to his office I met Margaret Shields and advised her of my intention. She decided to join me. David was working at his desk. I said: "We thought that we should tell you that we want you to win." He smiled, his worried look vanished and he lent back in his chair, relaxed, as if a great weight had been lifted from his shoulders. Our assurance seemed even more important than I had imagined.

So we became a united Cabinet, in part because we all had a stake in the leadership and because the wounds from the earlier internecine conflicts were slowly healed. But not completely! Helen Clark's exclusion from the Ministry outside Cabinet was an unfortunate remnant of the old 'A' and 'B' teams.

We were also united because of David Lange's leadership of the Cabinet. His chairmanship was dynamic. He grasped issues quickly with his formidable intelligence and he injected humour into our proceedings. He was just superb.

The Prime Minister invariably began proceedings with some humour, much of which perhaps shouldn't be repeated here, even though we had two women ministers. We would have a chuckle, perhaps a bit of discussion about the episode of "Yes Minister" from the previous night, and then it was down to the morning's work.

The Cabinet also kept its secrets. The decision to appoint Paul Reeves as Governor General to succeed David Beattie was an oral one, discussed and made entirely without paper. It was made towards the end of 1984 and remained a complete secret until the formal announcement in April 1985.

I recall being in Washington in January 1985 at the time of the second Reagan inauguration. John Wood, the current Ambassador, was acting lead of mission at the time in the interregnum between the departure of Lance Adams-Schneider and the arrival of Bill Rowling. He organised a round of meetings with officials, some of them quite senior, and also arranged for Helen Paske and me to attend Joe Allbritton's Inauguration Day party at Rigg's Bank (where the New Zealand Government's banking was done).

It was a very cold day—so cold that the parade was cancelled and the swearing-in conducted under the dome of the Capitol Building. There was a genuine fear that some of the cheerleaders might perish in the cold. So the party went on at Rigg's. At some point the door to our room opened and Archbishop Paul Reeves came in to join our New Zealand group. We had a great afternoon. He knew he was going to be Governor General and so did I. He also knew that I knew. Helen Paske didn't. So the party went on.

Helen Paske and I kept our secrets from our separate (journalistic and political) professions, as many other families in this town need to. When I came home from work on the day Paul Reeves' appointment was announced, however, she just fixed me with that well-known interviewer's glare and said *"You Bastard!!"*

Another oral decision we made, as I recall, which remained a complete secret, was to invite the then Dutch Prime Minister, Ruud Lubbers (now UN high Commissioner for Refugees) to help facilitate a solution to the difficulties with France that flowed from the *Rainbow Warrior's* bombing. This eventually resulted in UN Secretary General Perez de Cuellar announcing the settlement.

This brings us to the nuclear issue and its importance in defining the period. Colin James has described the 1984–87 period as radical and revolutionary. I agree. In the context of our history and society they were revolutionary times. And the dramatic changes were aided immensely by the nuclear policy. The nuclear policy, including the Oxford debate and the *Rainbow Warrior* incident, helped make the Government very popular. Often in history a revolution has been saved by an invasion, with the populace rallying to the national cause. So it was then.

The nuclear issue gave the Government the political capital to successfully introduce a range of policies which, collectively, amounted to a revolution in the name of the Lange Government, This is not without its irony, of course, given David Lange's earlier hesitations over nuclear matters and his later ones over economic policy.

The Cabinet, however, was not involved in the process that led to the breakdown in relations with the United States, the saga of the USS *Buchanan*. George Shultz, US Secretary of State, believed that he had been given a commitment by David Lange to fix the apparently irreconcilable differences between our no-nuclear policy and the US policy to neither confirm nor deny the presence of nuclear weapons on its ships. The Prime Minister drove the policy on this issue, directing both military and Foreign Affairs officials to come up with a solution. We knew nothing of this. Nothing! Frank O'Flynn, Minister of Defence, was kept out of the loop even though his senior officials were talking to the Americans. We recall him saying that he knew "something was going on, but I didn't know what it was".

In Washington in January 1985, being there principally for discussions on employment programmes and without knowing any details about the Prime Minister's attempts to resolve the issue, I met officials (including Paul Wolfowitz), and discussed the Government's nuclear policy in general terms. We talked about such things as the genesis of the policy being in French actions, not American ones, and the fact that it was supported by a majority of the population, and was a policy for the South Pacific. The discussions, as far as they could go, went quite well. Indeed, some people in the United States Government seemed to think that Canberra was more of a problem for us than Washington on this issue. Not for long.

Ministers simply did not know that our officials (and American ones) had produced the *Buchanan* as the solution. It was a ship like our own frigates and highly unlikely to carry anything nuclear. It was intended that it sail from Japan to New Zealand. But the Prime Minister by not working through the Cabinet system, had not built the political base in the Government for the proposed visit. We were a Cabinet that kept its secrets and this should have been a Cabinet decision. We could have been trusted to help achieve the best outcome.

At the moment of the crisis the Party forced the hand of the Government and the *Buchanan* visit was cancelled, thus effectively ending ANZUS and souring relations with the United States for a long time. The Americans were angry because they believed that the Prime Minister had given them an undertaking and he had failed to deliver. It would have been better by far to have taken the approach Helen Clark took recently over Iraq, by being clear about our position and sticking to it and by doing that through the Cabinet system. Other governments respect that level of frankness.

For the purposes of this discussion, therefore, the nuclear ships issue and the falling-out with the United States was caused by a failure of the Cabinet system. This was the only time in the 1984–87 period when it failed, regardless of the merits of the final decision, because ministers weren't involved in the issue until too late to support or influence the Prime Minister. But it made the Government popular! The country loved it. The outrage at the bombing of the *Rainbow Warrior* later in 1985 made the policy even more popular. All of which helped to make a united Cabinet and Government.

In the knowledge of later events, it is astonishing now to see how close David Lange and Roger Douglas were in that first term. David's return from Fiji to stand by Roger after a Budget leak was the most public example of that loyalty. The Prime Minister saw his Minister of Finance's survival as being essential to the integrity and survival of the Government.

Disagreements existed within the Cabinet, however, over whether the new State Owned Enterprises should remain in public ownership or be (at least partially) privatised. Many of us wanted the state's commercial activities to be run as businesses, to be more efficient and profitable, but to remain under public ownership. Others wanted to sell. But that debate was put off for a later day.

Prior to the 1987 Budget a range of proposals were presented to the Cabinet for their consideration. The Prime Minister began to think that these were part of a secret agenda of the Minister of Finance. I believe that Roger Douglas put them up as genuine options for ministers to choose between. He knew how to push hard for a favoured policy but he also knew how to accept a majority against him. Relations between Lange and Douglas, nevertheless now became somewhat strained by contrast with the total unity that had earlier existed.

The Government was easily re-elected in 1987 and I became the Speaker for the 1987–90 period. I deliberately took no part in the Government's decisions and no longer attended the Caucus meetings. I also advised the Opposition of this and spoke to the National Party Caucus about how I wanted the House to run, answering questions from its members.

I felt it was important that the Opposition knew that it could trust me not to know of the Government's strategies and tactics in advance and that I would deal with issues entirely on their merits. And I did. There was trust and good behaviour. The result was that not one Member of Parliament was ordered from the Chamber by me for any reason in those three years. None came near it.

I offer this view from the Speaker's Chair at the start of the 1987–90 Ministry because, in contrast with the 1984–87 Government, the unity of the Cabinet did not endure. From my position I was able to see a triumphant government and clearly defined 'A' and 'B' teams in the Opposition in the closing months of 1987 just as there had been in the Labour Party in the 1980–83 period. One only had to listen to Merv Wellington and Ruth Richardson follow each other as Opposition speakers in debate to understand its deep divisions. And, virtually in a moment, it all changed.

The Wall Street Crash of October 1987 resulted in the December package, agreed upon by the Government. The Prime Minister, acting alone, without consulting the people he needed to rely upon to carry the day, publicly resiled from his Cabinet's decision in January 1988.

This is not the forum to debate the merits of the economic issues, only to consider the role of Cabinet. It was bypassed by David Lange in January 1988, just as it had been over the *Buchanan* business three years earlier. The Prime Minister should have raised these matters through the Cabinet's processes. It's what they exist for. His unilateral actions caused a massive falling-out with his principal supporters, without whom he would never have become Leader. It led to the defeat of 1990.

From my perspective in the Chair, when the House resumed in 1988 a sea-change had occurred in the body language of members. The energy and spirit had gone from the Government and the Opposition was buoyant. It was like night and day.

I'll delve no further into that period now but return to the 1984–87 Cabinet. It was, and history should see it to be, the most talented this country has witnessed. United, youthful, energetic and quite superbly—incomparably—led by David Lange, it dealt decisively and radically with the catastrophic circumstances it inherited. In so doing it created a popular revolution. It was the watershed that built the basis of the country we know and enjoy today.

GEOFFREY PALMER
Working with David Lange: a personal recollection

On 3 February 1983 David Lange was elected Leader of the Parliamentary Labour Party by the Caucus and I was elected his Deputy. From then until David resigned as Prime Minister on 8 August 1989, we worked in double harness, both in Opposition and in Government. These were five and a half tumultuous political years. Whatever else can be said about that time in New Zealand politics, it cannot be said that little occurred. During the period we led the Labour Party, no MP worked with David Lange more closely or more constantly than I did.

Lange and I were almost the same age. He was born on August 1942 and I was born in April of the same year. Being close contemporaries gave us, I felt, a shared understanding of the New Zealand development through which we had both lived.

David and I were both lawyers, although lawyers of a different type. David, with an LLB and LLM from the University of Auckland, had been a brilliant criminal advocate. I was an academic lawyer from Victoria University of Wellington who had done postgraduate work in the United States and taught there. Although we were lawyers of different backgrounds and approaches, I always felt the shared profession made it easier for us to communicate and work together.

David was not as interested in the ideas of the law as I am—it was the involvement of people with the law that interested him. His practical knowledge of the criminal law gave him a real feeling for what it was like to be down and out. He had real compassion for people to whom life had dealt a bad hand. His experience in the criminal law gave him an uncanny appreciation of the motivations of the people with whom he dealt. He was the most astute judge of character of anyone that I have ever known.

In Labour Party terms, David came from that group who had wanted a change in leadership, leading to the effort in 1980 to unseat the then Labour Leader, Bill Rowling. This effort, although it had narrowly failed, left wounds within the Caucus. I came from the group of Rowling supporters. But in truth neither Lange nor I were much interested in or participants in the dark arts of political plotting, either then or later. He did not campaign for the deputy leadership either. David Caygill organised that.

David Lange was very much a person from Auckland—I was from the South Island. That balancing factor was important in politics then as it is now. Both Lange and I had been elected in by-elections, a political consequence of which is to give candidates much more national exposure and political oxygen than results from being elected as a new member in a general election. We had both been selected as candidates from big fields—in David's case, 16, and in my case, 18. We both came from safe urban Labour seats—Mangere and Christchurch Central.

In policy terms David was seen as something of a Christian socialist and that is not an inaccurate description of his interests in my view. Both of us were firm supporters of the welfare state and that remained in place all the time of the fourth Labour Government, despite the dramatic changes made to the economy.

David was, in my view, driven by a desire to make things better for people so that they would suffer less. His maiden speech in the House of Representatives on 26 May 1977 remains an accurate reflection of the social concerns that drove him in politics. In policy terms, what I wanted to achieve was more specialised and was spelt out in the book *Unbridled Power*, published just before I was selected as the Labour Party candidate for Christchurch Central, in July 1979.

When David and I were elected Leader and Deputy Leader, we had to decide how to organise our efforts and co-ordinate them. We took a single-team approach. We decided to run the Leader and Deputy Leader's offices in effect as one office, and that worked well. I recollect one of my early decisions was to move Margaret Pope out of the research unit into the Leader's office. She worked very well with David. He was never easy to write speeches for since he made spontaneous off-the-cuff speeches that soared and took off, with lashings of wit and exuberance. They were orations of a unique and magical style. The extempore nature of his speaking style added to its impact. He could always find the telling word or phrase. He did not like sticking to a prepared script.

It is interesting to dwell upon David Lange's great rhetorical gifts. He could inspire audiences of all types. His wit was quick, devastating and funny. He used humour more than any other political figure I have known or have read about. He was an avid reader of "Private Eye", but his humour was not derivative. It was his own sparkle. Humour can often be a disaster in politics, but not with David. He was hardly ever trapped by his own utterance as most politicians are. Not only was he funny, he was inspiring. He had the gift of making the audience believe—he could lift up their eyes to a wider vision where life could be different and better. As a public speaker he connected perhaps more with his wit and emotion than content. There was always within his speeches a sense of his own vulnerability and this gave them, I believe, greater persuasive power. Communication is the most essential of all the political arts and he was a brilliant communicator.

David and I had different styles of speaking. Mine was more analytical and didactic. It also had greater precision. Indeed, when he was away and I was Acting Leader, as happened so often in the first three years of our Government, he sometimes said to me "Geoffrey, do not be so precise and accurate. It does not help politically." Advocacy is for the hour. A speech does not linger long. I heard more Lange speeches first hand than most people—I always rejoiced in them. They were uplifting. David Lange was the best public speaker I ever heard. He had both charm and compassion.

Leadership in politics brings many more demands than those that are faced by ordinary MPs. Those demands swallow up one's family life. Perhaps the matter is best illustrated by the incessant programme of meetings, including:

- Caucus meetings
- Caucus Committee meetings
- Select Committee meetings
- Parliamentary sittings
- Ceremonial occasions
- Labour Party Executive meetings
- Labour Party Council meetings
- Joint Council of Labour meetings (these were easily the worst meetings that it was possible to attend in the days of Jim Knox)
- Election Strategy meetings
- Parliamentary Procedure Committee meetings of the Parliamentary Labour Party every morning that Parliament sat
- Electorate meetings; and
- Public meetings in the electorate.

In Government the demand is greater still, with Cabinet, Cabinet Committee and Executive Council meetings as additional burdens. Another feature is all sorts of time-wasting ceremonial functions; ministers often have to be on hand to greet visiting Heads of State and Heads of Government at airports and so on. In politics and in government, life is one long meeting and it is dangerous to be absent.

David and I divided up the work as best we could. I chaired the Labour Party Policy Council, dealt a lot with the Labour Party organisation, including the President and the General Secretary, chaired the Parliamentary Procedures Committee and endeavoured to take as much of the administrative load off David as possible. This was to allow him to focus on those tasks for which it was necessary for him to excel. Parliamentary debate and media appearances were the prime task for him. The Leader is the party's chief publicist. For such appearances, it is necessary to be fresh and lively. The grind of meetings can always prevent that unless matters are carefully paced.

In Opposition, our pattern of dividing up the tasks and executing them developed well. At the time Labour became the Government our pattern of working together was well established. After the snap election in 1984, I took much of the burden of organising the transition given the fact that David had to concentrate on stating our position on the devaluation crisis which attracted an enormous amount of publicity. There were also a lot of behind-the-scenes-lawyering activities in which I was heavily engaged at that time.

As Deputy Prime Minister, Leader of the House, Minister of Justice and Attorney-General, I concentrated on running the Government's legislative programme. In the second term I dropped being Leader of the House and became Minister for the Environment. I also ended up devoting at least half my time to the political fire-fighting duties that afflict any government. There are always crises, mistakes, political embarrassments and untidiness to be cleaned up and put right. It is necessary to have a lot of authority in order to intervene in other ministers' portfolios. That can only be done effectively by the Leader or Deputy Leader. There were many difficulties to sort out: conflicts between MPs, conflicts between ministers and officials. While I dealt with these matters, it was always in close consultation with David, and never without his approval. I hardly ever wrote him letters. We talked together constantly and he was very easy to consult with.

David had me attend the Monday meetings with the Prime Minister's advisory group before Cabinet, and this was very helpful. He also authorised the Director of the Security Intelligence Service to brief me. Between David and me there was total trust and total co-operation. We met together frequently to discuss issues—there was hardly a day when he was in New Zealand that I did not speak to him, often many times. Sharing a bench in the House was helpful in that regard. We worked together on Cabinet portfolio allocation. These decisions are never easy and always produce several seriously dissatisfied and grouchy ministers.

Politics is an unusual field of endeavour in that everyone in it thinks they are terrific and can do anything. Merit is hard to define in politics. This illustrates a wider point and is often not appreciated by the public. Every MP has succeeded in being elected to Parliament, so each MP is successful in his or her own right. Thus, often they are disinclined to accept instructions or leadership. And the leadership has no power over backbench MPs to hire and fire them. Furthermore, getting rid of MPs who should be got rid of is extremely messy and difficult and only to be undertaken in the most extreme circumstances. Sanctions that apply in many other spheres of life are not available to political leaders.

David took two major portfolios in addition to the prime-ministership. In the first term it was Foreign Affairs, which meant he was absent from New Zealand a great deal. He was an excellent Foreign Minister and made a big impact on a world that had never seen a New Zealand Prime Minister like him before. The impact of his speech at the Oxford Union on the nuclear issue was, in my view, the defining moment of his prime-ministership. But the travel exhausted him and caused added strain for me since I was Acting Prime Minister all the time he was away and sometimes Acting Foreign Minister as well.

My major recollection from that period is sitting in my Beehive office long into the night and signing out hundreds of letters to members of the American public who had written applauding the Government's nuclear policy and David's role in articulating it. I got to wondering if so many Americans approved of what we were doing, why was it that the United States was giving us such a hard time.

David took the Education Portfolio after the 1987 election. I was always of the view it would have been better for him to concentrate on the prime-ministership with only minor extra portfolios. But David was always easily bored and wanted some ordinary portfolios of the type that other colleagues had. It gave him a sense of achievement. I must say, however, he never altogether felt comfortable with Foreign Affairs' officials, who always seemed to be trying to steer him back to received orthodoxy on the nuclear-free policy.

As Prime Minister his style was collegial, not controlling or interventionist. He did not attempt to run other ministers' portfolios, although he was interested in what they did. Often they talked to him as a matter of courtesy. But he was no control freak; he preferred to leave it to me and his staff to tidy up or fix up things that had gone wrong. As a style it brought its own rewards in loyalty from ministers. It was in the character of classical Westminster Government where the Prime Minister is *primus inter pares.* But David was frequently not interested in the detail of particular policies. He was no policy 'wonk' in the way that many people who go into politics are. He became easily bored at Cabinet Committee meetings from which he often wandered away, yet his command of the big picture was always superb. In a crisis he was great—clear, decisive and resolute.

There were two occasions when I did not accept his own preferences in relation to my portfolio allocations. When he wanted to make Frank O'Flynn Attorney-General in 1984 I strongly resisted that because the Attorney-General is in charge of the Parliamentary Counsel Office and I did not relish having the legal portfolios split. Furthermore, I wanted the job and it was the only job in Government that I really wanted. I prevailed. David was quite understanding of this demand, but I don't think he was pleased by it. Then, after the 1987 election, David wanted me to be Minister of Education. I refused, so he took the job himself. He did this because he wanted the second term to be dominated by the social policy agenda in the same way that the economic agenda had dominated in the first term. That was a matter upon which we both agreed. Unfortunately it did not take place in the way we had envisaged, particularly because of the 1987 sharemarket crash and the policy consequences in economic terms that that produced.

David was an easy person to work with. I cannot recollect that we ever had cross words. We had a good understanding of each other's strengths and weaknesses. David had a particularly acute appreciation and insight into the characters of other people. He was remarkably observant and insightful about people. He could predict with accuracy how many would react to a particular issue. He had an uncanny intuition about people, in my experience. David was interested in people and he had an extraordinary range of friends and acquaintances. He had many, fascinating insights about them all.

In private he could be cutting about other people and their attitudes in a way that was at the same time wounding but very funny. He was as witty in private as in public and his wit was so quick. This made him entertaining to work with. He could liven up Cabinet meetings with anecdotes that would keep ministers highly amused. I remember one story about an encounter he had with the Crown Prince of Tonga in which that person had worn a pith helmet equipped with a propeller driven by solar power. He also wore a monocle, not a common sight in the South Pacific. David's description of these facts, coupled with his account of what the Crown Prince had said, dissolved the Cabinet meeting into stitches of laughter for at least 10 minutes.

My own sense of humour is rather drier, and I had learnt while teaching at university in the United States that humour did not travel well and it was important to be careful with it. I shall never forget trying to explain to the Americans why it was that David gave a weekly press conference. Often his witty quips at these conferences created enormous misunderstanding amongst the American diplomats.

David disliked difficult meetings with colleagues and frequently avoided conflict by not telling them how profoundly he disagreed with them. But he had the gift of causing all his Caucus colleagues to have confidence in him and how matters were being handled. Any Caucus contains a wide range of abilities and personalities. But the Labour Party Caucus from 1984 to 1990 was particularly diverse. Look at the number who attained leadership positions in other parties that grew from the Caucus: Jim Anderton; Richard Prebble; Peter Dunne and Ken Shirley. MMP has had the effect of narrowing the range of diversity in any one particular party because there are now not just two, but several parties.

Lange was a good Chair of both Cabinet and Caucus—crisp but inclusive. The business always moved along quickly. David became bored easily and did not encourage exhaustive and detailed discussions. Some ministerial colleagues bombarded him with letters about issues and this annoyed him. Sometimes he would become dispirited, but he usually quickly recovered his good spirits.

David had some unusual interests. He found it hard to resist riding on fairground roller coasters. That and his interest in motor racing, at which he was surprisingly good, always seemed to be a reflection of his restless character, when there needed to be a sense of danger or crisis in order to bring out the best performance from him. He was always a little on the edge. His health was never good and he had to be hospitalised for a heart condition in the Government's second term, an event requiring my urgent return from overseas. He was also fond of technology. He used his computer to talk to his staff long before that became common. There was always something of the little boy about David.

In a long professional life I have worked with many people with abilities but with no one easier to work with than David Lange. He was a very quick brief— sometimes too quick. We worked well as a team and we divided the tasks between us in a manner that produced a seamless sort of government. We were never close friends in a social sense. David was, in my experience, something of a loner. He often seemed vulnerable and he was always restless, but he secured my enduring respect for how he went about the tasks of a leader. And he was a generous person with whom to work. The devotion that he engendered from people who worked in his office is proof of the fundamental appeal of his character. He was the best parliamentary speaker of my time in Parliament. He could inspire an audience both inside and outside Parliament in a way that a good jury advocate can, but he was much funnier.

The battle over economic policy between David Lange and Roger Douglas destroyed the fourth Labour Government. That was sad and unfortunate. I devoted a lot of effort to trying to defuse the conflict and failed. There were faults on both sides. But it did not diminish the regard in which I held David. David for me is a real human being—warm, passionate, visionary and vulnerable.

No one can capture the essence of David Lange. He is too complex and has too many layers for that. I sensed he did not have too many support systems around him in politics and I never understood why his wife, Naomi, would not come and live in Wellington when Labour became the Government in 1984. I believe he found true happiness with Margaret Pope and came to be at peace. He resigned the prime-ministership because he had had enough. I was not pleased at the time, but I do not blame him now. He gave New Zealand everything he had, and it was a lot.

ROGER DOUGLAS
How we did it

It is not my intention to dwell at any length on the economic policies put in place during the first term of the fourth Labour Government. These are generally well-known and if not, there is plenty of literature. Rather, I intend to spend most of my time on how we managed to achieve what we did—what was important in political and economic terms and to some extent what was not particularly important.

POLITICAL ASPECTS
The first important point was that by 1984 there was general agreement within Labour's economic Caucus team about the programme of reform required. This agreement did not extend as far as the New Zealand Labour Party Council and some Caucus members, for example Anderton, were violently opposed to the policy.

Treasury and the Reserve Bank, with little to do under Muldoon but tinker, had both worked hard to develop a comprehensive economic strategy, and in some ways, more importantly, had determined what needed to be done to implement that strategy.

THE CRISIS
By 1984 New Zealand was without doubt in serious trouble: New Zealand's twin deficits were massive; our foreign exchange reserves had been squandered; and our creditors were seriously worried about us.

This presented the new Government with the opportunity to implement the policies we already knew were needed. We were further helped in this process by the fact that some significant lobby groups were in general agreement (e.g. Federated Farmers and the New Zealand Roundtable) with what we intended to do.

The crisis and the way Sir Robert Muldoon behaved on the Monday immediately after the election allowed David Lange to gain almost instant credibility in his new role as Prime Minister. The contrast of the two men was there for all to see that Monday night.

The Government was blessed with a young, able and generally remarkably united Cabinet, whose motto became: "We will do the right thing" no matter what. This also turned out to be remarkably good politics.

Another important factor was the almost 100 percent agreement between the members of the finance team of Caygill, Prebble and myself on what needed to be done and how best to achieve it. This proved to be the case on an ongoing basis during our first term in Government. Add the active involvement of Lange and Palmer on some important issues (e.g. SOE legislation), also de Cleene (on tax), and you had a formidable team. The importance of the process can not be underestimated—most issues had been thoroughly tested before they went to Cabinet and then Caucus.

My practice of having members of my staff, including my press officer, Bevan Burgess, sit in on the decision-making process also helped, in that they understood not only what we were doing but why, including why we favoured one particular option over another. This helped immeasurably with presentational aspects of the policy changes.

Undoubtedly Lange's ability to communicate with Labour voters was at times vital. His work at the 1984 Summit also proved invaluable in setting the scene for my first Budget in November of that year.

Educating or generally bringing up to speed the 17 new members of the Labour Caucus was another important factor in our success during those first three years. A number of those new members, heavily influenced by Anderton, started off opposed to the general direction the Government was taking on economic issues. After attending a number of Wednesday Club meetings where they were exposed to the arguments supporting the policy direction the Government was taking, a substantial majority came wholeheartedly on board. The work of Peter Neilson and David Butcher among backbench MPs was particularly important.

Less important from my perspective, but perhaps vital for some, was the nuclear ships issue. All I can say is that with or without it, I would have adopted the same economic approach. Whether the nuclear ships issue distracted potential critics and made my job easier I will leave for others to judge.

The first Budget set the programme for the next three years. This was necessary because of the length of time needed to introduce some new measures, for example the Goods and Services Tax.

From my perspective, the following approach was important in establishing credibility—clarity about what we wanted to achieve in various areas was critical to making progress. In other words:

Goals were primary. Until one forms some coherent view about one's destination, it is pointless to plague oneself with questions about how to get there. In most cases setting the right goals was not the real problem; rather, adopting the means for achieving those goals was the real issue before us.

Having a clear vision of what we wanted to achieve enabled us to think in new and fresh ways. Without goals the danger is that a particular means can come to be seen as the primary objective of the exercise, not simply one of several means to achieve the established goals.

For many, tax-funded schools and hospitals are the only means of providing universal service and as such are seen as the primary objective of the exercise, not quality education or health care for everyone. The means have become the end. In the economic area we avoided that trap.

Quality decision-making was vital. Having clear goals invariably led to quality decision-making, for example financial market reform, the goods market, taxation, state-owned enterprises. This approach of going for quality decisions involved accepting the initial costs upfront in exchange for the good times that would come a few years later.

Many of us came to realise that if a solution made sense in the medium term you needed to go for it without qualification because nothing else would deliver results that would satisfy the public. My first Budget taught me that consensus among interest groups on quality decisions only develops after they are taken and/or start to deliver results.

Appoint good people. Success in many areas was as much dependent on people as it was on policy, for example state-owned enterprise reform. Without people like Roderick Deane at Electricorp, Harvey Parker at New Zealand Post or Alan Gibbs at Forestry the reforms would simply not have been anywhere near as successful as they were (a lesson not learnt by the Bolger or Clark Governments).

Packaging reforms into large bundles was not simply a political gimmick; it was in fact the key to being able to sell the changes politically.

Large packages did two things. Politically this provided the flexibility needed to demonstrate that the losses suffered by one group were offset by worthwhile gains in other areas for the same group. Economically it was the right approach. The economy operates as an organic whole, not an unrelated collection of bits and pieces. In other words, it is the interaction of policies that matters, rather than any one policy on its own.

Speed is an essential part of any reform programme. When reform is delayed for many years, the short-term costs which start day one are considerable, while the tangible benefits may take years to appear because of the time-lags that are part of any system of reform. If action is not taken fast enough, support for the reform process can collapse while the reform programme is only partway through and before the results are evident.

Removing privilege (removing subsidies, import licensing etc.) but reminding people that this was not our only objective, was at the core of our policy approach. The essential argument was that Government is not there to protect vested-interest groups, be they manufacturers, teachers, farmers, trade unionists or health workers, at the expense of the public. Rather, it was the Government's role to ensure that vested interests could only thrive when they served the general public effectively.

Experience showed that once we had removed a sector's privileges and made it clear that the clock would not be turned back, that group started to focus on removing the privileges of other groups that were holding up its own costs. This dynamic helped greatly in moving the reform agenda further forward.

Credibility. The key to Government credibility during this period was a consistent approach to policy and communication—without it people would have refused to change until the clash between their old behaviours and the new policy imperative had imposed huge costs.

Credibility takes a long time to win but as we saw in our second term it it can be lost overnight. Confidence then collapses and the costs of any adjustments rise.

Letting people know where the reform programme was heading was an important part of the process as it let people know how much time they had to adjust (e.g. GST, lowering of tariffs). In this context the process of change often involved consultation. Having announced our intended direction we then asked for public feedback on specific issues. The confidence of the community was also increased by the use of experts from the private sector, respected for their experience and capability. This approach was welcomed by both decision-makers and opinion-formers in particular, as it contrasted so nicely with the former Government's approach.

Don't blink, public confidence rests on your composure. The first three-year term of the Labour Government involved ministers in some of the most radical decisions announced to the public for 50 years or so. In these circumstances, public confidence in and co-operation with the reform programme could be undermined by the least twitch. Research showed that people became hypersensitive to any signs of uncertainty in the politicians responsible for a particular reform.

Fairness to those least able to cope was a vital ingredient of the programme of reform, for example making lower-income families better off as a result of the change to GST was vital to its acceptance. What constituted fairness—what would deliver real results for low-income people—was where Lange and I finally fell out. We agreed on the goals; we disagreed on the means to achieve those goals.

We might have been able to work the issues through had we each better understood and accepted how the other operated. For my part, having determined the goals I was always prepared to look at all options (means) to achieve them. Hence my 1987 Budget proposals/options paper included a radical option (15c in the dollar, etc.). I enjoyed debate, I didn't necessarily think I would always win but having all the ideas on the table, in my experience, generally led to a better overall outcome.

Lange generally disliked this approach, and I did not realise how much at the time. He had a set of boundaries (i.e. ideas about what he saw as constituting fairness) which he would not go beyond. When Michael Bassett told me that Lange believed I had gone mad shortly after my Budget Options Paper had been put before key ministers I should have gone and discussed the issues with him immediately. Lange, for his part, should have spoken to me directly. Maybe, just maybe, things would have worked out differently.

In the end the most important factor to ensuring the reforms happened could well have been the politicians within Cabinet who had answered the question 'Why am I in politics?' by deciding: "I will do the right thing no matter what the political consequences."

This was in marked contrast to conventional politicians who generally ignore structural reform because they think they are in power to please the people and pleasing people does not involve making hard decisions. They use the latest polls to fine-tune their image and their policies in order to achieve better results in the next poll. Their adherence to policies which focus on immediate problems rather than the country's future opportunities, brings cumulative difficulties. It becomes increasingly clear to people that the problems governments claim they are solving have not been solved and the opportunities to do so have been thrown away. Such governments are, in the end, voted out.

GRAHAM SCOTT

One adviser's view of the economics and politics of economic policy

I can only highlight a few points that seem to me the most important in understanding the economic policies of the first term of the Lange Government. I will highlight the economic situation inherited by the Lange Government, evaluate some of the key policy successes, failures and omissions and conclude with a comment on the legacy. I will go into more detail on the record of the first Lange administration in managing the issue that snookered the Muldoon administration—wage fixing and the emergence from the freeze.

THE ECONOMIC SITUATION INHERITED FROM THE MULDOON GOVERNMENT

If the economy that Sir Robert inherited from the third Labour Government in 1975 was "shattered", as he put it, then it was still shattered when it was inherited by the fourth Labour Government in 1984. Fiscal policy had been thrown into crisis to support the freeze and the tax–wage trade-off. The 1983 Budget speech admitted that the fiscal position was unsustainable. Interest-rate policy had been neutered in the cause of the freeze so that monetary and exchange-rate policies had also been surrendered to the cause of the freeze. Enormous pressures were building for wage and price adjustments. The 'Think Big' investments were falling apart financially. All this was done in the name of 'common sense'.

As a thumbnail, New Zealand in 1984 looked pretty much the way the Asian economies looked before the crisis in the late 1990s—but without the high growth rates and with worse fiscal policy. Warning signs were everywhere and the announcement of the snap election provoked a financial crisis that had been brewing all that year.

In summary, the incoming Labour Government was faced with:

- A fiscal deficit that was too large to be removed by incremental changes in taxes and expenditures under existing policies;
- Public debt and overseas borrowing that were getting to uncomfortable levels and were structured wrongly in terms of risk management;
- Monetary and exchange-rate policy that was technically eccentric and lacked credibility in the markets;
- A highly distortionary freeze on prices, wages and interest rates that was falling apart politically;

- A looming fiscal problem in social policy due to the unaffordability of National Superannuation and pressing priorities in other social areas;
- A system of public management that was bound up in pointless regulations, inward looking, self-sustaining and not sufficiently motivated to increase efficiency and effectiveness;
- A state sector that was deeply engaged in activities for which it was ill-suited and created large demands for fiscal support in many different ways that were inefficient, ineffective and inequitable;
- Feeble mechanisms for accountability and a serious lack of transparency about the activities of government and especially, their financial implications;
- A mendicant private sector accustomed to maximising its income as much by lobbying as by efficient business practices.

There were items on the positive side of the ledger such as the progress with CER and other measures, but these pale beside this list of problems that were passed on.

My perspective on and analysis of this situation was captured in the Treasury Briefing Papers to the Incoming Government in 1984, which I was responsible for preparing as the assistant secretary for the economic policy divisions. These papers extended and rested on a stream of increasingly well-researched advice going back to the 1978 Treasury briefing. Much of what was in the brief had been discussed in the Cabinet Committee on National Development chaired by Rt Hon. Sir William Birch in the early 1980s.

There is no need to go into details of what the 1984 briefing papers said. They were published at the time under the title *Economic Management*. The essential messages were that:

- In economist jargon the markets for goods, finance, foreign exchange and labour were in disequilibrium.
- This had occurred because the Government had violated accepted principles for assigning policy instruments to targets for which they have comparative advantage. Crudely put, this is akin to bringing down helicopters by throwing hand grenades at them—it is ineffective and self-destructive even though hand grenades are very effective when used for the purposes they were designed for.
- As a result, a bad trade-off between growth and stability had been struck and the stability that had been bought was transitory.
- The prescription in the briefing papers was to redesign the role of the Government in these markets in search of a better net benefit from government intervention than was being achieved and a better trade-off between incentives for efficient resource allocation and hence economic growth and macro-economic stability. Given that the State was, in our view, seriously over-extended, this typically meant drawing the State back from where Muldoon had situated it or where it had historically been, especially in the case of State enterprises. Crudely put, the goal was to get the Government out of things it was no good at, such as hands-on management of commercial enterprises, and improve its performance in the places it remained by doing things better, differently or both.
- Our advice was also to attend to the inadequacies of the system of public-

sector management through clarifying goals, providing better information, strengthening incentives to perform and delegating managerial responsibility.
- We were also concerned with the challenges of getting out of the freeze on wages, prices and interest rates.

This advice lined up pretty well with the advice of the Reserve Bank in its areas of responsibility and there were many other sources of advice to the incoming government.

My perspective on the challenges that the Government faced in 1984 and the choices of action it had, have not changed generally, although there is a lot of detail in the advice that I would approach differently today mostly from lessons learned about the practicalities of implementation of large-scale policy programmes.

THE POLICIES

The flood of policy initiatives that the Government took in its first term are thoroughly documented elsewhere and there is a huge amount of literature on what the Government actually did. It has fascinated both the critics and supporters for twenty years.

My candidates for the major initiatives that worked, those that did not and what was overlooked are as follows.

The policies that worked in terms of the goals set for them at the time were:

- GST
- Other tax reforms to broaden the tax base and improve incentives
- Removing agricultural subsidies, including cheap Reserve Bank loans
- Corporatisation of government commercial activities
- Floating the currency
- Rationalising and reducing the incoherent morass of interventions in the financial markets
- Removing loop holes from the income tax system
- Addressing tax expenditures—fiscal subsidies delivered by tax exemptions
- Expenditure reviews
- Although not implemented in the first term of this government, I put the public-sector reforms, for which much of the advice was developed in the first term, high on the list. Some the performance improvements that these later produced were:
- 25 percent drop in the prices of standard administrative services
- drops in processing welfare benefit applications from weeks to over-the-counter service
- addressing captured advice, such as in air transport regulation.

While some senior colleagues felt that the drive to improve performance and accountability weakened traditions of free and frank advice, it seemed to me to depend on which policy area one was in and one's view of just how free and frank advice had actually been in the past. Defence policy advice was a particularly difficult area in which to get clarity on strategic objectives after the collapse of ANZUS and it took a lot of effort there to get agreement on strategies, performance goals and budget classifications.

My list of the policies that were inadequate, did not work, were overlooked or delayed is:

- The introduction of the tax surcharge on superannuation
- Postponing consideration of social policy expenditures to the second term in the hope that economic policy and social policy could be addressed separately once the economy was producing a fiscal growth dividend
- Slowness in getting to grips with the need to reform competition policy
- Inadequate labour market policies that slowed the transition to a more flexible policy framework
- Failure to close the holes in the corporate tax system faster than the vandals could cut new ones.

THE DILEMMA OF THE LABOUR MARKET AND INDUSTRIAL RELATIONS
I want to take a few minutes to comment on some aspects of labour market regulation and industrial relations reform.

Muldoon finally snookered himself in his wages and incomes policy as he was unable to achieve the political arrangements that his policy depended on. He was counting on the leadership of the union movement to use their influence to limit wages growth in exchange for tax concessions. The leadership was unwilling to co-operate in this and was unable to as the constituent unions would not surrender their autonomy for setting wages to the central authorities. Neither were they interested in contributing to the success of Muldoon's strategy even if they could.

So with a Labour Government in power and addressing the same problem of disequilibrium in the labour market, we get a test of whether its supposedly better relationships with the unions enabled it to succeed where Muldoon failed. Or was it a policy that was bound to fail under either government?

The Government was apparently influenced by the Australian examples in setting up the Summit Conference in 1984. The very essence of Australian-style summitry was the deep relationship between the ACTU and the Government. In New Zealand the picture was different. While there were cross-overs between the Labour Party and the union movement, many key union leaders were not powerful figures in the Labour Party—although some were. The most influential figure in the union movement, Ken Douglas, belonged to another party altogether. Some of the unionists who were most influential in the Labour Party were not important figures in the union movement.

Further, the Federation of Labour did not have the power over the constituent unions that the ACTU had at the time in Australia. Ken Douglas and other key players at the time have told me what a disciplined grip the union leadership in Australia had over its affiliates, including its aggressive left, and what a contrast this was to the New Zealand situation. Powerful unions here had made it clear to the FOL headquarters that the days of Skinner and Muldoon doing deals over wage movements were over for good. Jim Knox never had the authority of the man he succeeded as head of the FOL in that respect.

After the election the Government extended the freeze for a few months and implemented a rule under which the unions were free to renegotiate wages 38 months after the last time they had done so, in 1981. The effect of this was to repeat the pattern of the last wage round with the traditional leaders in the front bunch—the Electrical Supply, Metal Trades, Drivers and so on. In 1985 the Beehive took a close interest in the settlements that ended up at an acceptable level of around 10 percent. But when the paid rates in Auckland began settling at higher rates than the public sector it became a problem.

Around the time of the 1986 wage round the Higher Salaries Commission announced a large catch-up settlement that trickled down to lower levels. Teachers refused an offer around 20 percent and went on strike. The dispute went to compulsory arbitration with the Government offering 28 percent and the teachers demanding 34 percent. The tribunal split the difference at 31 percent. The attempt at an orderly exit from the freeze was failing. This had the effect of conditioning the senior ministers to the need for fundamental reform in public-sector wage fixing and set the stage for the State Sector Act as well as spelling the end of compulsory arbitration.

Both Treasury and the Government were concerned that the wage increases would confront tightening monetary and fiscal policy with adverse employment consequences. There were high-level meetings between the Government and the unions but they were ultimately fruitless. Treasury advisers rather half-heartedly advised the Government that a brief return to central controls of wages was an option. I doubt that the idea was taken seriously by the Government. The ministers concluded that deals with the FOL over wage fixing would not work, but nor would a return to controls. The stage was set for a rise in unemployment.

The same political relations between unions and government affected the reform of other regulations in the labour market and industrial relations. There were strong differences of opinion about what was needed here. There were some changes, including removing compulsory arbitration, but the bigger picture is that there was no political framework that would have permitted deeper reform in a deeper way to the labour market institutions that Muldoon had frozen, even if the ministers had agreed on what that should be.

A managed thaw and an extensive modernisation of labour market institutions largely eluded the Lange Government just as it had the Muldoon Government.

THE LEGACY

These economic policy reforms of the Lange Government have cast a long shadow. Three governments have since been elected with what they saw as strong consensus against doing such things, although one of them actually did. In my view when the Bolger Government spent much of its political capital and Hon. Ruth Richardson spent not only her political capital but her political career to arrest an alarming deterioration in the fiscal outlook in 1991 and then went on to institutionalise fiscal responsibility in an act of that name, they did the country a great service. This also brought down the curtain on the era of reform that the Lange Government began.

OECD reports confirm that in the eleven years to 2002 the New Zealand economy grew by 0.5 percent above the OECD average for the first sustained period in decades.

In the measured technical terms of the Treasury, a new generation of advisers there believes the reasons for this are that:

> Institutional and policy reforms since the early 1980s are likely to have raised New Zealand's steady-state level of per capita GDP and the speed at which New Zealand converges to this steady state. The lags in this process mean that the full effects of these changes are likely to still be emerging (The Treasury, New Zealand Economic Growth, April 2004).

In plain language, it was a significant and lasting achievement. However, the report goes on to argue that changes in policy settings are needed if a further improvement of the same magnitude or a bit more is to occur, which is necessary if the Government's growth goals are to be achieved.

There are signs that the political system may be equilibrating at last to this reasoned view of the economic legacy of the Lange administration and its remarkable finance team.

In conclusion, and on a more personal note, I hope the era in which economic policy programmes are defined in terms of their distance from those of the Lange Government is drawing to a close. History may not reflect well on the stream of speeches lambasting the "failed policies of the 1980s and 1990s"—although some criticisms of the policies are valid. All policy programmes have unintended side effects: things go wrong, and governments eventually lose their coherence, tire and die. New Zealand was fortunate to have such a talented Cabinet at such a critical moment—one that was willing and able to make fundamental changes to our economic policies and institutions.

DAVID CAYGILL
Industry policy

Much has been written concerning the general economic policies of the fourth Labour Government: its pursuit of financial deregulation, the floating of the dollar, taxation reform, its approach to state-owned enterprises and so on.

In this paper I concentrate on one narrow aspect only of the Government's economic actions: the area of industry policy. I do this for several reasons: first, because this area has been considered less often in the past; second, it was the area for which I had personal responsibility between 1984 and 1987; and third, there were some differences in the approach taken in this area as compared to that employed in the wider fields of macro-economic management. I thought it might be fruitful to explore these differences as well as to record the major actions taken and their rationale.

INDUSTRY POLICY DEFINED

First a brief word of background to the area I mean to cover. During the 1980s there was a flurry of debate over the appropriateness of countries adopting industrial policies.[1] By industrial policy I am referring to "the activities of Government that are intended to develop or retrench various industries in a national economy in order to maintain global competitiveness".[2]

The term 'industry policy' was often used pejoratively to imply a degree of intervention in, or targeting of, specific sectors, with the aim of encouraging growth within those particular industries. It was also used to encompass a wide variety of measures, including tax breaks, research grants or incentives, regional development assistance and direct subvention payments. In this sense it may be said that the fourth Labour Government did not have an industrial policy. Far from encouraging such forms of assistance, in the causes of fiscal necessity and neutrality we set about reducing them.

Perhaps in one other sense the existence of such a policy may be questioned. That is, there was nowhere a single coherent statement of Labour's approach to industry. As we will see, the Government's approaches to industry focused largely on the removal of barriers to competition, both at the country's border and within New Zealand, but one could look in vain for an overall outline of the anticipated impact of these measures, or, indeed, for a clear statement of what lay ahead. Instead a pattern of decisions accumulated as review followed review, and gradually—inexorably—the nation's manufacturers were exposed to competition they had not felt for 50 years.

Here I seek to tell the story of what happened in the first three years of that Government. I offer an insider's perspective, and hope to identify both the key decisions and their rationale.

MACROECONOMIC POLICY

While my focus here is on the policy changes of particular moment to industry, undoubtedly the decisions which affected industry more than any others were those that imposed change on the economy as a whole. The initial devaluation and the floating of the dollar, for example, set international prices on a market basis without the risks previously involved in a fixed exchange rate. The reduction in government borrowing and hence interest rates, as the Government sought to restore balance to its fiscal accounts, and financial deregulation gave business easier access to cheaper capital. The transformation of the tax system, both the lowering of marginal tax rates and the introduction of a comprehensive indirect tax in GST, reduced its tax burden. The long-drawn-out battle against inflation had a favourable impact on wage and other costs. The corporatisation of the Government's trading activities lowered the cost to manufacturers of inputs such as coal, electricity and rail freight. And changes to the labour market, although smaller than what was to follow later, were also useful.

In many cases, while industry was troubled by the opening of its markets, its principal concerns lay not with what was happening at the micro or industry level, but with macro New Zealand policy and indeed the international arena. While the author was involved in these areas, they are not the focus of this paper. However, they undoubtedly shaped the environment in which industry policy changes (principally the removal of price controls and import licensing and the reduction of tariffs) took place.

THE STATE OF MANUFACTURING IN 1984

Like much of the rest of New Zealand in 1984, industry was uncertain but expectant. The previous decade had seen continuing advocacy of economic deregulation from the likes of the Planning Council, and tentative steps in that direction. For example, the tendering of import licences had been announced in 1979, but did not begin until 1981. Industry plans had been put in place by the Tariff Review Board and the Industries Development Commission. There was a growing sense that New Zealand's destiny lay outside its shores.

By 1981–82 manufacturing exports were claimed to be 14.6 percent of turnover,[3] but I suspect this figure includes meat processing because the same paper claims manufacturing's contribution to total exports at 30 percent. More typical export ratios were 10 percent. And the conviction that one needed a domestic base before attempting to export was still widespread. In other words, while New Zealand industry was beginning to lift its sights beyond this country, the task of reorienting industry to the larger opportunities overseas was still in its infancy.

Of key significance was the fact that CER had been negotiated in 1982. The treaty came into force on 1 January 1983. This led to much anxiety amongst manufacturers. Some industry leaders (notably Earl Richardson and Don Rowlands) saw the ultimate removal of trans-Tasman barriers as an opportunity rather than a threat.

Richardson, in particular, made a connection between opening up to Australia and the wider reduction of import barriers. To open New Zealand markets to Australia, as CER required, but to remain protected against other countries' exports would, he argued, "hand our market to Australia on a plate". Correspondingly, if New Zealand exporters were to take advantage of opening access to Australia they would be competing there against the rest of the world.

So New Zealand cost structures would need to be addressed, and this would have to include addressing import barriers. On many occasions in the next six years the requirements of CER would be used to justify a wider opening to the rest of the world, on the footing that if manufacturers were having to face competition from Australia, then they could just as easily (or at least justifiably) face competition from everywhere else.

The use of CER in this way, to put pressure on New Zealand's wider import barriers, depended crucially on the fact that the CER Agreement did not require any preferential margin against third parties. Apart from some minor provisions, neither Australia nor New Zealand had made commitments to favour its neighbour over anyone else. They had merely agreed to lower barriers against the other. Another way of expressing this point is that CER was a free-trade agreement, not a customs union. There was no commitment to establish common external tariffs. In the early 1980s there was indeed some suggestion that CER might later develop into a customs union, but this talk was to be rejected by the New Zealand Labour Government—rightly in my view. Any prospect of retaining common barriers against third parties would have been seized by manufacturers (on both sides of the Tasman) as a way of avoiding adjustment.

The extent to which New Zealand industry was protected by high tariffs and import licensing had been established earlier in 1984 by the Syntec report into "The structure of industry assistance in New Zealand". This concluded:

- the average effective rate of protection for the manufacturing sector was in the vicinity of 40 percent.
- About 25 percent of New Zealand's total imports were subject to import licence. At least half represented components, equipment and materials.
- While import duty approximated only five percent of the total value of imports, it was approximately 16 percent as an average rate of duty on dutiable goods.
- Export incentives were a pre-tax subsidy equivalent to $433.5m in 1982/83. There were 11 different programmes or forms of assistance or subsidy.

Other studies reached similar or related conclusions; for example, BERL (reporting to ManFed in November 1985) summarised their conclusion this way: "Reducing import protection has two major effects for households: lower prices (and) reduced money income (lower wages). The two offset one another—with a small net benefit accruing to households through the price benefits being a little larger." (Given that conclusion it is perhaps unsurprising that the copy of this report on my files is labelled "Confidential—not for publication.")

In June 1985 Ralph Lattimore, a lecturer in economics at Lincoln College (as it then was), wrote: "A clear picture of the structure, conduct and performance of major industries and policies ... is not available. The inertia and vested interest in the status quo makes it most likely that the past policy cycle will repeat itself at a large cost to society as a whole ...". He noted that the farm sector was a notable exception (to the lack of a clear picture).

Reflecting on changes made since the change of Government, Lattimore commented: "In contrast to the change in agricultural policy, import policy continues to be negotiated. Sectors with Industry Development Plans and the oil refining industry will not be subject to general policy changes." This was perfectly true. Instead we dealt with industries one by one, starting with the motor vehicle industry.

1984

The "big bang" with which the fourth Labour Government commenced has been well described by others. The freezing of the exchange rate, followed by the devaluation and the removal of financial controls made an impact that resounded throughout the country and for long afterwards. Indeed, its surprise created the mythology that much of what followed was unplanned, in the sense that the direction of the Government was set by those initial events in a way which remained beyond the control of a majority of ministers, let alone the Caucus. This is nonsense. It does not do justice to the thinking which had preceded the elections, nor to the robustness of Cabinet debates after them. But to some extent it is true that at an early stage new ministers at least were feeling their way. A good example of this occurred within the trade and industry portfolio, where the events of 1984 set a path for what followed. The first to be noted were fiscal decisions incorporated in Labour's first Budget. In August 1984, Cabinet agreed that the Export Performance Taxation Incentive was to be phased out between 1985 and 1987, i.e. over the same time period as had been previously agreed in relation to Australia. This meant that the value of export incentives was halved from 1 April 1985, halved again from 1 April 1986, and withdrawn altogether from 1 April 1987. By September 1987, export assistance to manufacturers in total amounted to $22.5m, compared to their gross earnings of $33b.

Much of the rest of that first year was taken up with two industries that had been under review by the previous government at the point of the snap elections: motor vehicles, and wheat and flour.

THE MOTOR VEHICLE INDUSTRY

This industry had been under review since 1981. The terms of reference had asked the Industries Development Commission to "recommend a development plan for the motor vehicle industry which meets the Government's objective of *retaining* (my emphasis) the motor vehicle assembly and automotive component manufacturing industries, improving its efficiency, and ensuring that future investment within the industry constitutes an efficient use of resources from the national viewpoint ...".

The Commission had reported to the Government in April 1983 (a year after the original deadline) and the previous Government announced its decisions on 25 June 1984, just three weeks before the snap election. So Labour found itself reviewing the review. We also consulted with our new Australian colleagues, who had expressed an interest in this matter before the elections. (Lionel Bowen, the

Australian Deputy PM, rang me during the election campaign to indicate their desire for such talks. He was most gracious when his name meant nothing to my busy campaign office!)

In December 1984 the results of the further review were announced following negotiations with Australia which took place in Melbourne with my counterpart Industry Minister Senator Button. Highlights included the doubling of access for New Zealand motor vehicle components into Australia and the reduction of sales tax for most vehicles and motor cycles (offsetting the impact of the July devaluation). Tariff and licence-free access both ways across the Tasman by 1995 was agreed to. In other words, motor vehicles were brought under CER.

More fundamentally, from a longer-term perspective, the review announced gradually increasing access for imports of built-up vehicles, components and parts and accessories (i.e. from non-Australian sources) and the phasing down of tariff rates on the CKD ("completely knocked-down") packs from which New Zealand cars were assembled. Tariffs on CKD packs were to fall from 45 percent to 15 percent over four years. It was at this time also that the rules were changed to allow import licences for both new and used vehicles (though the real flood of second-hand cars didn't occur until after the removal of import licensing in 1989). Motor vehicles were also removed from price control.

Although the Australian Labor Government was also engaged in broadly similar economic changes, there was a significant difference in approach to the motor vehicle sector (and indeed other industries) between the two countries. Australia attempted to rationalise motor vehicle production down to a particular number of assemblers. New Zealand at this stage had 10 companies running 14 plants. We took no view as to the number of plants or models that ought to be available. (The difference is strikingly paralleled by Australia's approach to banking deregulation, where Paul Keating similarly sought to limit the number of banking licences, whereas New Zealand left that to be determined by "the market".)

Although outside our period of interest, the Motor Vehicle Plan was reviewed again following the elections in 1987 and motor vehicles were removed from import licensing altogether as from 1 January 1989, i.e. only six months later than goods not covered by industry plans, a step that had been almost inconceivable five years earlier.

WHEAT AND FLOUR

I don't intend to deal in detail here with agriculture, which in many ways faced adjustments as great as, or greater than, industry. This was not my primary focus. However, I watched with admiration the efforts of Colin Moyle, especially the programme that in effect reviewed farm mortgage liabilities farm by farm after the removal of farm price supports reduced farm values and equity. The story of this programme has been little told and is today much less well understood than, for example, the fact of the removal of SMPs, but is far more remarkable and important.

The reason farming survived the removal of subsidies as well as it did was because farm debt was written off, not just by the state-owned rural bank, but by private lenders as well. In many ways the removal of subsidies was the easy decision, driven as it was by the need to restore balance to the country's budget. Dealing with the consequences of that decision was much more challenging and time-consuming, and not the least of the consequences was the constant pressure from the farm sector for a speedier opening to lower-cost imports.

Where I did find myself interfacing with the rural sector was over the review of the wheat and flour-milling sector, which, to my surprise, came under Trade and Industry because of the "industrial" connotations of milling flour. This review was underway at the change of Government and was one of my first orders of business. It was also affected by CER, because of its implication that by 1995 Australian wheat would be able to be imported duty free.

It wasn't the duty that was the problem. In 1984 no one could import wheat at all, other than the Wheat Board. And no one could mill flour without a licence from the Wheat Board, who then purchased all flour. But anyone could grow wheat, which the Board was obliged to purchase—and, as one might expect, wheat was grown in the strangest of places. Wheat was grown in Southland, for example, on land which today is used far more productively for dairy cattle. The result (which didn't matter while no one could compete) was often poor-quality wheat and flour. Indeed the standard flour was described universally as FAQ, which stood for "fair average quality". "Everything goes" might have been more accurate.

Bearing in mind particularly the impending prospect of duty-free competition from Australia we decided to phase out import controls over four years and the requirement to operate through the Wheat Board. Farmers were more apprehensive of the power of local flour millers (especially Goodman Fielder) than they were of Australian competition, which they saw as a distant threat. In relation to Goodman's perceived monopoly powers, the stronger provisions of the forthcoming Commerce Act were a useful response (see below).

However, almost as soon as controls were eased farmers were asking for their removal to be accelerated. It appeared that a situation where some farmers could bypass the Wheat Board and some could not was more awkward or inequitable than complete freedom. So a further review was conducted. This led to the passage of the Wheat Board Amendment Act 1986, which provided for controls on the production and marketing of wheat to end on 31 January 1987, at which point the Wheat Board went out of existence.

Later the tobacco growing industry was similarly reviewed and exposed to competition from imports—much to Bill Rowling's consternation.

To complete the record of my involvement with matters agricultural, I should also mention the review of town milk supply. Reform began with the abolition of the consumer milk price subsidy, announced in the 1984 Budget. Then we commissioned a wider report from the Industries Development Commission. While this was still being debated, in October 1986 I announced the removal of controls on milk packaging, allowing the sale of milk in cartons for the first time. This greatly encouraged the sale of milk by supermarkets, leading eventually to the removal of the obligation to provide home delivery. (The Milk Board was abolished in 1988 along with the Poultry Board.)

THE COMMERCE ACT 1986

Much of 1985 was spent revising the previous Labour Government's general competition legislation (i.e. the Commerce Act 1975). This proposal stirred up considerable controversy, not so much in Parliament as amongst policy advisors. Its revision was driven in the first instance less by any sense that it would contribute to a wider programme of reform, than by the sense amongst Trade and Industry officials (at least) that it was in need of renovation.

The amended legislation proposed two major changes. First it altered the administrative structures used to oversee mergers and monopolies. The investigative and administrative functions which had previously rested with an independent civil servant, the Examiner of Commercial Practices, were combined with the quasi-judicial functions of the Commerce Commission.

Second, and more substantively, the previous law was amended by deleting provisions which had seldom been used, such as the powers to require compulsory disinvestment by monopolies, and provisions against "profiteering" that were, arguably, both ill-defined and over-bearing. The new Act also changed the basis on which mergers were to be approved and restrictive trade practices scrutinised, to come into line with overseas terminology and practice.

In many respects the changes closely followed the Australian Trade Practices Act 1974, although there were significant differences that to some extent have remained contentious, notably the decision to require prior approval of mergers (whereas Australian scrutiny operates ex post). The Act also included a provision repealing price control on many items, e.g. sheet window glass. It eventually came into force on 1 May 1986.

As ministers debated these proposals, Treasury in particular expressed strong reservations. They were not unhappy, I believe, with the Bill's administrative changes, but rather with the new emphasis on anti-competitive behaviour and the acquisition of dominance in markets. Treasury's concern was "to ensure that the rules focused ... on the issue of contestability and did not become confused with past approaches to competition and efficiency (e.g. market concentration) which were based on an inadequate understanding of economic behaviour".[4] Or, to put the matter in the language used by the Reserve Bank: "Where markets are contestable there is no need for interference."[5]

Two views were in contention. To some extent they were different views about the future, and to some extent they were different because of a different starting point or analytic framework. One saw trade liberalisation, the review and reduction of business regulation and a more business-like approach to state enterprise as enhancing competition. The other view saw this reduction in regulation as increasing the risk of "private regulation" and hence as a justification for stronger controls.

In the end the decision to proceed with the new Commerce Act had less to do with competing approaches to competition policy and more with the impact that these changes might have on the other reforms then underway. That is to say, the key question was how to manage the transition to a more open and competitive economy.

I saw a modernised, and in some respects stronger, competition law as a useful lever to prise open the many regulated sectors. In March 1986, for example, in a note to Sir Ron Trotter responding to the NZBR's concerns at the bill, I wrote:

> Wheat farmers, flour millers, dairy workers, egg producers, milk treatment station proprietors and petrol resellers have all placed reliance on the Commerce Bill as a precondition to deregulation of their sector. On the other hand, lawyers, real estate agents and sharebrokers have all been influenced in their decision to voluntarily deregulate by the prospect of the Commerce Bill.

The revised Commerce Act was followed by the Fair Trading Act. This replaced the previous law governing misleading and deceptive trading conduct and unfair trade practices, contained in the Consumer Information Act 1969 and other statutes. It also took a step towards legal harmonisation with Australia, following their Trade Practices Act 1974. Both new laws provided new rights to bring private actions. (Although these have subsequently been little used, at the time I thought them a useful safety valve.)

IMPORT LICENSING

Now let me turn to the broad programmes which occupied most of my time and that of my advisors, as well as that of interested parties: namely, the reduction and ultimate elimination of New Zealand's exceptionally high levels of border protection in the form of import licensing and tariffs. The phase-down and ultimate removal of import licensing was perhaps the Government's single most important industry policy change—on a par with floating of the currency in the broader economic sphere. Unlike the float, however, there was no single dramatic decision. Rather removal of protection was conducted by painstaking reviews of each separate industry and a seemingly inexorable move in only one direction. Gradually the volume of goods subject to import licence tendering increased. In turn, the premium levels disclosed in each tender round were then used to assess the "need" for continued licence protection.

Import licence tendering was first announced (by Sir Robert Muldoon) in the 1979 Budget. It was introduced in 1981, but by 1984 was still in only limited use. This greatly expanded under Labour, until eventually licensing was removed altogether. But for a time the tendering of import licences was a major activity of the Trade and Industry Department—just as price control had been previously. Many refinements were introduced: to the payment of deposits, the cancellation of unused licences, and the availability of "continuity" licences between licence periods. By February 1987 we were up to Tender Round 43.

In March 1985, 340 categories of goods were placed on licence on demand; that is, licences were freely available for anyone who applied. In September 1985, decisions were announced covering both import licensing and tariffs, flowing from a series of meetings with the Manufacturers Federation, Federated Farmers, the Retailers Federation and the Bureau of Importers and Exporters.

From 1 July 1986, items with average successful premiums of 7.5 percent or less in the two previous rounds of general tendering (i.e. in 1985 and 1986) would move to licence on demand. LOD would then operate for one year (rather than two as previously intended). In 1986 the decision was taken to eliminate all import licensing outside industry plans on 1 July 1988. And by October 1987, only footwear, clothing and motor vehicles lacked import licensing end dates. (An end to import licensing of motor vehicles was announced in the December 1987 'flat tax' package and footwear and apparel were also dealt with in the second term.)

In June 1987 I wrote to *Business Week* in response to an article by Alan Blinder (then Professor of Economics at Princeton) advocating the auctioning of import quotas. The article had made no reference to New Zealand (or Australia, which had a similar means of allocating tariff quotas), so I pointed out our experience of the past six years, concluding: "the tender system has proved effective both as a means of allocating import licences and as a means for dismantling a form of protection which we believe to have outlived its usefulness".

TARIFFS

Now let me turn from import licensing to New Zealand's other form of protection, namely tariffs. In September 1985 we announced that all tariffs above 25 percent were to be reduced on 1 July 1986 by five percent and again on 1 July 1987 by 10 percent. I believe these were the first across-the-board tariff reductions in New Zealand's history. Early in 1988 there was to be a further review of tariff policy, by which time it was envisaged that import licensing outside industry plans would have substantially disappeared. I said: "The Government has chosen a middle course between the views of manufacturers (who had argued for more time to adjust to CER and the phase-out of import licensing) and farmers (who had argued for faster reductions in tariffs)."

Part of the Economic Statement made to Parliament on 12 December 1985 dealt again with import protection. Tariffs on goods not made in New Zealand were reduced to zero as from 1 July 1986. This affected about 500 products. After this, I was deputed to have further discussions with Man Fed with a view to further tariff reductions on products of particular interest to agriculture. These discussions took some time. The relationship with manufacturers was understandably not an easy one. Many were deeply suspicious of the Government's ultimate intentions. Much discussion took place over just how far the Government intended to go. For example, in June 1986 the President of Man Fed called for "an expression of final Government intent on the cutting of import protection for manufacturing. We want to know where it's going to stop. What's the bottom line?"

On the other hand, three months later Sir Lawrence Stevens was writing to the Prime Minister: "Earl (Richardson) and I were pleased to learn from Mr Caygill that in fact there is no 'bottom line'." This was in the context of their concern that the Government may have already fixed 'the bottom line' for tariffs and that this may not be adequate. Through all my many meetings with industry, Federated Farmers and Treasury kept up equal pressure to move forward.

INDUSTRY PLANS

In this work we were greatly assisted by the advice in particular of the Industries Development Commission. This was chaired by Ted Tarrant. It had been set up in 1975 by the Rowling Government, replacing the Tariff and Development Board. It undertook a programme of individual industry studies. By 1984 it had studied about half of the manufacturing industries.

Ted's advice to the Economic Summit Conference that year and privately to me was: "Do not think in terms of efficient and non-efficient industries. Within every industry you can find inefficient companies and efficient ones." At the conference Tarrant pointed to four factors standing in the way of progress: the cost of distribution, including transport; many parts of the economy were overmanned; the lack of sufficient skills in many parts of the workforce; and finally, "our reluctance to change".

The industries covered by industry plans (of which there were still 16 in March 1987) were addressed individually. But all industry had an interest in the outcome, not just as a signal of how they might be treated when their turn came, but also because many manufactured products are inputs into other products. So as import licence and tariff protection was reduced those who were exposed to greater competition became all the more concerned to see the cost of their inputs fall.

Many industry plans had arisen because in the mid-1970s a tariff review committee had been unable to recommend tariffs for the industries concerned which would provide a similar level of protection to that afforded by import licensing. Many plans were small (e.g. margarine, cement) and their reviews proceeded with little fuss. So, for example, electric motors came off import licence on 1 September 1986 at the conclusion of the Electric Motor Industry Plan. Other plans covered ceramics, plastics, textiles, footwear, glass, starch, canned fruit, and wine.

A good example of the plan review decisions relates to the cement industry. In New Zealand (as elsewhere at that time) there were just two major players. They were keen to be removed from price control. The unions who represented their workforce were not. On this occasion I met with all the parties and announced that from 1 August 1986 cement would be simultaneously removed from price control (notwithstanding the advice of the Commerce Commission, which recommended its retention) and import licensing, and import tariffs were to be set at zero. I also counselled the unions that if the industry did not play fair they should let me know. They did not come back to me.

PRICE CONTROL

At the time of the Economic Summit Conference no fewer than 36 goods and services were under price control—apart from the general price control imposed by the Muldoon "freeze". This separate form of control applied, for example, to cement, window glass, drugs, apples and pears, bananas, canned foods, eggs, neutral spirit, oranges, sugar, frozen vegetables, aluminium, metal pipes, ceramic tableware, milk, motor vehicles, pharmaceuticals, butter, steel, steel pipes, steel wire, flour, bran and pollard, natural gas.

One by one each of these was reviewed and each was the subject of a recommendation to the Cabinet. By 30 April 1986 there were just nine items remaining under price control. On that date window glass, apples and pears, canned foods, frozen vegetables, metal pipes and pipe fittings (other than those made by NZ Steel), wire, ceramic tableware, sugar, wheat broking and manufactured gas were all removed from price control.

Butter was removed from price control on 1 August 1986. We also revoked the

Butter and Cheese Marketing Regulations 1948, removing controls on the wholesale distribution of butter. (Why there were ever controls on the distribution of butter was something I never discovered.)

We also repealed the Margarine Act 1908. Yes, there was such a law, just as there was a margarine industry plan. Indeed, not only was there a Margarine Act, but also Margarine Regulations, promulgated in 1940, which amongst other things required the Minister in considering an application for a licence to manufacture margarine to take into account the likely effect on the demand for butter. The Minister could fix the maximum quantity of margarine that could be manufactured in the premises being licensed. Repeal of the Margarine Act was announced in April 1987, at same time as tariffs were reduced and import licensing increased, to be phased out altogether by January 1990.

By April 1987 the only items still under price control were a number of steel items and wholesale natural gas. Steel went off price control with its import liberalisation, but natural gas stayed under control until the 1990s.

REPEAL OF THE ECONOMIC STABILISATION ACT

One of the highlights of the 1984–87 term, at least symbolically, was the repeal of the instrument by which previous governments had done so much damage, the notorious Economic Stabilisation Act 1948. The review of regulations made under it and its ultimate repeal had been a specific plank of Labour's 1984 Manifesto. Once again, rather than announcing any sweeping reform, each of these regulations was reviewed on its own merits and each in turn was repealed.

I well recall the case of the Economic Stabilisation (Return of Bread) Regulations. Strangely, these had been drawn to my attention by a constituent, who came to see me with the unusual complaint of harassment at his workplace. Apparently he had "potted" one of his workmates for breaching the regulations; that is, for selling bread on a "sale or return" basis. This is when I discovered that the 1972–75 Labour Government had outlawed this practice in an effort to conserve wheat, or perhaps from a desire to reduce the need for its importation. Such policy objectives no longer seemed appropriate and the Cabinet agreed to solve my constituent's problem (not that I presented the issue on this basis) by repealing the prohibition.

By 1986 only five Orders in Council under the act remained. It seemed time to turn to the underlying statute. Accordingly, a bill repealing it was introduced. I sought in vain to excite some interest in Parliament: "The Government believes that the type of regulatory control epitomised by the previous use of this act has no place in modern and effective economic management. No Government should pretend to achieve solutions to its economic problems through repressing the symptoms. The bill (I argued) removes one of the last symbols of the failed policies of the past." In response only three submissions were made to the Select Committee and no one wanted to appear. The bill was reported back unchanged. The last remaining regulations still in force were repealed as it came into law.

THE EXTENSION OF CER

Another major focus of activity was the negotiations with Australia to extend CER to include the sectors originally (and quite sensibly) left for later consideration when the Treaty was agreed in 1982, i.e. steel, motor vehicles, apparel, textiles, footwear, tobacco and sugar. Australian interest lay initially in addressing motor vehicles and steel. But although motor vehicles were the subject of early progress, Australia went cold on steel. It seemed that they were uncomfortable about NZ Steel, whose support from the New Zealand Government, they argued, was an unfair subsidy. This was ironic given how reluctant we were to spend another cent on the plant. Ultimately the prospect of its sale removed the stumbling block. Meanwhile we tackled each of the "TCF" (textiles, clothing and footwear) trio in turn, and eventually tobacco, and sugar. The first five issues (i.e. cars, steel and TCF) were pursued with Australian John Button and the latter two with his countryman John Kerin. Both were excellent to deal with.

Several opportunities arose to pursue these matters in the context of Australian reviews of their own industry plans. For example, in November 1986 we reached agreement with Australia (following Caygill/Button negotiations) for the inclusion of apparel in CER (at same time as the Australian TCF plan was released in Canberra). The quantity of New Zealand apparel exports New Zealand exporters were entitled to send to Australia was increased by $A10m (from $A13.7m) as from 1 January 1988. New Zealand granted the same amount of exclusive access for Australian clothing exports to New Zealand. Both tariffs and quantitative controls were to be eliminated by 1995 (i.e. the original full CER implementation date).[6]

Another difficult issue was the removal of preferences offered by the Australian state governments in favour of domestic bids for their government contracts. This latter issue was taken up by officials and ministers, in particular at the Australian Industry and Technology Council meeting in Brisbane in November 1985. In effect this was a meeting of State and Federal Industry ministers plus New Zealand. At that meeting Australian ministers agreed in principle to the elimination of their state government purchasing preferences on an inter-state basis from 1 July 1986. New Zealand foreshadowed reciprocity, i.e. it was willing to treat Australian bids as New Zealand if we got the same treatment in reverse. Thereafter we sought and ultimately obtained New Zealand participation in their National Preferences Agreement.

The Australian use of bounty (subsidy) payments was even more problematic. By 1984/85 these had reached $A264m. Most bounties applied only to production sold on the Australian domestic market (but nevertheless these affected the ability of New Zealand exporters to compete in Australia (e.g. steel, yarns) and constituted inputs into exports to New Zealand). Three bounty schemes, namely shipbuilding, electric motors and computer hardware and software, extended to direct exports. A joint working group of officials met at the end of 1986 and produced a combined report. Ultimately, in my view, bounties were phased out because of the distorting effect they had within Australia and because of their fiscal cost, rather than because of CER considerations.

MISCELLANEOUS MEASURES

This completes this sketch of the major policy changes adopted in pursuit of the objectives of raising the efficiency off New Zealand industry and thereby enhancing the country's economic performance. Along the way a number of smaller steps were taken to modernise procedures or reduce inequities. For example, the Industry Safeguards Bill 1986 regularised the approach to dumping and countervailing duty, i.e. the response to overseas subsidies and market imbalances. It replaced the previous Emergency Protection Authority and followed a similar arrangement in Australia. Also in 1986 New Zealand accepted the GATT Anti-dumping Code.

The DFC was reconstituted as a company under the Companies Act. The Industrial Design Council was given a final grant (of $650,000) for 1987/88 and told to act "under a commercial mandate". The Standards Association was encouraged to pursue commercial opportunities, i.e. told to operate on a reduced government grant.

Fruit Distributors Ltd lost their monopoly import rights over pineapples, grapes and some citrus fruits (bananas and oranges came later).

And we commenced work to be completed in our second term, e.g. the deregulation of petroleum distribution and the Marsden Point Refinery's import monopoly, and the domestic purchasing and import monopoly of the Apple and Pear Board (and its tax-free status).

I am conscious that this survey has still not addressed many areas. For example, I have said nothing here of the wind-down of the Think Big projects, even though they were certainly substantial industrial plants. Partly this is because Roger Douglas largely addressed these matters and partly because the main rationale for reform was the need for fiscal savings, although there were undoubtedly wider efficiency benefits as well.

Nor in respect of tariff policy have I mentioned the SPARTECA agreement with the Pacific Islands (in effect a one-way free-trade deal that obliged New Zealand to accept island exports duty free, whilst imposing no reciprocal obligation). This agreement encouraged some manufacturing to relocate to islands like Fiji, but was not a significant component of our own reform programme.

Similarly the review of the Generalised System of Preferences (that provided for lower tariff rates on goods from developing countries) was a matter of concern to New Zealand industry, but was not a significant aspect of our own approach to industry policies.

Let me finish instead with a story that attempts to put a human face on these abstract policy decisions. In May 1986 a doctor in Hastings wrote asking for an import licence to replace his three-year-old Volvo that had recently suffered fire damage. He needed a car to sustain his practice, but as he and his wife had six children it needed to be a Volvo station wagon. New ones weren't available in New Zealand and he wanted to bring one into the country? As on many such occasions, the task of replying fell to my able and hard-working under-secretary, Peter Neilson. His reply was very correct. It observed that in the past the answer would have had to be "No", but now a private individual could access the licence tendering scheme. He noted that the premiums had fallen from 27 percent to just four percent in the latest round.

And the final word should come from the Prime Minister. At some point in these tumultuous years David Lange wrote: "The main thrust of the Government's economic policy is to provide an environment in which the responsibility for decisions rests with the parties involved." Exactly.

KEN DOUGLAS
What were the real issues?

Of the four million population of our country, approximately 1.2 million were not born at the time of the 1984 General Election. That to me is sobering, in that how will those 1.2 million people view the fourth Labour Government now or in another 20 years?

We all have difficulty in making such assessments because of the interconnection between the immediate influences of the pre-1984 election period, the Muldoon era, the changing global conditions and the fact that many elements of change are still evolving. Nothing exists in isolation, and so with politics. My aim is not intended to look for blame, but to understand.

Even before election day the Lange Government had created huge expectations. These expectations were largely based on the very real experience of the previous nine years. What was real was that the economy was not only in stagnation but in danger of imploding. Muldoon had slowly but finally offended everyone and all sections of society. He not only attacked and scapegoated unionists and communists but also journalists and, finally, significant sections of the National Party's own electoral base. His time proved that a strong dictator image did not sit well with the New Zealand psyche.

David Lange was seen as a 'breath of fresh air' in the body politic of New Zealand and people flocked to hear and see him and to join his party. There was a very real surge of people suddenly becoming interested and invigorated in politics. Muldoon's National Party was publicly perceived as having no solutions.

- The 1981 Wage–Price Freeze had become the mechanism that pushed the economy into virtual stultification.
- The 1982 Wage–Tax trade-off was rejected by the Federation of Labour and the Combined State Unions.

A long-term Wage Reform working party was established to attempt to:

1 Find a mechanism to come out of the Wage Freeze and
2 To construct an alternative to the concepts of:

- A centralised wage-fixing apparatus;
- Compulsory arbitration; and
- The rigid relativity system that was the core of the Industrial Conciliation and Arbitration Act.

What is often overlooked in examining developments in New Zealand's industrial relations is the fact that the combination of the Industrial Conciliation and Arbitration Act, the Economic Stabilisation Regulations and the General Wage Order provisions were the instruments of government control of the whole internal economy. They provided the mechanisms that set the process for price escalations for all regulated industry changes, contract adjustments and service charge variations.

Some people have suggested that the 1984 election was a surprise and that Labour was not ready. I don't agree.

Lange's election as Labour Party Leader was a conscious preparation for an election as soon as possible (replacing Bill Rowling). As early as 1981–82 the Joint Council of Labour (made up of the Parliamentary Labour Party leadership, the Party leadership and the Federation of Labour National Executive) had started work on identifying critical points of a policy framework for an election. The change in the Labour Party presidency from Anderton to Margaret Wilson was similarly an element of that preparation and the significant revitalisation of the Party's structure. There are other examples that could be found as well as the public media record.

I have found it instructive in preparing for this paper to refer back to specific key documents in attempting to unravel the analysis required.

I have already referred to the Wage–Tax trade-off proposal. The second document that is relevant is the official 'Labour Party Election Policy Release'. This document was very widely distributed and became the core reference for identification of the post-election intentions of the fourth Labour Government. In short, it was the Party's promise of what it would do.

Popular mythology is that Brother Roger hijacked the Cabinet and governmental process. I do not subscribe to this hijack theory. Direct participants in that Cabinet have spoken about the unity, purpose and direction of the Cabinet. I don't believe in conspiracy theories or that the process was driven by inherently evil people.

I make this point because in late 1983 the Federation of Labour Research Officer, Gary Bevan (Alf Kirk had gone off to David Lange's Office) had a series of discussions with Doug Andrews, Lange's Economic Advisor, from which he developed a report to me in early January 1984. That report was startling. He had, after drafting the report, gone back and checked the detail with Doug Andrews, who confirmed its accuracy.

This became known as the 'Bevan Report' and set out the detail of what was to become known as 'Rogernomics'. This report caused a furore inside the Federation of Labour as to what it meant and became the only major point of difference between Jim Knox as president and myself. When reported to the National Executive there was similar confusion, anger and frustration. Many of the executive, including Knox, did not want to believe it and openly espoused that it was a fabrication.

Likewise many union leaders, because of the nearly three years of the Wage Freeze, were desperate to want to believe that Labour would save them. In my view herein lies much of the subsequent problem of the trade union movement.

A meeting of the Joint Council of Labour was scheduled for early March and Knox reluctantly agreed at my insistence to have the matter tabled there. Margaret

Wilson was in the chair and she agreed that it was necessary to get its authenticity and status resolved.

At the meeting, which was attended by the President, Secretary and Industrial Liaison Officer of the Labour Party, David Lange, Geoffrey Palmer, Stan Rodger, Roger Douglas and one or two other shadow Cabinet ministers—Lange and Palmer proceeded to perform a two-actor farce:

Lange—"Have you seen this document Geoffrey?" "No David I have not," replies Palmer.

"David have you seen this document?" asks Geoffrey. "No Geoffrey I have not," is the response.

Jim Knox was quick to give me a "told you so" nod and supports David Lange's response, "Well that's behind us now" (reaching behind him to put his copy on the servery behind his chair).

Lange then proposed a special working party be set up to draft agreed policy principles for an economic rebuilding programme. After some debate as to whether or not the Labour Party should be included, Roger/Palmer from the parliamentary team, Peter Harris from Combined State Unions and myself from the Federation of Labour were appointed. The group met regularly for the next three to four months either at Peter Harris's house or Stan Rodgers' office.

Whilst the policy principles developed by this group were reflected in the official Labour Party Election Programme, they were never able to be put into effect because of the events surrounding the so-called 'monetary crisis and devaluation debacle' over the days following the election day outcome.

These events led to some interesting insights into the complexity of David Lange as a personality. Nobody can doubt the intellectual capacity of Lange. He was exceptionally quick in working through critical issues to their core components and reaching a conclusion on what needed to be done.

The first insight occurred in a late night meeting in the Prime Minister's Office (about 2 am) in about October 1984. We had been engaged in a quite intense argument over the economic programme and what was being proposed. Lange quite belligerently pointed out to Peter Harris: "Understand one thing. Anyone who tries to come between Roger [Douglas] and me makes an enemy of me for life."

The second insight was some few weeks later, again in a late-night discussion. Lange with considerable exasperation said to me, "Look, what Roger [Douglas] does with the economy is fine by me provided he doesn't damage our social policy programme".

Both statements seemed to hide an understanding of the natural dependency of economic consequences and the importance of the process needed to build a strong consensus (with popular support) for a sustainable rebuilding of the economy driven by strong social democratic imperatives.

His subsequent "it's time for a cup of tea" was a rejection of the Douglas mantra TINA (there is no alternative) as a smash-through approach. In my view this realisation imposed itself upon him because fundamentally he is a humanist. He was not prepared to ignore the damage to people that was wreaked across New Zealand society.

I asked a question regarding the pre-election speech when Roger Douglas referred to the need for a major devaluation, as to whether this was a collective view of the Labour Party or an individual initiative on his part? Interestingly, I didn't get a direct answer. Everyone realised that once implemented, such a devaluation would completely negate the Labour Party's own policy publication, let alone the work being done by the Joint Council of Labour working party. Roger Douglas explained when questioned about this part of his speech that "it was a typist error". Well, I don't believe in fairies at the bottom of the garden and I don't believe that it was not deliberate.

Once started, the damage was done. The outflow of currency and the holding offshore of foreign exchange earnings that triggered the currency crisis was the single most important act taken to destroy all expectations of the new Labour Government.

David Lange's explanation that this was imposed on his government (made at the meeting with the Federation of Labour/CSU to agree to extend the Wage–Price Freeze in late July 1984) and blaming Muldoon's intransigence for the crisis, ignores the primary role of Roger Douglas.

In fact, working papers show that the specific question of the exchange rate had been discussed between us but had been agreed to be dealt with later. I don't doubt that Treasury had been pushing for some time for such an approach, but Muldoon could not have responded because the economy was locked down by the Wage–Price Freeze, so what mechanisms could have been used?

A review of subsequent documents is also instructive in attempting to understand something of the complexities of the first term of the fourth Labour Government. For example, in April 1985 Roger Douglas, as Finance Minister, spoke to an audience of European Bankers organised by the Frankfurt Bankers. In this speech he not only spelled out the detail and programme of 'Rogernomics' but identified the 20 percent devaluation, privatisation, flat tax and GST as key elements in moving to the deregulation of the finance system.

It is worthwhile noting that not even the Reagan or the Thatcher reforms had ventured so far. No wonder the international banking institutions saw New Zealand as something of a world phenomenon that attracted international inspection as if New Zealand was a colony of white mice in a mad scientist's laboratory.

In June 1986 David Lange's speech at the Macintosh Memorial Lecture in the United Kingdom had several sections of interest. For example, reference is made to the agricultural reforms—the removal of Supplementary Minimum Prices, but Lange ignores the cost of change. The plight of hundreds of young farmers caught in the vice of over-valued land and their productive value suddenly and traumatically reduced, not only bankrupting them but also driving many to suicide. This particular feature was studiously ignored by our media.

Similarly the dramatic and instant removal of business subsidies that wiped out 50 percent of the country's manufacturing base and 290,000 well-paid (relatively speaking) jobs. The implementation of policy reform was devoid of consensus, and it ignored social and economic adjustment considerations. It reflected the political adage that 'the means are justified by the end'.

It was, in my view, *Stalinist*. It completely ignored a fundamental social democratic value that the process of political change has to reflect the values of the objective end itself, otherwise you never arrive at the intended destination. Joe Stalin did not achieve a workers' paradise because the methods he used were in essence anti-worker. Roger Douglas and David Lange never achieved the social objectives of the reforms because they similarly butchered large sections of the economy and the population along the way.

In the same Macintosh Lecture, Lange emphasised the protection of social services. He listed the basic principles as:

- A reconstruction of public finances
- A fairer tax system
- A planned approach to growing and raising foreign exchange
- An investment programme to get New Zealand working again
- A price and incomes policy that protects the lower paid and looks towards stability of living standards.

My question is 'were these principles delivered upon?'

Finally, a short comment regarding relationships between the Federation of Labour and the Government. They were despite the tensions – positive.

- Roger Douglas was good and keener to engage, than some. He was intellectually vigorous.
- David Lange acted as the Chairman of the Board (or more correctly, in my view as the Captain of the *Titanic*), and was singularly unaware of the consequences of the course he was steering.
- Geoffrey Palmer was, as the driver of the legislative programme, the navigational helmsmen and with Stan Rodger he was prepared to give regular time and energy to consultation and dialogue.
- Stan Rodger played a huge role in assisting the Federation of Labour (and CSU) in understanding the complexities of the Government initiatives and in Government demonstrated the exceptional capabilities that had established him as one of the foremost leaders of the Public Service Association before entering Parliament.

Most meetings were positive, except when Richard Prebble was in attendance. I actually liked his style, but it was blunt – often excessively so. He was the brawler, and he was the henchman of the Finance troika. He was the deliverer of the ultimatums and the clean-up man.

Tragically, from my perspective as part of the leadership of a significant section of the trade union movement who in the main wanted to make a serious and positive contribution to rebuilding our economy, this was unachievable.

Our leadership, my leadership if you like, could not deliver the required union membership support in a coherent and a progressive way. The fact that the Labour movement collectively has never seen itself as a cohesive movement of mass action, capable of developing a consensus that was able to be turned into a popular political programme, was our Achilles' heel.

This collection of recollections is an important start in developing and gaining an objective understanding of the Lange legacy. But it only begins to expose the fundamental philosophical differences within the Labour Party, the Parliamentary Labour Party and the trade union movement. In my view this was because the whole environment was contaminated by our own (trade union) history; the reality of the Muldoon Government inheritance; the fast-changing nature of global politics and the emerging global–regional economic integration.

So what were the lessons? It is too early yet to make a comprehensive assessment. We have yet to uncover more objective factors. This has been a good start by at least beginning to get rid of the personalities camouflage and the mythologies that were created to hide the real issues of what must be recognised as an amazing if not the most fascinating period in New Zealand's political history.

GARY HAWKE

Bliss at dawn – social policy in the first term of the Lange Government

In July 1984 I was on leave in Australia, and in the following few months I followed events in New Zealand from a distance. I was amused by rumours which I knew to be untrue and I read the Treasury Briefing Papers in the Snowy Mountains, finding them to be more orthodox than I expected so that I was surprised by the intensity of the *Opening the Books* controversy. I thought official and academic economists were talking past each other.[1] Treasury economists were unaware of how far they had departed from what had become unquestioned assumptions about the framework in which the New Zealand economy was discussed. Academic economists were unaware of how much they resented the fact that they had not contributed to what was obviously useful new thinking. Some of them fell into the trap of assuming that there was one true model and they were its guardians. Discussion at the annual Economists' Conference in February 1985 was foolishly vitriolic.[2] I was in a middle position, trying to argue that the issue was misconceived and that we should concentrate on analysing the economic situation rather than claim exclusive value for any specific analytical approach. As usual, this position attracted criticism from all contenders.

This is somewhat typical of the position from which I viewed the events of 1984–87. I had been a member of the Economic Monitoring Group of the New Zealand Planning Council for some years, and was appointed to the Council by the Muldoon Government. I took up that position when I returned to New Zealand at the end of 1984 and was appointed by the Lange Government to be chair of the Council in 1986. Throughout 1984–87 the Council sought to be an independent and neutral commentator on New Zealand's economic, social, cultural and environmental development. I certainly found the vigour of the intellectual debate after 1984 refreshing, as I did the sense that anything could be attempted if it could be shown to contribute to efficiency and equity in New Zealand—hence my title.[3] I never experienced any restriction to a single line of argument as has been claimed in some accounts of the 1980s. I thought the slogan TINA, 'There is no alternative', to be an amusing bit of Pommie journalism, and when once asked about it by a journalist responded with the reply (from a similar source), "I'm TANYA, the alternative not yet available". Real debate lay elsewhere, in issues rather than in whether anything could be argued. I was working closely with Henry

Lang, especially from the beginning of 1987, but we occupied adjacent rooms at the University before then, and I knew perfectly well the deep uncertainties and anxieties of those who thought that much of their lifetime's work could be undermined. I have a letter from David Lange on his resignation, certifying that he did not regard me as among the "New Righters"—which can be a credential or a skeleton, depending on context.

In any case the Planning Council tried to keep to a neutral position, clearly looking forward. I think it a mistake to associate the Planning Council with a view that became common in journalism in 1984–87, that our problems were all our own fault, and that nothing had been got right before 1984.[4] The Planning Council was associated with many efforts to find middle ground, achieving the ends sought by some policy initiative while avoiding some costs which advocates of the initiative considered inevitable.[5] The ministerial member of the Planning Council was David Caygill, with the result that I have never been able to take seriously as an historical account Roger Douglas's writing about policy formation as "crash through or crash", keep the pace up so as to keep opponents on the back foot and so on.[6] I have no doubt that it appeared like that to some who were negotiating with the Minister of Finance and his staff, but for the most part, more typical was David Caygill's "marshmallow theory"; search for soft centres, apply pressure, and if it gives, press harder and if it still gives, eat it, but if there is resistance, turn to another chocolate."[7] The Planning Council was involved in assessing softness. I think we had some success in advising where and how policy objectives could be achieved, and were thanked by nobody.

Towards the end of the 1984–87 period, we ran a conference on income distribution which led the Governor-General, Paul Reeves, to fear that we were getting too close to opposing government—although my information from close to the PM suggested that he had no such worries and that, as is so often the case, censorship was anticipated but the constraint was actually self-censorship.[8] An academic participant, Charles Crothers, commented during the conference that just as the Planning Council under Frank Holmes had been early in promoting "more market", a greater reliance on markets relative to direct government provision, so it was early in a countervailing move.[9] I welcomed the thought of being early, but I saw "more market" as an attempt to find a better balance of efficiency and equity, not a shift from welfare state to market economics, and it was still balance that we were seeking. In particular I had no interest in reversing any of the policy initiatives of 1984–87, but I was interested in evolving conceptions of the welfare state. Could we do more to promote the welfare state as enhancing income-earning capacity and so independence, in opposition to its common conception as a safety net for the disadvantaged?[10] That was the policy question at issue, not silly arguments about "New Right" and dismantling familiar fabrics of society.

Notice the implication that fundamental questions of social policy were on the agenda before the 1987 election. There is a conventional view that social policy was deferred while for its first term the Government focused on the economy. There is some basis for that view. The period 1984–87 was notable for floating the exchange rate, fully funding the deficit, removing subsidies for agriculture and industry, reorganising public enterprise and preparing for reorganisation of the public sector. The principal achievements were the SOE legislation, State Sector Act, Labour Relations Act, and preparation for the Public Finance Act which followed in the second term. There were explicit suggestions, eventually, that the first term had to be got through, so that there would be an opportunity for "social policies directed to those in need" in the next term.[11]

However, the critical issues of social policy were raised as economic policy was developed. The relative reliance on monetary policy and fiscal policy in the search for economic growth without inflation involves a choice between income distribution objectives.[12] (Different groups are affected by the choice of instrument. Countering inflation through fiscal policy would have required a reduction in public expenditure and the incomes of groups like teachers and nurses would have suffered. Choosing monetary policy raised interest rates and reduced the incomes of exporters like farmers and the incomes of those who depended on investment projects such as building contractors and labourers.) The introduction of GST provoked a lot of discussion of social policy objectives, essentially a lot of woolly thinking about the impact of GST on food and clothing versus analysis of the distributional consequences of GST and other tax and benefit changes. This particular issue was a major one among party activists throughout 1985, with the Government apparently in difficulty at several regional Labour Party conferences although the national conference supported the Government.[13]

There is a strong element of party politics in this. As the 1987 election loomed, there was a tendency for the Government to drive itself into corners. Russell Marshall was reported to rule out user-pays in education, and while the report was later corrected to his expressing opposition to a form of user pays which amounts simply to requiring students to pay more, the slogan of 'user pays' was not conducive to public debate about efficient allocation of resources and appropriate institutional arrangements.[14] It is a useful instrument to start analysis, not announce policy conclusions. There is good reason to analyse who uses education, but that leads immediately neither to increasing student fees, nor to exempting students from fees. Not all party spokespeople were as sophisticated as Russell Marshall, and anyway what was heard was not always what was said. It was readily apparent that Lange's statements about not requiring people to pay for health care and not having 'user pays' in education could come to haunt him in the next parliamentary term. His words could be read as consistent with different management of health and educational institutions in the interests of efficiency and equity, but it was obvious that people would claim that they were betrayed in the same way as national superannuitants made that claim after the 1984 election.[15]

There were, of course, many issues which various people thought important. As the 1987 election approached, euthanasia and abortion were taken as a challenge in some Roman Catholic circles.[16] Throughout 1984–87, homosexual law reform was a significant topic of debate, and even though the legislation was a private member's bill, that distinction was not always observed—certainly homosexual law reform was treated as a matter of government policy in the Timaru by-election of 1985.[17] For much of 1985, the prospect of a rugby tour to South Africa was headline news. At the beginning of the year Lange nominated it as the major topic of 1985, while suggesting that any improvement in living standards was at least two years away.[18] This was not diversionary tactics; the point was that different people attached different importance to different topics, and the rugby union issue was a sensitive one for many. Lange's staff tried very hard to persuade the rugby union, and school principals may have been more concerned about the future of school rugby than about any other issue in education. The Rugby Union could not be persuaded, but a court challenge to Rugby Union decision processes provided an unexpected solution, even if it was undermined to some extent by the "private" Cavaliers' tour.[19]

New Zealand was becoming a more litigious society. As Deputy Prime Minister, Geoffrey Palmer was much occupied with the rule of law, and especially with the Bill of Rights. He regarded it as far more important than economic policy while I wondered why he found it so exciting, and why he accepted that economic rights were less significant than civil liberties—so pleasing neither Geoffrey on the one hand nor the Business Roundtable and others who took a traditional approach to entrenched constitutional rights on the other.[20] Given the range of topics which the Government was addressing, it is not surprising that as early as 1985, Palmer was commenting on how the Government was having difficulty communicating with the electorate.[21] We were to hear that lament much more often throughout 1984–87 and later.

Many of these social issues separated the political leaders from their trade union constituency. There was a sense in which the government conceded compulsory unionism in return for acquiescence in reform elsewhere, but Stan Rodger told me that the deal was specifically in return for union reform.[22] He hoped that a modern union structure would become a reforming agent. But his notion of a modern union structure—large unions capable of bargaining directly with employers, understanding the employment relationship in a modern economy, and looking for mutual agreement rather than sharing out a fixed resource—was a mixture of the outdated and idealistic. He had some allies; in early 1985 Rob Campbell was advocating a revival of the radicalism of the 1930s, not by a return to the past but by changing the employment relationship, as had happened with annual holidays, redundancy and other elements.[23] But for many, if radicalism was sought at all, it was the radicalism of the past. It is often not realised how important the wage round of 1985 was in reshaping economic policy. The Government stood back and insisted that employers and unions negotiate without a government-approved "figure". The Government accepted Treasury advice to "take it on the chin" and not surrender other instruments in what would probably be a forlorn effort to reach a deal which would "stick".[24] Despite hesitations, from institutions like the IMF as well as from politicians,[25] the Government stuck to its guns and a major institutional shift was implemented.[26] This was discussed as an aspect of economic policy, but it was also a significant development in social policy. By not following the few progressive leaders such as Ken Douglas,[27] unions lost their role as agents of social change. The Planning Council attempted, in *Labour Market Flexibility*, to find a middle course, and so did the Government in its Labour Relations Act at the beginning of the 1987–90 term. But trade union leaders appreciated the attractions of the balance then offered only after the Contract of Employment Act of 1991.

Despite this range of issues, and the importance of areas like trade union reform, I am here concentrating on the conventional core areas of health, education and welfare. I do not pay much attention even to superannuation and retirement policy. It did not seem so important to me twenty years ago. Like Bob Jones, I thought it inevitable that the Government would use a surcharge once Lange ruled out all other options before the 1984 election and I was surprised that what I took to be rhetorical if not demagogic language about broken promises gained any traction. I had yet to learn that the precision of academic discourse was not greatly prized in political debate. In early 1985, I thought that the courage of the Government's approach and the problems it created for the National Party outweighed any unpopularity its actions attracted, although I also noted that some good observers thought that the unpopularity was greater outside Wellington.[28] On the whole, my judgement was justified. Grey Power was noisy, but superannuation did not become a major issue until 1990. There was, however, one area outside the conventional health, education and welfare trilogy where events which were really important for New Zealand's social development occurred between 1984 and 1987 and with which I will deal. That was Treaty policy. Before turning to specific areas, however, I want to reflect further on how important 1984–87 was in setting directions which still continue to preoccupy us. The underlying issues were about the integration of social and economic policy.

INTEGRATION OF SOCIAL AND ECONOMIC POLICY
Integration of economic and social policy was far from a new idea. The form of words which was used in 1933 to describe the objectives of the Reserve Bank was "economic welfare of the Dominion" once the Bank could no longer be said to be preserving stability of the exchange rate.[29] From any time after 1945, with the creation of the United Nations and its covenants of social and human rights, the phrase "economic and social" would have come naturally. The Great Depression of the 1930s, and the experience of the Second World War encouraged belief in the efficacy of governments, and governments were expected to improve the experiences of people in general. They were to be helped to earn incomes—government had economic aims—and unattractive employment outcomes were to be modified—governments had social aims. The two were always related. Initially it was thought that the more governments could mould economies so as to generate harmonious societies, the less social policy intervention would be needed. However, social trends proved to work in the opposite direction. Education and health spending rose inexorably, and so did policies which redistributed income to specific groups such as solo mothers.

The idea that economic and social policy should be "integrated" simply evolved between 1945 and 1984. Successive New Zealand governments sought to promote economic change. One significant instrument was the National Development Conference in 1969, which sought to change the way domestic industry was helped. This had implications for how social policy was implemented but that was realised only slowly. Henry Lang said that the fundamental purpose of the Task Force on Economic and Social Planning in 1976 was to integrate social and economic policy. The Planning Council which was created in 1977 and chaired by Frank Holmes, who had also convened the Task Force, reflected this intention. It also, under the leadership of Rangi Mete-Kingi and initially Ann Delamere, took a particular interest in Maori affairs and began to think in terms of "economic, social and cultural development". (The Maori Social and Economic Advancement Act of 1945 may have been among the first official joinings of "social" and "economic" in New Zealand, but Maori, as we shall see below, were far from satisfied with how their interests were approached. I do not think the specification of "cultural" had any suggestions of separatism; certainly that was not the view of many Planning Council members under the leadership of Frank Holmes 1977–82 or indeed later.) A separate Social Advisory Council, intended to be somewhat wider in its scope than the earlier Social Development Council co-existed with the Planning Council until Geoffrey Palmer's QUANGO hunt in the mid-1980s, which also claimed the Environment Council so that the purposes of the Planning Council became monitoring "social, economic, cultural and environment development". That phrase has now been fossilised in local government legislation. It means nothing more than our collective objectives, and in other historical circumstances could well have specified educational, artistic or (non-denominational) spiritual development.

There was, however, more than terminology to "integration of economic and social policy" between 1984 and 1987. During the Planning Council's first five years, 1977–82, through its studies of *Planning Perspectives, Taxing Issues. Investment Issues* and a set of public-sector studies, it sought always to embrace social issues as well as economic ones. So it did later, and the *From Birth to Death* reports, later continued by Judith Davey and the Institute of Policy Studies were direct forerunners of the *Social Report* now published by the Ministry of Social Development. Social issues loomed larger elsewhere too. The McCaw tax committee which in the early 1980s advocated a shift to indirect taxes, paid more attention to distributional consequences than had committees which had made similar recommendations in the preceding 50 years.[30] This was partly because of progress in data and techniques, but it also reflected growing interest in social policy. It could, however, be said that despite the genuine interest in integration, there was investigation of the social consequences of economic policy and interest in the economic implications of the social change being experienced but little substantive integration.

Between 1984 and 1987, the Planning Council, which was chaired by Ian Douglas until 1986 when I succeeded him, was well aware of a strong sense that the major change in economic policy which was being implemented needed to be accompanied by a change of thinking about social policy. Ian Douglas explicitly articulated this to me on my return from Australia, and he attributed to David Caygill a specific request that the Planning Council should advise on what was desirable.[31] Of course, the change in economic strategy was not immediately understood. At the end of 1985, I detected a gradual acceptance that we had moved away from traditional thinking about export-led growth[32] (a change which is still, in 2004, far from complete as is apparent from Andy West's recent statements about educational policy). At the same time I thought we could see that New Zealand was discarding old ideas of "backbone of the economy" and coming closer to what I had found in Australia in 1984, a view of farming as one activity among many, differentiated most by the importance of the weather in determining the patter of its output cycle.[33] That was a long way of seeing agriculture as the most important driver of the economy. Nevertheless, it was only slowly appreciated that we had adopted a major new economic strategy of using international prices to direct resource allocation within New Zealand. And of course, there was political expediency, and also genuine concern to "share the burden" fairly. This was what underlay Lange's quip towards the end of that year that perhaps the Government would provide some relief to farmers, although Treasury was advising that he should give nothing but bible tracts.[34] (The Government's package a month later was fully in line with the economic strategy and not a retreat.[35]) So we had to think about implications for social policy while still seeking to understand the economic changes themselves.

The Planning Council attempted to respond to the Government's challenge in *Social Policy Options* (1987). The Council had quickly discovered that defining social objectives was not easy.[36] We have rediscovered this several times since, most clearly in the attempt to create a Social Responsibility Act analogous to the Fiscal Responsibility Act. The latter can use criteria which have real substance while leaving room for different collective preferences to influence fiscal policy which is why it has survived transitions between successive governments. In social policy we do not agree on the desirability or otherwise of key social trends such as the level of divorce and reconstitution of families, or the substitution of market transactions for community volunteering. These difficulties were apparent to any who tried to define social objectives in 1984–87.

There were several key issues. One was selectivity and universality. This could be reduced to the tautological—all transfer payments should be available universally to those who were defined to be the targeted beneficiaries—but that was to belittle a significant development. There was a long history of seeking to avoid the attachment of "stigma" to social welfare recipients. Those who argued for a more selective approach to social welfare often ignored this history.[37] When David Lange was persuaded that the untargeted nature of family benefit made it an inefficient use of public expenditure, I was led to note, "he could at least show some awareness of the nobility of the concept of removing selectivity and ensuring the dignity of the benefit recipient when all this was planned in the 1930s, even if National Super has gone too far and forced a retreat".[38] The concept of "stigma" was anachronistic. Social welfare was "de-stigmatised" as it expanded in the early 1970s, with ACC and the DPB. The language of a "right" to welfare had replaced the idea of charity to the disadvantaged—Nash's "First charge on the wealth of the nation should be the aged, the sick and the poor". National Super, almost by *reductio ad absurdem*, destroyed the acceptability of distributing to all and achieving redistribution through progressive taxation. The expenditure was seen as wasteful and the tax was regarded as burdensome rather than reasonable. Handing out benefits only to immediately repossess them was called "churning", and it could not be defended as a way of avoiding stigma once social change made receipt of welfare benefits respectable and not in need of justification. (Perhaps it was aided by changes in social objectives of women, for whom "dependence on the state" was no more unacceptable than "dependence on a bloke".)

Universality was only one topic of debate. Another was preventive versus remedial. There was obvious sense in building fences at the top of cliffs rather than running ambulances at the bottom, but such analysis could take us only so far. The fence might have to be very large and unsightly, conflicting with other objectives. And the ambulance service did not welcome the thought of redundancy or even significant slimming down. Many such ideas and issues floated around. Was an approach to economic policy of "more market" being applied without thought to social policy?[39] "More market" was often lost in the rhetoric of surrendering to "market forces" although it was always obvious to me that the issue was the respective roles of government and market, collective and private, and direct or indirect control of market transactions rather than a choice between government and market.[40]

In dealing with questions such as the balance of universality and selectivity, or preventive and remedial, "efficiency and equity" was a useful phrase for stating high-level objectives, but it gave little help in carrying analysis forward, let alone providing answers. "Efficiency" was problematic enough and was usually exchanged for "efficient and effective" which reflected mere terminological confusion,[41] and "equity" was even more difficult. Within the Planning Council, it was analysed as access and opportunity, but even there it was often confused with equality.[42] Much social policy was arbitrary: Dennis Rose created "a very useful image when he wondered what we would be doing if we had decided to provide cars rather than health-care as a social service; we would presumably now have an industry run by professionals wanting the latest gadgetry and only a little less ready to wave the fear of people dying because of a less than perfect output.[43] On the other hand, the members of the Planning Council with a social policy background could point to real difficulties in the analytical approaches of economists; there was at least tension between treating individuals as such while using households as the unit of assessment for taxes and benefits.[44] And wrong political conclusions could be drawn when discussion was prematurely treated as concluded—Dennis was far from wanting government to withdraw from health-care as he began to explore the extent to which access and equity depended on public activity.

Rapid change was hard to comprehend. Why had occupational licensing become unacceptable? To some, it was obvious that optimal resource allocation would be facilitated by a distinction between certification of quality and barriers to individual choice, and that claiming to know better than other people what is good for them should be done only with care. Others thought they had been doing a social service for many years by training or educating students to qualify for an occupation.[45] Even those attuned to change were challenged; New Zealand had a tradition that people in employment should be able to manage without explicit subsidies so that it was easy to think instinctively that new policies of family care should be no more than transitional. But the social change towards two-income families created an argument for using transfers to support children, whether or not their parents were working. Roger Douglas was genuinely responsive to social change, despite the scepticism about his claim to be following the ideas of earlier Labour leaders.[46]

The integration of social and economic policy was actually most apparent in the choice of the balance to be struck between monetary and fiscal policy as the Government sought to get inflation under control. As we noted earlier, the distributional consequences differed markedly,[47] but there was little discussion at that level of analysis or abstraction. There was more enthusiasm for the integration of economic and social analysis in principle than there was in learning the concepts and techniques of another discipline so that economic and social implications could be addressed as a whole. This was most apparent in debates over unemployment, especially in small towns heavily dependent on a single employer who was affected adversely by the economic restructuring—freezing works in Patea or Wairoa, or forestry in central North Island towns. Maori were often heavily represented among those who were affected adversely, as is now surfacing in claims to the Waitangi Tribunal.

Integrated social and economic analysis led to the conclusion that there was a case for facilitating movement from one source of employment to another, recognising that this was easier for the young and those without family commitments. Further analysis was needed to ensure that the problem was properly identified and to get a sense of the extent of the problem. Much of the social concern in localities reflected not the actual impact of restructuring (which was less than expected), but feelings of uncertainty, and indeed feelings of rejection as people were forced to confront the reality that what they had been doing with great conscientiousness was not a sensible use of New Zealand's resources. They grew trees, which neither sustained land nor produced usable wood; they assembled TV sets superbly, but merely made more costly what was available without their effort. They had been literally wasting their time, and no amount of soft-soap and euphemism could change that reality. But that was not to say that they had not contributed to society, let alone that they were to blame for the situation in which they found themselves.

It was very hard to make progress when advocates of intervention were only too obviously seeking to use (or even create) opportunities to reverse the whole thrust of the Government's policies. Political advocacy got in the way of policy development. The language of integration of social and economic policy was often used to disguise efforts to change policy altogether. And the only effect of that was to limit the effort devoted to facilitating adjustment, for fear that it would not be distinguished from a retreat on policy in general. It was often difficult to get any kind of meeting of the various parties, let alone any meeting of minds. As well we were discovering that the Official Information Act precluded the old formula of open agreements secretly arrived at.[48]

Far from being a period when social policy was in hibernation, awaiting the second term, the years between 1984 and 1987 saw key changes in how the role of government was conceived. The issues then defined have preoccupied social policy in the last 20 years. Some said, and continue to say, that the policies associated with Roger Douglas assumed a theory of society which was at odds with the values of traditional Labour (or even of New Zealand society). Others say that some interpreted the values of New Zealand and of the Labour Party in a way which was incompatible with the social change which New Zealand had experienced. Unfortunately, the debate could not be focused on that essential issue, and nor were there many people seeking to do so in a constructive way.

MAORI ISSUES AND THE IWI RENAISSANCE

The importance of the years 1984–87 for Maori development is less underestimated than it is for other aspects of social development. Even so, much more happened than is conventionally believed.

The usual story focuses on extension of the jurisdiction of the Waitangi Tribunal from 1975 to 1840 and the victory of the NZ Maori Council in the Court of Appeal as a result of the way the Treaty was written into s.9 of the State-Owned Enterprise Act. Geoffrey Palmer's response to Koro Wetere's advocacy of what was needed to achieve fairness was the key to the former element. Section 9 of the SOE Act was clever legal drafting to prevent a challenge to the reorganisation of government-owned business in pursuit of efficiency of resource use, especially in forestry. (Crown property was available to settle Treaty claims upheld by the Waitangi Tribunal. The property of an SOE might not be, and the formation of SOEs might therefore be challenged and delayed.) Not for the first or last time, a quick legal solution proved to have far-reaching consequences.

This conventional story is correct, but it is so selective an account of what happened between 1984 and 1987 as to be a distortion. Those years also saw major developments in what continues to exercise us—especially the claims of iwi as distinct from Maori.

The party-political nature of governments had a very direct impact on Maori policy machinery. National Governments usually had no effective common membership with Maori leadership, although some Maori leaders had longstanding personal or family links with the Party. There were National MPs in general electorates who were Maori in ethnicity, such as Ben Couch and Rex Austin, but standing as Maori leaders could not come from such a source. National Governments relied on the NZ Maori Council, a statutory body whose spokespeople were intermediaries between Maori and Pakeha rather than Maori leaders (although some individuals had mana as the latter too). With the election of a Labour Government, the Maori Council was sidelined. The four Labour MPs for Maori electorates provided a direct channel between Cabinet and Maoridom, especially with Koro Wetere as both Minister of Maori Affairs and a Maori leader (within Tainui). In Pakeha terms, the Board of Maori Affairs, an obscure organisation including the four Maori MPs and concerned with land management, became influential and supplanted the Maori Council, but the formalities were unimportant. Maori leadership worked through Maori channels to the Cabinet.

The Maori element in New Zealand public life and history was never as remote as is now often alleged. Those who complain that they never heard at school about the Treaty of Waitangi mostly reveal that they were not paying attention when Maori elements in New Zealand history were taught. There were large elements of romanticism in *Our Nation's Story* and even in Condliffe and Airey's *Short History of New Zealand* from which teaching materials were often ultimately derived. Romanticism was a significant element in making accessible to schoolchildren the history of other elements of New Zealand society too, such as the role of Magna Carta and the Bill of Rights in creating our parliamentary institutions and legal protection of freedoms. There is as much romanticism in current understanding of the Treaty, and not only among schoolchildren. (One might wonder whether "romanticism" is quite the right concept for how lawyers distort history, whether it is venerable authorities like Coke appropriating medieval events to promote parliament relative to the king, or eighteenth-century lawyers creating Cabinet government, or the current New Zealand Treaty jurisprudence, but there is certainly a common process of distorting history.)

There was, however, a distinct "marae history"—accounts of the past in discussions on marae throughout the country—which kept history alive and part of modern iwi. Raupatu, or confiscation of land, and other land losses which were believed by Maori to be unfair, was central to it. In Northland and in some other areas, the Treaty was central, and in the 1980s, the Treaty became at least a symbol for other iwi too, although not without some thoughts of a preference for reliance on the doctrines of indigenous rights that were emanating from North America and the United Nations. (Some iwi had previously referred to the Treaty as "that Nga Puhi thing". The slogan, "honour the Treaty", which could seem vacuous, had many connotations.) There was a strong belief that Maori should be assisted to manage their affairs in a Maori manner, continuing the adaptation of imported institutions which had been going on from the early nineteenth century, but retaining what was regarded as important from within Maori culture, especially the continuity through time of the iwi. Throughout the 1950s, 1960s and 1970s, there were memories of the Maori war effort. Participants thought they were promised that self-reliance would be facilitated after the War as well as during it. For Pakeha, the Department of Maori Affairs delivered on the promise whereas for Maori it provided paternalism rather than self-reliance even when its heads were Maori. The Government of 1984 gave a new opportunity to create a solution to longstanding grievances. The Waitangi Tribunal was a mechanism, not an answer.

The strongest positive elements were Maori efforts to decide how Maori development should be managed. An initial hui taumata of Maori and government leaders launched a loose concept of "development decade". It was followed by many hui and conferences regionally and by interest groups.[49] Ironically, given recent developments, there was discussion in 1986 of "closing the gap" and the Planning Council cautiously suggested that "narrowing" was a more plausible objective.[50] Robert Mahuta of Tainui and the Centre for Maori Research and Development at the University of Waikato directed a series of studies for iwi of what their resources were—especially their human resources—and what constituted a sensible iwi plan for development.[51] There was always much concern with the role of government. A motif in Bob Mahuta's thinking was that so much could be achieved if the government funding of responses to failure—welfare benefits and costs of maintaining Maori in prisons—could be converted into "positive funding"—into investment projects for development of human and other resources. The objective could hardly be opposed; the difficulty was always in implementation. Those in receipt of "negative funding" could not be wished out of existence or directly converted into agents of development projects.

How should Maori relate to government? Towards the end of 1986, Ngatata Love, a prominent Maori thinker with expertise in public management, thought that the Maori Council was in limbo, and the various trust boards too specific in their purposes, too diffuse in their nature, and lacking in administrative support. He thought that some new creation was needed.[52] Naturally, the Department of Maori Affairs, under the leadership of Tamati Reedy, thought that it was perfectly capable of responding to all opportunities and challenges. It formed a Steering Committee for the Development Decade, in which the Planning Council participated. The Council's attempts, especially through the work of Dennis Rose, to find a form of "planning" that was consistent with the economic policy being implemented had a natural fit with Maori aspirations. What was sought was not a government direction of economic development but a process of consultation about collective objectives, identification of conflicts and as much agreement as possible on trade-offs. The search was for understanding of the path from where we were to where we wanted to be. But there was a good deal of scepticism among Maori of the capabilities of the Department of Maori Affairs, and the Steering Committee was sometimes far too much a body of sympathetic Pakeha.[53]

Eventually the Department of Maori Affairs lost its position and was replaced by a Ministry of Maori Development while an Iwi Transition Authority was established to facilitate the transfer of many responsibilities to iwi. That outcome had not been inevitable. A ministerial advisory committee of Bert Mackie, Denise Henare and Ngatata Love argued for a national development board and regional boards between the Government and iwi.[54] Concern for management and accountability could easily point in that direction, but intermediate structures were hard to reconcile with Maori custom. Iwi varied in their capabilities, but some could function in a much more independent manner than is implied by national and regional boards, and organisations such as the Maori Council and the Maori Women's Welfare League would be Pakeha devices unless they had to argue with iwi for their funds.

The principal argument was within Maoridom. Beyond debate about the extent to which there should be a structure intermediate between government and iwi, there were arguments about penetration of Pakeha institutions versus the creation of parallel Maori ones. The Planning Council facilitated Maori submissions to a review of universities, but had little to contribute to questions such as whether there should be a Maori equivalent of the review committee or indeed of the University Grants Committee and the Planning Council itself.[55] Whatarangi Winiata was a key exponent of the need for distinct parallel institutions; he had some success with the Anglican Church, but it was well on the way to being essentially a private institution of interest only to its members, and the case was very different for public institutions with powers of legal coercion and taxpayer finance. Robert

Mahuta was a major exponent of the strategy of penetrating Pakeha institutions, while relying on traditional Maori means for preserving Maori culture. It was a strategy much easier to implement in areas like the Waikato with the thriving Tainui culture, than it was in places with largely immigrant Maori populations like Christchurch and Wellington (although Ngai Tahu eventually succeeded with it in Christchurch). Locating the centre of gravity of Maori opinion was not easy; I was distinctly surprised at the extent of Maori support for the first Rabuka coup in Fiji.[56]

However, not all the argument was within Maoridom, especially once the Maori loans affair hit the headlines. Maori leaders, including officials and even Koro Wetere, got too close to financial deals with overseas financiers of dubious respectability and reliability. Given the difficulty of switching government expenditure from 'negative funding' to development finance, offers of cheap money from abroad were tempting. But there are good reasons for public service rules about financial procedures even if they could sometimes be constraints on initiative. Those deeply imbued with the history of Maori development and those immediately engaged in the debates of the mid-1980s knew about the Ngata affair of the 1930s;[57] it was well-known that Kara Puketapu, Tamati Reedy's predecessor at the Department of Maori Affairs, had had difficulties with government procedures before his early retirement from the public service. The history could work in either direction. It led some people to be more understanding of the difficulties in trying to combine public service processes with effective action for the Maori community. For others, another mistaken departure from proper official behaviour had to be combated. Even though foolish, let alone illegal, commitments were avoided—the scepticism of people like Ngatata Love with management experience helped politicians and officials to avoid serious mistakes—there were people in senior positions who felt that the errors which had been made should have resulted in more sanctions. Roderick Deane, who was then State Services Commissioner, certainly expressed such a view later, although his initial response was less condemnatory. Perhaps the best response was that of Henry Lang who argued that the mistake in dealing with con-men should be acknowledged, and attention turned back to Maori development.[58]

While the Maori loans affair was very prominent in the media, a great deal was being achieved in allowing Maori more self-management in the delivery of social services. A training and employment-placement service, MAccess, operated alongside the mainstream Access programme. Through Mana Enterprises, schemes for assisting Maori business were promoted through the Department of Maori Affairs. Programmes within the Department of Social Welfare were also achieving significant change. There was naturally more attention paid to the problems being experienced, and especially the way that Maori were bearing a disproportionate part of the cost of restructuring of industries such as the railways and forestry.

Nevertheless, at a meeting of the Planning Council at the beginning of 1987 Robert Mahuta talked of how 1986 was far from the disastrous year for Maoridom portrayed in the media. In his view, the development of Hui Taumata, the economic commission, the ministerial review of the Department of Maori Affairs,

MANA enterprises, MAccess, the extension of the Waitangi Tribunal to 1840, and the foundation of Maori sections within the Ministry of the Environment and Department of Conservation made Maori people see 1986 as one of the best years since 1840.[59]

The decision of the Court of Appeal in the State Owned Enterprise case certainly had an impact on Treaty issues thereafter. The general story is well known. Deputy Prime Minister and Minister of Justice, Geoffrey Palmer, acceded to Koro Wetere's advocacy that it was desirable to respond to the marae history which had persisted throughout the twentieth century and permit the Waitangi Tribunal to investigate historical grievances. The Government itself should attempt to reconcile Maori values with Pakeha processes. The whole approach was to seek to avoid creating new injustices, but Crown assets might be used to redress proven injustice. The Government's corporatisation process, and even more any privatisation process, could reduce the assets available for this purpose. In a little considered move, s.9 of the SOE Act provided that the Act did not over-ride the principles of the Treaty of Waitangi. The Court of Appeal ruled that the Government was therefore required to recognise a relationship in the nature of a partnership with Maori and find an agreement before corporatisation of forestry proceeded.[60]

The Waitangi Tribunal had become influential before the Maori Council case. In 1986 it issued a judgement that the Treaty of Waitangi required the Government to preserve the Maori language and that as the education system and the broadcasting services were failing to do so, the Government had an obligation to act.[61] This undoubtedly gave an impetus to changes in schools, although much more important were arguments within society and education circles generally that eventually emerged in the Picot Report. It also eventually led to Maori Television Services, although the initial effort through agreement between Aotearoa Broadcasting and TVNZ failed, and in any case, radio was always much more effective in promoting te reo.

The Waitangi Tribunal tried very hard in 1987 to develop an approach in relation to historical claims of hearing grievances, acknowledging wrongs and finding a path forward in which iwi could function as progressive and dynamic social units within the modern New Zealand economy and society. It attempted to meld history and law. It was a bold experiment—one that eventually failed—but the boldness and effort should be acknowledged. It was always surrounded by more or less irresponsible rhetoric such as the claim that corporatisation was the ultimate land-grab, something which sounds ironic now in the wake of the similar debate about foreshore and seabed. But there were strong voices that the demand for compensation should not be a demand for retribution and that ancient grievances should not be replaced by new ones.[62] Responsible leaders agreed with Tamati Reedy that if you said you wanted perfect biculturalism or nothing, you would get nothing.[63]

Chief Judge Eddie Durie was explicit on his approach when in 1987 he launched a Planning Council publication, George Asher's *Maori Land*. Its preparation involved input from people who were or were becoming well known—Eva Rickard, Joe Williams, Shane Jones and others. The report itself was an early effort towards establishing the current status of Maori landholding and elucidating links between landholding and current policy issues (including the legal status of whanau, runanga and iwi). Durie argued that the Treaty showed that government policy was that no tribe should be left landless, and that the spirit of partnership required the government to provide an endowment of land or other resources, returning places of spiritual value where this was possible, but looking to the future rather than to past wrongs. He asked, "Does the reparation approach in any event create more problems than it solves?" and was very pragmatic in his approach to problems of development versus respect for the past. The focus was on iwi development.[64] This was as true of Waitangi Tribunal findings as of Chief Judge Durie's (rare) participation in public debate; it became less dominant in later years as he formed the view that the Government was not responding sufficiently energetically to Tribunal findings.

Changes in Maori participation in policy and service delivery were proceeding well before the Maori Council case. Debate and negotiation took time. In the view of Maori participants, Labour, Education, and Social Welfare departments resisted loss of control of resources to Maori Affairs. On the other hand, some iwi authorities were reluctant to accept that their capabilities were not as great as those of others. And the Department of Maori Affairs had limitations. What to some people was an accountability device, was to others a barrier between the Government and the iwi authorities.

Equally, the significance of the Court of Appeal decision was not immediately as self-evident as might be inferred from the symbolic role it played later. Tainui leaders considered that most of its impact had been anticipated in an earlier private letter of undertaking from the Government to Tainui. What the Court decision did was revive the fortunes of the Maori Council relative to the other institutions in which Government–Maori relations had become concentrated.[65]

The Court of Appeal decision was important for the way it foreshadowed the shaping of policy debates in legal terms throughout the 1990s. We can also see the key debates which are still with us: the nature of iwi as institutions in a modern society and economy, and the extent to which urban Maori preserved traditional institutions. Sir Robert Mahuta, as he became, was a member of the Planning Council, and between 1984 and 1987, I had no doubt that the terms 'Maori Renaissance' and 'Iwi Renaissance' could be used interchangeably. Equally, however, we knew of the effectiveness of the Waipareira Trust for service delivery. Iwi were not frozen in concrete; Ratana had established itself in the 1920s and 1930s as a Maori organisation for the morehu, the dispossessed, and it co-existed with traditional structures. So did the Maori Women's Welfare League and a later Congress of Iwi included both those organisations. The Maori Council was more problematic because it was undeniably a Pakeha creation. It had to establish Maori credentials, which it did more easily and more fully in some regions and contexts than others. Most New Zealanders were unaware of the extent of the debate within Maoridom; people who the mainstream media took to be Maori leaders were often mediators rather than leaders; many statements and actions which were taken to be by representatives of Maoridom were attempts to use relatively new institutions to participate in traditional Maori governance processes or to create alternatives to them.[66]

Debate within Maoridom had many nuances. Central in the debate, nevertheless, was the extent to which Maori should first develop their own institutions and capabilities before engaging in national affairs. This was often discussed in terms of 'biculturalism' and 'multiculturalism', the focus being the extent to which bicultural approaches would permit Maori to engage in multicultural processes. The positive elements were beyond the comprehension of many commentators and of many Pakeha, both those who wanted to make no distinctions among Maori and other minorities and those who adopted a patronising cringe towards the tangata whenua.[67] Much depended on local circumstances. Tainui was well placed to rely on iwi institutions to maintain Maori culture, while penetrating Pakeha institutions to facilitate participation in the modern society and economy. Hence its emphasis on endowed colleges as a means for assisting Tainui youth to attend Waikato and Auckland universities. Where iwi institutions were weaker, often divided among distinct iwi, or where hapu and whanau were less likely to be cohesive, and especially when many Maori were immigrants and resident within the rohe of another iwi, the building of distinct Maori institutions was a more attractive strategy. All of these characteristics were present in the Wellington region. In response, Te Wananga o Raukawa followed a strategy of self-reliance and Victoria University of Wellington found it difficult to find a basis for collaboration.[68] (Not that reaching out was universally sought, and much more was involved in each specific case, as is obvious from the differences between the University of Canterbury and Lincoln University.)

After 1987, the Tainui and Ngai Tahu settlements, and smaller ones, created entirely new contexts for some iwi. Others continued to be dominated by their grievances throughout the 1990s and beyond. The ideas of 'partnership' and tino rangitiratanga reverberated in many contexts. Ways of making services, especially education and health, more accessible to Maori continued to be explored. Sensible ideas were stretched into claims for special treatment. There was always opposition to what could be portrayed as the Government being "soft on Maori"[69] and right up to the Orewa speech of the Leader of the Opposition in 2004 and doubtless beyond, attempts at analysis were met by abuse rather than argument. But that had always been the fate of those seeking to give Maori a place in New Zealand public life too. Between 1984 and 1987 significant progress was made in defining and progressing all the issues which remain significant.

SOES AND CORPORATISATION

Corporatisation of state trading activity and early debates about privatisation and reform of the public service featured prominently in the 1984–87 term of the fourth Labour Government. They were mostly treated as part of economic policy, an essential part of the general thrust toward guiding New Zealand resources to where they could contribute most according to relative values established within the international economy. That formulation, conventional enough among economists, reminds us of the challenge to ideas of 'insulationism' and exerting local control over international price trends, ideas which had been central to the first Labour Government. They had given way in the face of international experience in which material well-being resulted from participation in the world economy. Remnants of desire for self-sufficiency persisted in political movements such as some forms of environmentalism and old-fashioned protectionism. They were elements of resistance to economic thinking, not components of economic thinking. Social thinking had not progressed as much as economic thinking.

As was perceived by Colin James, already in the mid-1980s among the most experienced and best of our social commentators were vast gaps in attitudes. Many Labour Party activists saw (and see) government activity as something which is good in itself, while they saw (and see) 'the market' as something which lacks heart or soul. The very distinction of government and market in such terms is misguided; any market depends on some kind of authority for enforcing its contracts and all regulatory authorities are met with creative responses as well as obedience. But political debate can proceed without much attention to logic or history. When Roger Douglas rejected privatisation but talked of government operations becoming more efficient and market-oriented, he was puzzled by the lack of enthusiasm in party circles; it resulted simply from incomprehension. Only a few could ask whether what Douglas proposed involved paying too high a price in terms of a compassionate and humane organisation for mere material goods and services. That was a significant issue which would have been difficult enough to debate, since what is "compassionate and humane" requires material support, and "material comfort" is often valued more highly than we are willing to acknowledge. Understanding the choices available and striking a balance was always going to be difficult, but the debate was rarely joined.[70]

It was necessarily diffuse. Even those who thought of government activity as generally compassionate could not be entirely unaware of some inefficiency. Roger Hall's *Glide Time* and its television adaptation, or the mostly gentle but disparaging treatment of people from "the government" by Fred Dagg were far more influential than any scholarly studies. The critical division was between those like the existing State Service Commissioners and many public service leaders who thought that incremental reform could eliminate inefficiency and waste and those who believed that there was adequate evidence that nothing but a radical change could make the kind of difference that was needed for an efficient public sector and economy. There were plenty of specific differences of view. The Minister of Energy, Bob Tizard, thought that "Treasury going berserk" was the only explanation for suggestions for corporatisation in the energy sector;[71] the arrangements for broadcasting required deep analysis of the concept of 'public sector broadcasting' and the role of collective processes in maintaining and disseminating culture while also recognising that TV was part of a competitive entertainment industry.[72] On the less elevated topic of home delivery of milk, there was much regret at the loss of a village tradition, while many, often those who expressed that regret, preferred the convenience and lower cost of collecting cartons from supermarkets in their own cars.[73]

The process of corporatisation was led from within the public service by public servants who wanted a more effective public service. It was not imposed by politicians. Older public servants often regretted the loss of what they had valued, and change was resisted within the public service as elsewhere. It was often resisted even more by academics who thought that innovation in the public service should be directed by their particular disciplines.[74] Opponents of change in the PSA leadership were undercut by their own members, who saw the desirability of making organisations such as the Post Office more efficient and freeing them from the controls of the State Services Commission.[75] The debate was more intense but not essentially different when it moved on from state trading activity to the core public service. Allegations that the central public service was being ambushed were at best an exaggeration. No later than mid-1986, Wellington debates were occurring about how a modern public service would be constructed from first principles and what that suggested about the direction of reform given that history had to be taken into account, and there were public reports of these debates.[76] Although public announcements of government decisions were deferred until after the 1987 election, and although Stan Rodger has said several times that his response was that the changes proposed could either be implemented or be made the subject of formal consultation, but not both, any surprise was only to those who had chosen not to hear the clear evidence that radical reform of the public service would be attempted.

The core argument was about the role of government.[77] In the mid-1980s, it was often debated in the language of 'devolution'—who has the best information? Who has the strongest incentives to get the decision right? Who reaps the greatest reward or bears the greatest cost according to the outcome of the decision?[78] This was not the standard way of exploring the role of the state, and it opened up many arguments. When it was applied to constitutional doctrines and central government functions, it raised questions about traditional concepts such as ministerial responsibility.[79] When it was applied to mechanisms for service delivery, as in the fields of health, education and social welfare, it was often hard to distinguish from decentralisation, which was conventionally conceived as the delegation of defined tasks without a transfer of decision-making responsibility. It was also frequently confused with the idea that somebody else should pay for decisions taken locally. There was considerable debate over whether the development of service delivery mechanisms more attuned to Maori communities were part of a general process of 'devolution' or were an entirely different process related to the Treaty of Waitangi.

When the ideas of 'devolution' were applied to state trading activity, they raised questions about whether corporatisation was an equilibrium position or whether the only stable positions were privatisation and direct ministerial control exercised through government departments. Economists could readily agree that a critical question was whether the discounted stream of future income from state ownership equated to the price offered by private investors but that was not obvious to many in the business sector, let alone in the wider political community. Many could not believe that it was wise for Electricity Corporation to abandon a computer centre on which millions had been spent, and there were human-interest stories about immigrants who were specially recruited to work in it.[80] There were similar stories about equipment that was specifically built for New Zealand telephone systems but which was scrapped in favour of cheaper (and reliable) off-the-shelf commercial imports. Business decisions require more than everyday 'common sense'. There were problems in competing views even within the business community; economists' insistence on pricing assets by looking to future earning capacity did not always sit easily with business ideas of recovering past costs, and inducing business decisions which accorded with best use of resources was not easily distinguished from hobbling managers with crippling debt.[81] Early debates tended to be about the value of capital market monitoring, but by mid-1987 it was also recognised that government was not a commercially-minded shareholder. Expositions of official policy which treated the Government as a holding company and SOEs as subsidiaries were only partially convincing.[82]

In later years, the impact of governments being more risk-averse than many in the community and so inhibiting diversification of businesses and development of new products became even more prominent in the relevant debate. Between 1984 and 1987 public debate tended to remain centred on the difficulty of distinguishing social objectives. The basic SOE model proposed to distinguish social from commercial objectives and make the former the subject of explicit agreements between governments and SOEs; the social objectives would be financed by taxpayers as such rather than by the customers of firms which happened to be SOEs or by taxpayers as involuntary shareholders in SOEs. The framework made it less likely that social objectives would be defined and pursued, especially by a government which faced extreme fiscal pressure, and there were few explicit utilisations of the framework.[83] Furthermore, it proved impossible to keep social and commercial objectives in separate compartments, especially when in the course of privatisation of both Telecom and Air New Zealand, "golden share" arrangements were used.

The core reason for believing that corporatisation was merely a prelude to privatisation was that corporatisation did not allow capture of all the gains from capital-market monitoring and single-minded shareholders. The core reason for believing that corporatisation was an equilibrium form was that governments have multiple objectives and have to be content with messy compromises. There were also ideological arguments about the desirability of co-operative behaviour as a political objective versus enhancement of freedom through the institution of private property. The argument with greatest support among relevant senior public servants was not that corporatisation was a prelude to privatisation but that it was a temporary phase while the business was exhaustively and rigorously evaluated so that the best possible partitioning could be achieved between what should be subject to ministerial direction—which should be brought back within a departmental structure—and what should be commercialised—which should be privatised. There was also some support among the relevant officials for seeing SOEs as permanent institutions; there was, for example, argument from within Treasury to see the Reserve Bank as within the SOE structure, and the argument was always about a permanent or at least long-term status for the Bank.[84] Ironically, those who took a conservative stance on issues such as whether SOEs should be treated as part of the public sector, rather than as commercial entities, in contexts such as the appropriate application of the Official Information Act strengthened the hands of those who saw SOEs as transitional. But eventually, the question was determined not by argument but by political exhaustion.

There were, therefore, plenty of issues about the role of government and the nature of society which were posed by reorganisation of state trading activity. There were still more when other parts of the public sector was subjected to the same search for the best institutional forms for achieving social and economic goals. Reorganising the Department of Scientific and Industrial Research and then replacing it with Crown Research Institutes challenged traditional ways of thinking. Not many would defend taxpayer funding for comfortable and unquestioned pursuit of individual interests, still fewer, for idleness, but the line between that and public support for the noble and valuable pursuit of knowledge was not easily drawn. "Public science" was not as longstanding as many thought, most of it having originated after World War II rather than being an outgrowth of earlier modest activity.

The notion of scientific research as the source of economic growth was equally recent, and only marginally true. After World War II lobbyists seeking to retain government funding that had been part of the war effort created the myth of a sequence from pure research, development in laboratories and on commercial scales, creating applied technology and so generating economic growth. It was never taken seriously by historians of science as explanation of the relationship between research and economic and social change. (This was all as true internationally as in New Zealand.) Insistence on rigorous analysis rather than uncritical acceptance of convenient myth baffled many who thought that expertise in an area of science was all that was required to determine how government revenue should be applied to that area. Not surprisingly, debate was intense, feeling ran high, and there was some unfortunate disruption of good research.[85] The relevance for social policy is not so much the issues of organisational design themselves, but another challenge to existing ideas about how society should be organised. Traditional lines of authority, the persistence of specific cultures which were "entitled" to support from public funds, longstanding recognition of respectability and social worth—all were questioned.

Most economists saw the issue as one of institutional design. Many joined me in seeing the role of the state in terms of a beehive; an arrangement whereby individuals pursued their own activities within constraints which ensured that they served the common good. Human societies, of course, are constrained less by physical infrastructure (despite some apparent exceptions in urban roading issues) than by the restraints of social mores and by rules on behaviour. These may be most effective if they are indirect and do not appear to impose requirements on individuals. This was no more than an application of the core of economic thinking which began with Adam Smith's attempt to state under what conditions private action motivated by self-interest would lead to a socially optimal outcome and which remained the motivation of the seminal work of Arrow and Debreu in the 1950s, and beyond. This view was not shared by all economists, and it was shared by few non-economists. (Indeed, the most common external view of economics is that it is about minimization of government rather than optimal allocation of different tasks to different institutions, including governments.)

Public debate was usually at a less rarefied level. The most common argument against specifying the role of government and making it transparent was that future governments might then remove what would become the visible instruments of government action.[86] Fear of an unknown future was a much greater barrier to progress than the power of any entrenched groups. Devolution with transparency was, and was intended to be, a defence against any repetition of government intervention in secret as had been practised by Prime Minister Muldoon. This was clearest in the 1989 Reserve Bank legislation where great care was taken to give the Bank instrument autonomy while ensuring that ultimate control remained with governments which held a democratic mandate and which were prepared to argue their case to the public.[87]

Government policy between 1984 and 1987 posed challenges to those who thought that the role of social policy was to preserve traditional sources of comfort and to provide instruments for direct management through collective institutions and processes. It is hard to resist the conclusion that social policy debate was most fundamentally about the degree of control which should be exercised by the State. Focus on choice among public and private instruments for pursuing public purposes was lost.

One particular aspect of social policy was rendered powerless because of the struggle over the role of the State. Given the implications of the changes being made, there was a fruitful field for social-impact assessment. It was agreed that the changes being implemented imposed transitional costs which fell on some individuals and groups with particular severity. Government policy could ease adjustment problems. There was a trade-off to be struck between alleviating adjustment problems and merely prolonging problems, but social impact assessment could facilitate a sound approach to making that trade-off. Social-impact assessment was not, however, at all successful between 1984 and 1987. Treasury and promoters of economic change were accused of sabotaging social-impact assessment efforts. My observation, however, was that champions of social impact assessment were too often not assisting to define and implement the best possible adjustment path, but used what purported to be social-impact assessment to undermine and relitigate economic policy. Social-impact skills were simply wasted in a fruitless and misguided attempt to construct arguments which lay outside the expertise of those involved. Uninformed public debate was extended and professional skills were not applied to a significant policy area.[88]

There was a similar issue at a more central political level. Before the 1984 election the Labour Party debated the possible role of an investment agency. Some advocated a significant government body engaging in investment in industry, making up for the incompetence of private investors who neglected opportunities for socially valuable investment. Others advocated a government agency which removed barriers to private investment. This role was often described in terms of making "transparent" the reasons why investment was constrained, and the debate was often in terms such as "transparency agency". The debate was long and involved, and eventually ended in favour of something close to the latter position, with the Economic Development Commission being the result.[89]

The debate sometimes extended to the role of the Planning Council and the extent to which it overlapped with the Economic Development Commission. The role of monitoring and reporting on economic, social, environmental and cultural development was very different from the focus on regulatory review which the EDC came to have, but there were certainly areas of common interest. Throughout 1986, largely under the leadership of Dennis Rose, the Planning Council sought to develop a notion of transparent co-operative planning which was compatible with the emphasis on efficient use of resources at the heart of the evolving economic policy. The ideas included carrying the notion of optimal allocation of tasks beyond the government–private sector dichotomy into what was common to sectors or industries rather than distinctive for individual firms. There were echoes of the distinction between the pre-competitive phase of industrial developments which had long been the practice of the much-misunderstood Ministry of International Trade and Industry in Japan. And there were links back to the 'indicative planning' of the 1960s in Europe and of the National Development Conference in New Zealand 1969–74.[90]

Considerable efforts were made with specific industries such as the meat industry. But the climate was not conducive; employers and unions were too keen to protect their own interests. Even after the subtle Ken Douglas replaced Jim Knox at the head of the trade union movement, trade unionists insisted on confronting employers, and employers looked for quicker returns than any planning process could offer. The effort to focus on common interest shared the usual fate of conciliators between warring parties; it was lost between those who wanted to promote change without too much concern about adjustment costs, and those who wanted to use arguments about adjustment mechanism to regain control of economic policy from antagonists who had a much higher level of economic literacy.[91]

The core issues in social policy were therefore: what is distinctive about public sector? How respectable is the materialistic? And what social changes cannot be contemplated? These remained the core social policy issues in the later 1980s and throughout the 1990s into the twenty-first century. They were clearly identified in 1984–87. Social policy in the sense of what benefits should exist and at what rates were much less important than the way that government decisions about its role shaped social attitudes and values.

ROYAL COMMISSION
Although it was said that explicit attention to social policy would be deferred to the second term, preparations were well under way before 1987. A Royal Commission would be used to chart the appropriate path. By early 1986, ministers were reporting serious debate about terms of reference and personnel. Disagreements quickly surfaced. There was no doubt that a serious study of social policy was wanted, but what did that mean? Much contemporary discussion was in terms of 'social justice', but the meaning of that term varied greatly—it generally connoted nothing more than a wish to maintain a high level and wide range of collective responsibility. There were supporters of 'traditional values', either because they were conservative

politically or because they saw no reason to change from the inspiration of the first Labour Government of "the first charge on the wealth of the nation being the aged, the sick and the poor". In between, there were those who wanted to re-examine the principles of social policy in the light of social changes since the 1930s. This was probably the most influential position within Treasury, but Treasury was believed by some to be intent on destroying the welfare state and minimising collective action. There were plenty of positions to be considered, and they were multiplied by alleged or suspected positions.[92]

By mid-1986 Lange had agreed that the terms of reference should include "responsibility of the individual".[93] It might seem extraordinary that anybody could think that a serious enquiry into social policy would not include examination of individual responsibility, but precise wordings of terms of reference can be symbolic, as well as constraining for lawyers. The issue was whether the Royal Commission should be concerned with defining a future path towards more collective action or whether it should be an examination of how social policy should be adapted to changing circumstances with the same focus on first principles as was being applied to economic policy. Should it be asked to define a path or should it be a vehicle to preserve social policy from the radical change being applied to economic policy?

The immediate debate was less over concepts than over personnel. As an academic, I had spent many hours in committees of various kinds. I had therefore experienced (and probably ridden) many hobby-horses and suffered interminable discussions for the sake of discussion. However, most of the committee reports in which I had been engaged reflected genuine engagement with competing ideas and the dominant influences on committee reports were ideas and information. From the late 1970s I became more familiar with non-academic committees, and learned why so much attention was paid to their composition. What people brought to committees was often more important than what they did as committee members. Those who formed the Royal Commission on Social Policy knew this.

The senior officials advising the Prime Minister suggested to him that Auckland lawyer Ted Thomas would be a suitable chair, and once Lange satisfied himself that he would, those officials expected to fill the commission with the "usual suspects" and to recruit a suitable secretariat. But the process was far from smooth. Lange was not prepared to fight for what he wanted. He encountered strong pressure to exclude any Treasury influence. Ted Thomas was not satisfied that the membership of the Commission and the secretariat were sufficiently independent of government and political commitments and he eventually withdrew. In any case, Lange had become disenchanted with him. By October 1986, intense disputes between Cabinet and Caucus were creeping into the public arena. The membership of the Commission was announced late in October. The chair was Ivor Richardson, a judge of the Court of Appeal, and members were Ann Ballin, a psychologist with personal experience of physical disability, Marion Bruce of the Wellington Hospital Board who had personal and professional experience in providing services to those with disabilities, Mason Durie, a psychiatrist and Maori leader although not then as obviously so as he now is, and Ros Noonan, prominent in the Labour Party and trade unions and a former researcher in social history. It was always going to be a body which adjudicated on what was placed before it rather than an engine for a directed social enquiry. The Commission would engage in a 'greenfields' consultation exercise, and then distil wisdom. That the Commission was clearly going to be a minefield of competing political activists and community pressure groups meant that it had difficulty recruiting a professional secretariat too. It appointed as manager W.E. Dasent, a retired academic chemist and bursar with whom Ivor Richardson had worked as a member of the council of Victoria University of Wellington, and he tried to recruit and manage expertise in economics and social analysis. Later Len Cook, Government Statistician, provided professional direction and was added to the membership of the Commission, but it always had problems assessing the evidence put in front of it. Separating advocacy from analysis required more professional expertise than was available.[94]

I should acknowledge that there was tension between the Royal Commission and the Planning Council. We thought that our work on integration of social and economic policy, and our networks throughout the community could be useful to the Commission. We were suspected of wanting to control the Commission. I think the suspicion was misguided, although my colleagues shared my view that a simple process of listening to the people, adjudicating among competing views, and distilling a new basis for social policy could not possibly be done within the Government's time-frame. The eventual frustration of the Commission and its premature resignation of its mandate because the Government was making policy decisions while it thought it was still conducting the analysis on which those decisions should be based was the immediate implication of the Commission's initial choice of its mode of proceeding. But the view which prevailed was that anything which looked like Treasury's management of economic policy should be excluded from the Royal Commission, and that included the Planning Council.

There were nevertheless informal contacts about people who might do research for the Commission, there was collaboration on an income distribution conference, and when Ivor Richardson eventually agreed that there was sense in some common membership, Marion Bruce became a valued member of the Planning Council.[95] The Planning Council discussed the one substantive report the Commission produced: *Taxing Issues* offered a review of trends in taxation which did not advance beyond a Planning Council report of nearly a decade earlier and did not engage with the serious analysis of taxation which underlay the introduction of GST.[96] It advanced a ludicrous suggestion of a "carer's allowance" with little attention to eligibility criteria, let alone incentives.

The Commission issued thereafter only the *April Report* (1988) when it was obvious that the Government was not going to wait and the Commission, in Lange's phrase, "packed it in". The *April Report* is valuable to academic researchers as a compilation of reports about New Zealand society in the 1980s, although it gives an odd picture of New Zealand society since it depends so heavily on which particular interests thought it worthwhile to devote time and energy to making submissions. The principal inference of Commission staff was that New Zealanders were seeking "voice, choice and safe passage", to be consulted, to be allowed to decide among options, and still to have a high degree of security. Those objectives, so obviously in tension if not conflict, could be a useful starting point for a lot of analysis, but they clearly did not contribute much to policy design.

Taxing Issues referred to the New Zealand tradition of providing flat-rate benefits rather than replacing for the disadvantaged a proportion of the income to which they had been accustomed. New Zealand had developed its system (similar to Australia) when the relationship with the international economy had taken a specific form and when wage fixing was through central conciliation and arbitration. European economies, which often inspired advocates of 'social justice', had evolved along a different path after World War II as economic integration had proceeded. There was no real engagement with this disjunction. Len Cook ensured that the Commission was aware of demographic trends. An ageing population was shifting attention away from how to redistribute income to the aged, the sick and the poor and towards what the role of the State should be in facilitating the ability of people, individually or collectively, to shift income from the years of employment to the period of retirement. Little progress was made even in this area.

Politics got in the way of social policy. Between 1984 and 1987 the key issues of the role of government in redistribution and the means for making collective decisions were identified, but the Royal Commission on Social Policy did not make substantial progress towards answering them.

PICOT AND GIBBS

It was soon obvious that the Royal Commission on Social Policy was not going to produce a blueprint for the future of social policy. Government initiatives in all the major areas of social policy went ahead independently. In every case there was an agenda of issues from before the advent of the Lange Government that did not stop, and when the injunction to wait for the Royal Commission became less cogent, they began to get more traction. I was especially interested in education, and Henry Lang, with whom I interacted weekly in 1987, was especially interested in health. We tended therefore to take most interest in those fields; had Henry or I had other interests, social welfare would have loomed much larger.

My first involvement was with a dead end, although it was a dead end which still plays quite frequently. The Planning Council in the early 1980s was attracted by the idea of a coherent approach to youth policy and it entertained ideas emerging from educationists that students should be supported to the same extent as unemployed youth. Two officials from the Department of Education were seconded to the staff of the Planning Council and led projects on what an integrated system of youth allowances might look like.[97] There is an obvious appeal in the idea that somebody who was engaged in study should be no less rewarded than somebody who was simply unemployed, and even more appeal in the idea that unemployed youth should not be discouraged from increasing their skills and employability by being paid a dole if they did nothing and being left without support if they enrolled in an educational institution. But it is inadequate analysis; it takes too little account of different situations. Some young people are investing in future incomes. Paying them allowances while they do so is equivalent to paying somebody to divert all their income into investment and to rely on social subsidies to provide for consumption, while themselves enjoying all the benefits of the investment in future years. There is little case for that, no matter how skilfully the rhetoric of 'social justice' is deployed. Access to education should be explored and the nature and causes of youth unemployed should be investigated. Putting them together was, and is, a dead end. Advocacy of youth allowance can be seen as a high point of regarding the state as source of undifferentiated manna. (The right response to the wrong incentives created by paying the unemployed but not those engaged in education and training is to change the conditions of eligibility for unemployment relief.)

Not surprisingly, the Planning Council projects got bogged down in seeking to rationalise the complicated array of existing benefits rather than looking at principles. If the idea had gone further, it would have had the same effect as National Super did after 1975. It would have led to rejection of wasteful government expenditure rather than acceptance of what could be defended as an elaborate scheme of redistribution which avoided stigma by distributing widely but reclaiming from all but intended beneficiaries.[98] The idea, nevertheless, lived on—it was part of discussions of tertiary student grants in 1987[99] and it recurs frequently in student lobbying now.

The Department of Education had many ambitions beside a coherent system of student allowances. It wanted to resume work on the modernising agenda of the 1970s after what it saw as the years of the deadening hand of Merv Wellington as Minister of Education, rejoining education policy to social changes rather than being concerned with outdated institutions such as school flag ceremonies. Its director-general, Bill Renwick, was beginning what would soon become a distinguished contribution to rethinking the Treaty of Waitangi and management of Maori–Pakeha relations.[100] The Department was somewhat preoccupied with critiques about how schooling related to socio-economic stratification in the community. While this was fascinating to some academics and it impinges on significant policy issues, change came from elsewhere. Key drivers were the role of human capital in economic growth and the role of information in social and political life. Many department officials eventually concluded that because they dealt with a challenge from the left of the political spectrum they failed to see one from the right of that spectrum. But even in the mid-1980s it was a mistake to be preoccupied with political analysis which was old-fashioned (although it still preoccupies many educationists and political commentators twenty years later). The important challenges lay in society and the economy, not in politics.

There was clearly going to be a major enquiry into university finance. Treasury was concerned about the next quinquennial, the standard instrument for financing universities since the 1960s.[101] Leading politicians such as Geoffrey Palmer and David Caygill were interested in how universities were financed.[102] Audits or enquiries into the effectiveness of university financing were advocated, and debate was more over whether a wide or focused enquiry was desirable rather than about the principle of enquiry. Thinking stalled when it appeared that the topic might be part of a Royal Commission on Social Policy but that was no more than a delay.

The universities eventually acted themselves and set up a review which produced the Watts Report. Unfortunately, it looked not to the future but firmly back to the 1960s and a cosy arrangement among 'social partners'.[103]

The universities tended to see themselves as of major concern to the Government. In fact, policy issues were about education rather than institutions. Even when institutions were relevant, the management of polytechnics tended to loom larger in the minds of officials and ministers than did universities. Polytechnics had grown from the 1960s with a core idea of educating technicians—somewhere between the professions which were served by universities, and trades which could be accommodated by apprenticeships and on-job training. This conception was irrelevant by the 1980s, when the issue had become the the spread of human capital throughout the labour force. Polytechnics, with a narrow mission and subject to detailed control from a central ministry, could not make the required adjustments. The Department of Education was trying to find new institutional forms. Reports known as Young–Hercus and Probine–Fargher explored options. The Planning Council was included in these consultations and then I was invited to be a member of a small group of advisers who the Department consulted on such issues. In this capacity I learned about efforts to use polytechnics to assist with redeployment of workers displaced by such events as closures of major freezing works, the general search for "responsiveness" in education institutions, and the depth of commitment to making available educational opportunities for the emerging economy and society. The debate was a long way from what was dominating the news media.[104]

The venue for all these debates was seldom in the public eye. It was the Cabinet Ad Hoc Committee on Training and Education. It responded to youth unemployment as economic restructuring proceeded. Topics such as how social stratification in schools and suburbs impacted on the rights of young people to education were remote from the experience of those working with young unemployed and their need for remedial education. Concern in polytechnics to maintain a focus on technicians and not to be confused with trades training seemed precious and self-centred when contrasted with the need for life skills if young people were to be attractive to potential employers. As the need for remedial education became apparent, teachers reacted defensively to what they interpreted as attacks on them. Even searches for ways forward with no interest at all in attributing blame created resentment. Defensive responses deflected attention from the creation of income support for young people (conceived as a search for effective mechanisms for equipping people with the capacity to be employed, rather than as the distribution of manna from government).[105]

Practical issues gave substance to academic research and thinking about the place of education in society. The key issues were not generalised access of social groups to primary schools, but how to ensure that schools were effective in generating the learning needed for a modern society and economy. For those familiar with recruits for the schemes seeking to facilitate youth employment, Access and MAccess, there could be no doubt that schools were not succeeding. Debate about whether this was because of teaching deficiencies,[106] bad parents, or an unsympathetic society, let alone whose 'fault' it was, mattered much less than finding ways to change the unsatisfactory outcome. In the tertiary field, what was being worked out was not any recent decision about government's role in education, but the implications of decisions from 1945 onwards about mass tertiary education rather than supporting some education for professionals and finishing school for the well-off.

The principal debates among officials of the Cabinet Ad Hoc Committee were not about Treasury distorting the purpose of education but between officials of the Department of Education and the Department of Labour about the extent to which public funding should be tied closely to outcomes. The Department of Labour wanted to define outcomes for those on programmes like Access and MAccess and pay providers who achieved them. The Department of Education argued that funding should be conditional on compliance with established educational processes. There is a clear echo in arguments in the 1990s about the appropriate "tightness" with which funding was tied to student achievement. The debate was then properly moved forward by looking at where "tightness" and "looseness" was most appropriate. Even in the mid-1980s, the politics of left and right were discarded in favour of technocratic arguments about whether learning could be assessed separately from evaluation of teaching, and whether the funder should be concerned with teaching practice or leave that to institutions. This was the context in which thinking about measurement of social and private returns to education, the impact of barriers on specific groups such as Maori and women, the impact of examinations which selected students for further education rather than recognising what had been achieved, and other major educational issues were debated as more than academic topics.[107]

The debates soon spread into wider contexts. They did so in various ways. If more resources were needed to provide remedial education for young unemployed who had failed to learn in schools, could they be secured by shifting resources from schools where they were failing to achieve intended (or even promised) results? If assessment of social and private returns provided some information which was useful for apportioning costs of polytechnic courses between employers and taxpayers, did it also provide guidance on an apportionment of university costs between students and taxpayers? Such questions tapped into contemporary literatures overseas and theoretical discussions in New Zealand. Student loans and fees was such a literature, quickly appropriated in New Zealand by the Opposition spokesperson, Ruth Richardson, and the Opposition Research Unit, with its lively analyst Michael Laws.[108] There was plenty of discussion in universities too, and there was wider thinking in the usual Wellington policy community, including senior Treasury officials who anticipated political difficulties when parents realised who would be paying fees.[109] As in other contexts, the term 'user pays' was never more than an initial step towards identifying beneficiaries, no matter how often it was treated as the answer to a policy question. There is genuine policy content in worries about undermining of community reciprocity, and this was understood by politicians such as David Lange and Russell Marshall.[110] But the fine thinking needed on trust, reciprocity and an appropriate location of costs with beneficiaries was soon lost. Lange was vocal in opposition to 'voucher education', but he was responding to Ruth Richardson and not to the policy debates about social and private returns to education.[111]

Similar debates—wrestling with real social and economic problems in New Zealand, managing the political debate with overseas ideas, local thinking and much inherited prejudice—could be found in other areas of social policy. Indeed, the issues were even clearer in health. Medical pressure groups, especially health professionals, were stronger and more articulate than their counterparts in education. Furthermore, while teachers seemed to think that the world revolved around schools, and while it is true that everyone thinks they know about schools because they remember their experiences there, health tends to be a more pressing concern for most people as they deal with the cycle of children's ailments, parents' decline and the consequences of age. Health institutions were bigger and more public than education ones, and so there was a bigger immediate link with the changes in public management that were occurring in departments and SOEs. Key issues such as the 'provider/funder' split as a way of using incentives to make institutions more responsive to citizens were more prominent in health than in education. There was the same distinction to be made between the analysis of contemporary problems, and rhetoric about "managerialism" and "economic rationalism" undermining public institutions which were essential to civilization. Health activists were skilled at managing two public relations lines: the health system was on its last legs and would collapse in the absence of more public funding; and the health system was a triumph of public enterprise and should on no account be subjected to change. The chair of the Auckland Health Board, Frank Rutter,[112] coined the term 'shroud waving' for variants of the claim "if we are not given more money, people will die". The nurses' organisation was adept at recycling two press statements: one announcing a shortage of nurses who should therefore be paid more; and the other complaining about the absence of positions for nurses emerging from training so that hospitals should have more money to employ them. At the same time they consistently regretted the subjugation of nurses to medical staff with inflated egos. Occasionally rhetoric and analysis made contact.[113]

The health debate was more visible than the education one. Alan Gibbs was retained to chair an enquiry into hospital administration. Its proceedings were better known than an equivalent enquiry into education which was underway in 1987. This was the Picot Committee, which became the most important single influence on all the changes in the education sector in the 1987–90 term of the Labour Government and indeed through the 1990s. The Gibbs Committee and the Picot Committee had many similarities, but they had very different outcomes. Essentially, Picot was implemented, while Gibbs was discarded. David Caygill deliberately disrupted an IPS seminar to ensure that the Gibbs Report was sabotaged as it was launched.

Both committees were appointed by one minister and reported to another. Picot began with Marshall and reported to Lange, while Gibbs began with Bassett and reported to Caygill. These ministerial changes resulted from changes in political sentiment, but they do not easily explain the different outcomes. Both committees focused on administration rather than policy, but both used administration as a vehicle for exploring resource allocation, and finished with similar content, the central message being that institutional structures and the incentives they created should be revised. While they claimed to be putting to one side matters of professional expertise, both committees upset pressure groups. Education lobbyists followed their time-honoured strategy of 'absorb and ignore', while medical activists engaged in shroud waving.

The committees differed in presentation and publicity skills. Picot was a superb salesman, the master of a telling phrase which created empathy with his audience while he was making his point. He talked about "good people, bad system" which was about half true in both halves but which deterred an entirely defensive reaction by educationists. He talked about "local autonomy within national guidelines", with which nobody would disagree even if they had very different ideas about what should be in the guidelines and what should be subject to autonomous decisions. He presented himself as a simple grocer, and anybody who believed that was credulous. He had been a successful manager in the grocery business, but he had a long involvement in public affairs, with the Planning Council and in education institutions. He took responsibility for the report; he managed the committee's proceedings to ensure that the expert staff was well utilised, but decisions were made by members and he then talked only about what the committee had decided. Gibbs was a much more colourful character and the Gibbs Report was only a part of his public role—he was engaged in corporatisation of Forestry and he could always be induced to talk about privatisation and what he would like to do if he were not restrained by other members of the committee and its staff. He referred to the "Gordon Davies report", Davies being one of its key staff members, who knew a good deal about hospital management. The report was written in a way that could easily be challenged; it had a sophisticated comparison of cost levels among hospitals but it was often read as assuming that all else was similar.

There were, however, more than presentation differences. Picot dealt with bureaucracy and compulsory schooling. Gibbs dealt with the interface between primary and secondary providers and more generally with the interaction of public and private sectors. If the Picot committee had been required to deal immediately with post-compulsory education it would have had to grapple with the questions of public and private funding and its central messages would probably have had a more difficult passage. The really central social policy issues were around the balance of collective and private activity; Picot's brief circumvented some difficulties.

These two committees were working in 1984–87 and reported soon after that period. They set the directions for social policy development in 1987–90 although different mechanisms were used then, especially Cabinet Social Equity Committee Working Groups. They show that by 1987 social policy had moved well beyond scoping towards implicit decisions on many lines of development.

DECEMBER 1987 PACKAGE

The December 1987 package falls outside the period of the first term of the Lange Government, but it throws light on how social policy thinking evolved in that period. The 1987 election result seemed to me and to many others an "endorsement for Rogernomics"; Lange talked about the "maturity of the electorate's judgement", and many inherited conventional beliefs seemed to have been dispensed with. We could no longer believe that any incidence of unemployment would be fatal to an incumbent government—the inheritance of the 1930s, and the mythology about Holyoake personally knowing every unemployed person in New Zealand had given way to acceptance that a process of economic adjustment was unavoidable. The National Party's strategy of capturing secondary-centre seats through anxiety about youth unemployment failed. But there could be no sense of triumph. Economic adjustment was painful and there was some evidence that ministers were less popular electorally than other government candidates.[114] There were indications that the Cabinet was less unified than it had been, although it was some time before the depth of the split became apparent.[115]

The Government had indicated that it would move on areas such as education immediately after the election.[116] It did so across the whole of social policy, with Working Groups reporting to the Cabinet Social Equity Committee as the key instrument. The simple mechanism of requiring conveners to note dissenting views but mandating them to define choices for Cabinet rather than seek compromises broke many log-jams. Working groups on post-compulsory education (which I chaired) and on early childhood education joined the Picot Committee.

Any possibility of a smooth transition to a comprehensive approach to social policy soon proved ephemeral. The stock market crash of October 1987 brought a sharp dose of reality to dangerously euphoric financial markets. It took a very long time to adjust to sharp changes in asset values. Disagreements about the role of government intensified. Those who saw both a need and an opportunity to press on with radical change ran into determined opposition from those who sought to revive their interpretation of the traditions of the Labour Party and of the New Zealand welfare state.

The evolution of social policy between 1984 and 1987 ended, therefore, not in a new integration of social and economic policy adapted to the society of the 1990s, but in a break-up of the Government. The package of measures announced on 17 December 1987 (and abandoned by the Prime Minister in early 1988) was exciting for those who sought radical approaches, but appalling to those who thought familiar instruments would provide much-needed reassurance against the effect of the financial crash. The Royal Commission on Social Policy found reason for saying that its work had been pre-empted, and eventually Roger Douglas left Cabinet and the Government struggled to find any political coherence.

The political conflict was overt and can be understood, but there was a deeper policy debate. Education policy caused disputes as people struggled with change. Health policy was even more difficult because issues of private and social costs and benefits could not be displaced from centre stage. Most difficult of all, however, was social welfare—the appropriate approach to redistribution or the construction of benefit systems for the disadvantaged with costs distributed among taxpayers.

The December package was much as expected for those who recognised the logic by which social policy had been moving. It had, though, a key weakness. This was not the flat tax per se, although that was what attracted public attention. It might once have attracted derision as the kind of policy associated only with politicians like Joh Bjelke Petersen who indulged in romantic nostalgia, and it had got little support when discussed in a Planning Council analysis of taxation issues in the 1970s. By 1987, consensus analysis had moved quite a long way. (I learned about it from the Institute of Policy Studies projects on tax incidence.) Redistribution by progressive tax does not work in a world characterised by two-income families, long periods of retirement, health expenditure which is divided between discretionary cosmetic surgery and major disaster events, and education which is lifelong rather than for the young and which is the fundamental basis of economic growth. If social policy has to be built on planned and managed redistribution through expenditure, progressive taxation can be discarded in favour of the gains to economic efficiency from flat tax.

It was no longer necessary to undertake the difficult task of restraining the vehicles of tax avoidance which had meant that progressivity was more apparent than real. (By the mid-1980s there was a case for saying that progressivity applied to public-sector wage and salary earners and nobody else. The dentist who owned a kiwi-fruit farm and so avoided tax was typical rather than exceptional. Certainly there was evidence that tax incidence was more progressive after marginal tax rates were lowered than it had been before; that is, those with relatively high incomes paid more tax relative to those with low incomes when tax rates were lower and less progressive but there were fewer ways to avoid tax. Nostalgia was not a good reason for basing policy on progressive tax. The tax policy implemented in the 1980s was not concessions to the rich, but a wider tax base made possible by lower tax rates.) There were still issues to be pursued. Was the political context such as to give assurance that redistribution would be pursued? Otherwise changing to different instruments could be an excuse for abandoning the objective. In particular, for technical reasons, the flat tax would have to be at a lower level than the current average rate.

Redistribution therefore had to be more tightly targeted, and there would be constrained total government revenue unless there was significant economic growth. Views about the growth impact could reasonably differ, but the policy recommendation was based on the belief that growth would be faster, not that public spending should be restrained. That did not prevent suspicion that the package was intended to constrain the Government's expenditure plans by limiting government revenue. And even for those who believed that economic growth would permit expenditure plans to be realised despite lower tax rates, the ratio of collective consumption to private consumption would certainly fall. For those whose objective was not redistribution but a sizable public sector per se, the policy implications were unpalatable.

The redistribution included in the December '87 package was substantial, but there were analytical reasons for regarding the policy development as incomplete. The package included a guaranteed minimum family income scheme, but the analytics of using the tax and benefit system to ensure that family income in one year became the basis for establishing a floor to family income in subsequent years were not developed convincingly. The change proposed was great, including a departure from flat-rate benefits which were traditional in New Zealand (and

Australia), but uncommon elsewhere. Such a major change, ironically opposed by the Royal Commission on Social Policy in one of its few collective decisions, requires a long period of acculturation. It could be expected to find favour with proponents of 'social justice' but most of them did not begin to come to grips with the content of the December '87 package, being content to reject it on the basis of its origins. More important, beyond the point of principle, the mechanics of using the tax and benefit system to guarantee a changing minimum income in the face of fluctuating earnings were never properly evaluated. It was this incompleteness which was the key policy weakness of the package. But it was the politics of the initiative which undermined the Government.[117]

The fate of the December '87 package shows that there is a limit to how far leaders can get in front of their followers. It also shows that the question of how economic and social policy should be integrated was clearly identified in 1984–87. It is still with us.

The 1987 proposals are sometimes likened to the *Titanic*. At a simple level, the point is that a large ship sailing at full speed is difficult to manoevre. But the deeper lesson of the *Titanic* is that the technological edge can be sunk by a very conventional danger. There is clearly some weight in the analogy, but so there is in what has been said about other uses of the *Titanic* image: loss of the *Titanic* is not the only maritime disaster in history, and the tragic loss in 1915 of the Great Lakes passenger ship the S.S. *Eastland*, which capsized due to mismanagement at the cost of 844 lives while secured at its berth in Chicago is a much more appropriate analogy than the sinking of a state-of-the-art vessel by elemental natural forces in international waters.[118]

The choice was not between the approach to social policy that culminated in the December '87 package and a comfortable quiet life. The feasible alternative was a different process of change which was likely to have as many dangers, albeit different ones.

CONCLUSION

Henry Lang commented frequently between 1984 and 1987 that the "intellectual work has not been done". He was contrasting social policy initiatives with the introduction of where the analysis was extensive, extended over a long period so that the issues achieved wide familiarity, and where consultation was eventually focused on implementation issues. Even so, there was a debate about 'exemptions' which continues to dominate many memories of the mid-1980s but which was essentially a by-play to the policy development. Other policy initiatives were certainly less well prepared, but it is not always clear when it is right to describe the intellectual work as "not done" and when to acknowledge that it produced results which are uncongenial.

Intellectual work was certainly needed. Answers could not be found in wishful thinking about the principles of the welfare state in the 1930s. The problems of the 1980s could not be solved by any simple implementation of compassion. Nor could they be solved by a simple assertion of any textbook logic. The key issue might be stated as "Where do we go when economists' comments on things like the efficiency and equity of the health system are met with the assertion that communal acceptance of responsibility for health is the hall-mark of a modern civilised society just as the abolition of slavery was in earlier times?"[119]

My location of the key issue as economics versus non-economic thinking will naturally attract scepticism. There were different views among economists as there were among practitioners of other disciplines. Some public policy analysts were not dominated by any particular discipline, and yet I think the central question did rest, above all, on an understanding of economics. (I will, of course, eventually accept the verdict of historians, especially economic historians.)

What made economics pre-eminent was not any 'power of money' or obsession with the material. The belief that "economics was about only money" was misguided and crippled critics of government policy. Economics was crucial because the single most important issue was to adjust social policy to how people had come to behave in the fifty years after the 1930s, and economics deals centrally with incentives. There is a comic-book version of history in which Adam Smith is associated with minimum government and ideological commitment to 'the market', and there is a history in which Adam Smith was concerned with 'sympathy' as well as 'self-interest', with the institutions required to ensure that self-interest serves the public interest, and with the optimal allocation of functions between collective and individual endeavour. The history is known to few, whether economists or not, but it is this history which gave economics its pre-eminence in the 1980s.

The key issues were identified between 1984 and 1987. They are still with us.

HILARY STACE
Labour owes us – the 1984 women's forums

"It's not an exaggeration to say that Labour slid to power on our votes. To put it bluntly, Labour owes us."[1] This comment from the Public Service Association's Joanna Beresford at the Women's Summit in early October 1984 sums up the prevailing attitude of many women's movement activists. In July a new Labour Government had overturned three terms of conservative rule. Women, particularly those identifying as feminist, were idealistic, organised and ready for change. One of the first consultative acts of the new government was an economic summit, but its lack of input from women was the impetus for a women's summit held at Wellington High School in the first weekend of October. The meeting was open to all women and many women's groups had also been invited. The speaker quoted above called for "a fairer slice of the country's economic resources" for women, and also warned the audience "But a huge feminist effort will be needed to ensure that an economic and social strategy is developed and implemented that not only does us no harm but which also involves positive improvements."[2]

It is highly ironic that the speaker identified economic policy as the key to change. These women were fighting for inclusion in a consensus society, unaware that the fourth Labour Government would be remembered mainly for dismantling this consensus. While women's rights, human rights and anti-nuclear activists concentrated on social and foreign policy issues, several members of the new government, led by Roger Douglas, were quietly and efficiently creating a restructured New Zealand where the rules and battles would be quite different. As Helen Clark later said, "Like rust, Roger and the Treasury never slept."[3]

Nevertheless, major gender equity initiatives were begun in the first term of the fourth Labour Government and the new Ministry of Women's Affairs was intended to oversee their implementation. An unprecedented consultative process of prioritising the Ministry's programme was undertaken before its formal establishment. It is conservatively estimated that 12,000 women took part in the 21 forums that were held between October and December 1984.[4] Although officially consensus was achieved, few anticipated the intense debate this exercise unleashed. Reported and possibly embellished by the media, this was a battle between the "feminists" and the conservative "Christian" women, or those wanting social change and those fearing it. Like other defining issues before and since, the debate reflected an ongoing and vigorous discussion about New Zealand's identity.

It may be hard today to understand the feelings, both enthusiastic and fearful, that the impact of the second wave of feminism (starting in the 1960s) had aroused by 1984. We have recently seen similar polarisation around the civil union legislation. The United Nations declared 1975 International Women's Year and the following ten years the Decade for Women. In New Zealand many women's groups sprang up to promote various causes such as abortion rights or the political power of women. In response to public opinion National Governments had made some significant legislative changes such as the Equal Pay Act 1972, Matrimonial Property Act 1976, Human Rights Commission Act 1977 (outlawing gender discrimination), and in 1980, under its spokesman on Women's Affairs Jim McLay, set up the Advisory Committee on Women's Affairs (ACWA). The United Nations Convention on the Elimination of all forms of Discrimination Against Women (known as CEDAW) was signed in 1980 by former National MP Colleen Dewe as chair of ACWA.[5] But support for feminist causes was far from the Muldoon Government's agenda.

Power struggles were reflected in the Labour Party itself. Active women's branches started soon after the foundation of the Party. But by the 1970s many daughters of the Party founders were ageing and their activism reflected earlier times. The new Party women wanted to "make policy, not tea",[6] and in 1975 an elected Labour Women's Council (LWC) replaced the Party's Women's Advisory Committee (WAC). Anger at lack of policy input, dismissive treatment of the women's report and the growing number of younger active feminist women in the Party were significant reasons for change.[7] The defeat of the third Labour Government in 1975 and the ascent of the pugnacious Muldoon were other catalysts. While Labour was in opposition the LWC networked and strengthened through annual women's policy conferences. Due to their efforts the 1978 party conference voted to repeal the conservative abortion law, and in 1980 (largely from the impetus of trade unionist Sonja Davies) passed the Working Women's Charter, including controversial sections on abortion law, child care and sex education. Policies for a Ministry of Women's Affairs came out of the 1983 Labour Women's Conference chaired by Margaret Wilson.[8]

The snap election of July 1984 meant lack of time to prepare a full manifesto. But a brief Election '84 official policy release stated:

In all spheres—economic, social, cultural, legal and political—Labour will play a leading role in promoting and achieving equality for women.
Specific policies include:

- The establishment of a Ministry of Women's Affairs;
- A wide range of affirmative action programmes in the employment area, both in the public and private sectors and on statutory bodies;
- Greater recognition of the contribution of women who work at home and in the community;
- The promotion of a diverse range of quality child-care facilities adequately funded;
- Review of legislation as it effects women, including rape reform and the Human Rights Commission.[9]

The *National Business Review* of 2 July featured a snap-election special on women, by Virginia Myers. National MP Ruth Richardson wanted asset sharing between partners for tax purposes but her priority for the '80s was "encouraging more active participation of women in public life". Labour's Ann Hercus explained her party's policy of affirmative action, which was "aimed at removing barriers—particularly barriers of the mind—to promoting women on merit are very important ... so too are job redesign, job sharing, more flexible work hours, career opportunities for women in the public and private sectors."[10] The article also flagged opposition to CEDAW by groups such as Women for Life as potential flashpoints. Labour's intention to ratify CEDAW worried the Concerned Parents' Association and their July newsletter urged members to question local candidates.[11]

Soon after her selection as the new Minister of Women's Affairs, Ann Hercus was interviewed for Radio New Zealand on the proposed ministry and the role of women in society:

> It will have a minister sitting around the cabinet table where the final decision-making processes take place. The voice of women ... will be heard at the cabinet table. That means, for example, that every single bit of legislation will be monitored by the Ministry of Women's Affairs .... It will mean, for example, that the ability of our new government to appoint women—many more women—to the 800 statutory boards, commissions and tribunals, will be enhanced, because we will have a monitoring mechanism both within cabinet and without to ensure that that happens. It means that legislation of particular concern to women, for example, rape law reform, will be vigorously promoted, won't be allowed to slide off the back of the table in a legislative rush. It means that there will be, in my view, far more effective liaison with women's organisations, far more effective funding of women's projects, far more effective promotion and monitoring of affirmative action programmes.
>
> It's going to be small, it's going to be high-powered, it's going to be compact. It will be given adequate resources for its role as an initiator, a coordinator and a monitor of activities affecting women but I must stress it's going to be a small, high-powered and very active ministry. ... I believe the ministry becomes a very important symbol of a vast educational programme that I think has to be undertaken in this country across so many spheres.
>
> I think it is fair to say that many women are struggling to see themselves as equals but you know it's very hard–when you are told for generations that you are, in effect, inferior, then you come to believe it. If you are told that your rightful role is only as a carer of children or as a carer of old people then you come to believe that that is the only horizon for you and it's an undervalued horizon. If you are told, as a person in the workforce, that your job is first at risk because you are a woman, then you come to believe you are a dispensable part of the workforce instead of recognizing that the economy would collapse if women pulled out. I think it is hard for women to battle the prejudices that they're presented with, daily.[12]

New Labour MP Anne Fraser (later Collins) fought prejudice in her maiden speech by criticising the sexist comments from male opposition MPs during the swearing-in ceremony.[13] Muldoon's patronising response was "for my part I, I think, this morning I sat next to this lady on the aeroplane and did not know she was a Member of Parliament. That's how much notice I took of her swearing-in."[14] A few weeks later, retiring Waipa MP Marilyn Waring was the guest of honour at a Suffrage Day celebration at the Beehive. She described the life of a woman MP as a "private hell".[15]

In early October the Wellington Women's Summit, mentioned above, made the headlines for excluding men, including male reporters, although men ran the crèche (which the *Dominion* reported had about 30 children, including nine in nappies).[16] Several hundred women attended, and although angry about lack of input into the Government's September economic summit, they were "trying to cooperate with government consensus initiatives".[17]

Maori women had also been organising themselves. At the women's summit a Maori woman claimed that "New Zealand had never met the cultural, social, economic, spiritual or mental needs of Maori women" but "your ignorance has been excusable".[18] It is interesting to note that a few months earlier the YWCA made news by setting up a Maori and Pacific Island women's office in response to claims of racism in the organisation.[19]

An advisory group ran from August to December to prepare for the Ministry of Women's Affairs the consultative process to hear submissions and gather input. In order to include as many women as possible, forums were held throughout the country. Eventually (because of demand) 21 were held, including one for Pacific Island women in Tokoroa. Some parallel hui for Maori women were held in conjunction with other forums.[20] The numbers participating in this exercise in participatory democracy show unprecedented interest in social policy initiatives at this time. Attendance included about 400 in Invercargill, 100 in Blenheim and 1,500 in Lower Hutt at a particularly busy time of year.[21]

These one-day forums were organised jointly by the advisory group, Labour women MPs and local women. Groups like the Women's Electoral Lobby were actively involved.[22] Most forums featured a speech by one (sometimes two) Labour women. The participants then broke into workshops to prioritise the Ministry's programme, followed by a plenary session.

Much controversy centred around the issues themselves. By October the policy details incomplete at the time of the election, were finalised. The Government's view was that the forums were to assist with prioritising these identified issues. However, some women attempted to overturn or add new ones. From press reports abortion law, child care, sex education and opposition to the ratification of CEDAW caused the most outrage.[23]

The media reports started immediately. At most forums men were asked to leave after the initial speeches and this made good copy. The *Evening Post* of 3 November reported that the Minister herself was "pushed to the ground as angry women tried to evict a group of men" from the Canterbury women's forum earlier that day at Hagley High School. A man was later charged with assault.[24]

The *Dominion* report of the following Monday put the number attending the Christchurch forum at 1,000 and quoted a spokesman [sic] pleased at the diversity of women attending who had met to "discuss Government's policy on women and to set priorities for the new Ministry of Women's Affairs". The report added that the priorities decided included "the need for funding and support for community-based health programmes, input into educational decision-making, support for low-income families, minority and ethnic groups, disabled and rural women" and that women's groups wanted "effective communication with the new ministry" and that such meetings be held again.[25]

That day's *Evening Post* carried a report on long-serving MP Mary Batchelor's anger at the "intolerance" expressed at the forum. She claimed she had "championed"

FORUM TIMETABLE[26]

	Region/town held	Estimated attendance	Government speakers
27 Oct	Southland held in Invercargill	400	Ann Hercus
	Marlborough/Blenheim	100	Margaret Austin
	Taumarunui	60	
3 Nov	Canterbury/Christchurch	1,000	Ann Hercus, Mary Batchelor
	Whangarei/Northland	250	Judy Keall
10 Nov	Waikato/Hamilton	1,100	Anne Fraser
	Bay of Plenty/Tauranga	450	Judy Keall
	Taranaki/New Plymouth	400	Annette King
17 Nov	Auckland	2-3,000	Helen Clark, Judy Keall
	Wellington/Lower Hutt	1,500	Fran Wilde
	Otago/Dunedin	600-900	Ann Hercus, Margaret Austin
	Hawkes Bay/Napier	1,000	Anne Fraser, Whetu Tirikatene-Sullivan
	Manawatu-Horowhenua/ Palmerston North	1,200	Annette King
18 Nov	Rotorua	600	Annette King
24 Nov	Wairarapa/Masterton	300	Margaret Shields
	Nelson		Fran Wilde (but airport closed so didn't get there)
	Timaru	350	Helen Clark
22, 27, 28 Nov	Kaikoura	80	
1 Dec	Gisborne	250	Helen Clark
	Wanganui	500	Margaret Shields
15 Dec	Pacific women's forum, Tokoroa	60	Margaret Shields

women's rights for more than a decade but now, "Women are becoming too vocal. They want to have their cake and eat it too."[27] A couple of days later an unusually insightful *Evening Post* editorial noted "Some intolerance is inevitable as the move to free women is a revolution, and all revolutions provoke anger."[28]

Religious difference was behind a sensational report later carried by the *Evening Post*.

> Women described as very violent and abusive "witches" grabbed a two-year-old baby from its father's arms at the [Christchurch forum] ... because "he was a male and had to leave". The mother, 'who said she was not a feminist and did not support the [Ministry] said she believed the women were "witches" because one had a badge which said "witches heal" [and she said] "I think a lot of people don't realize the force of that side of the women's movement".[29]

The Taranaki forum was held the following Saturday, 10 November, and Doreen Bridgeman gave a personal account of another battle in the revolution:

> Afterward, liberal women felt crushed. With much head shaking, some described the forum as awful, others as unbelievable; one said: "We were massacred." It was the inevitable battle of white protestant liberal women against white protestant Christian women. Inevitable because it was the first chance for those women frightened or uncertain of women's liberation to voice their reaction and they did .... Their reaction caught the liberals by surprise. Women's liberation had been around since the 1960s; surely the reaction had evaporated by now?... The divisions became apparent in discussion .... What was surprising was the punitive attitude of conservative Christian women. Coupled with sheer lack of knowledge, fundamentalist beliefs gave new meaning to "Do unto others as you would be done by".... It was intolerant, immovable male chauvinism in skirts. It was the voice of women who felt their lives dangerously challenged by greater choice; who could not see themselves taking decisions; therefore, no woman should have choice and a role in the community which went beyond voluntary work and traditional stereotypes [CEDAW] "attacked the cornerstone of our society, the family" yet few, pro or anti had read it .... That epitomised the battle: tradition against change with no supporting evidence .... Strangely, the forum was seen as worthwhile. Calls for regular forums, not just on women's issues, were made. For the bulk of women in need, working class, other than European, it was yet another Saturday taken up by housework.[30]

A few days later an alternative women's forum of 450 at New Plymouth decided to send a petition against ratification of CEDAW to the Governor General. The *Dominion* reported that "Speakers opposing the convention claimed it would destroy family life, force women out to work and their children into childcare, and introduce genetic engineering". Some said "New Zealand would ... become a puppet of the communist-controlled United Nations".[31] Although the media gave the impression that conservative Christian groups led the opposition to Government initiatives, other groups also opposed policies such as CEDAW. The Country Women's Institute, for example, actively campaigned against it.[32]

Letters to the editor columns were full of the forums. An Anglican woman at the Hamilton forum expressed her anger at the conservative Christians.

> But for such sects to impose their views on society as a whole, to refuse to recognise any viewpoint but their own, is presumptuous, intolerant and repugnant. To oppose measures designed to help women who choose a different way of life is incredibly selfish, and the antithesis of Christian. I count myself fortunate to belong to a Church that encourages its members to think for themselves, both about their beliefs and about issues of vital importance to humankind. Within the framework of Christian values it is possible to be both liberal and a feminist.[33]

Five large forums were held on 17 November. After the Christchurch incident the

Dunedin organisers decided that men could have their say on a separate Friday evening session before some ran Saturday's crèche. One organiser told the *Evening Post* that they had not anticipated that men would be interested.[34]

At the Dunedin forum only the opening speeches by Ann Hercus and Margaret Austin were open to the media. Of groups opposing CEDAW Margaret Austin said: "One would almost think there was body of women in this country who are really anti-women."[35]

The Auckland forum was the largest and most abrasive. Organised opposition by conservative women's groups was evident, appearing to catch forum organisers unprepared. The press reported that 'Women for Life' members arrived early in large numbers to fill the hall, meaning adjoining halls were also required to accommodate the numbers. Disruption started early when the Maori welcome was interrupted by a person who called out "speak in English" and a group proceeded to sing the national anthem. Women for Life's Connie Purdue said that "… somebody started singing the National Anthem. Some Christian women, mistakenly believing the Maori welcome had finished, stood up to join in". Maryan Street [the chair] said "she could only assume the person was a Christian because the voice had come from an area of the hall where the Christians were sitting. It was possible the person could have belonged to some white racist group …." No vote was taken on ratification as it was already part of government policy and was thus 'non-negotiable and non-votable', but a second forum of about 1,000 who made up the overflow from the first had a vote 75/25 in favour. Mrs Purdue said "forum organisers had spread a lot of misinformation about Christian women at the forum. They had not arrived in busloads and there had been no predetermined plan to disrupt the Maori welcome."[36] (Connie Purdue, daughter of an early Labour Party feminist was formerly an active member of the Labour Party's Women's Advisory Committee.)[37]

Tuesday's *Dominion* quoted Prime Minister David Lange's belief that a far-right group was seeking to disrupt the meetings being held around the country. It also reported that Maori women were now calling for a separate ministry, but Ann Hercus thought this might be a reaction to the incident at Auckland.[38]

Labour MP Whetu Tirikatene-Sullivan further illustrated divisions in the Labour Party as she aligned herself with the conservative women, after a group of women protested against the first speaker, Anne Fraser. She said "I have already been challenged (by some Maori women) to express their concern about the ratification … especially as it concerns the family". She had been asked to "venerate the family and the homemaker …. There is concern from our women for what is referred to as a new religion of humanism which denies the existence of God." She said God was the centre of Maori culture. "There was concern," she said, "that the convention, which will be ratified as part of Labour policy, denied culture."[39]

The same day about 1,500 attended the Lower Hutt forum. Seventy lively workshops were held, including seventeen on CEDAW, although, as usual, no vote was taken. This time action against pornography was headlined and the press report also included: "Women who choose to stay home with their children, and women who choose to work, both received the support of the forum. Participants … want support and economic equality for parents who choose to stay home. They also want better child-care services for people who need them."[40] However, the Women's National Abortion Action Campaign (WONAAC) accused Labour of "toadying to the conservatives" for ignoring women's right to abortion at the Wellington forum.[41]

After the Palmerston North forum a letter writer impressed by the Maori welcome including the Lord's Prayer in Maori and English wrote: "The workshops were interesting and relevant to women .... one could say there is very definitely a conservative and Christian attitude applied to most of [them]. It was a good day, enjoyable and informative. Let us have more of them."[42]

On 19 November Lange announced Cabinet approval for the establishment of the Ministry with a maximum staff of 20. Its priorities would include "monitoring of government policies in terms of their impact on women, monitoring and initiation of legislation to promote equal opportunity for women and advice to the minister in implementation of the Government manifesto policy where this explicitly relates to women."[43]

MP Fran Wilde was prevented from attending the Nelson forum of 24 November by bad weather. A protest from one group that the forum and workshops remain open to the media caused the meeting to split, with about half going on to workshops. The breakaway group went to another hall and passed resolutions opposing ratification, abortion and sex education. The Police were called about a trespass complaint but no action was taken.[44]

The same day's forum at Masterton included three men, allowed reporters and was notable for a large number of older women. It apparently ran smoothly with no hecklers.[45] A letter to the editor that day noted that conservative women's groups often exclude men because of belief in segregation of sexes, and another "I would like to point out that men have had entire governments looking out for their interests for hundreds of years."[46]

Personal lobbying against ratification prompted Lange to comment:

> The prejudice, misconceptions and downright dishonesty in submissions from convention opponents was the worst he had seen in eight years of being an MP ... suggestions in letters he had received included allegations the convention would mean the Bible would banned in the home and that people would be obliged to engage in homosexual marriage ... I would have thought that New Zealanders would have been well placed with our history of human rights legislation to want to lend a hand to people internationally who want to see the role of women upgraded from being demeaned playthings of men or their stooges in economic terms.[47]

New Zealand ratified the convention a month later, on 20 December 1984, with the two reservations Ann Hercus had previously signalled (as economic conditions did not yet allow them): state-funded childcare centres and paid parental leave.[48]

The advisory group was disbanded in December after receiving a number of submissions, including a call for a separate Maori secretariat. This eventuated as the Ministry's Te Ohu Whakatupu. Legislation establishing the Ministry was passed in March 1985 and the first secretary, Mary O'Regan, was appointed in June and started in August after participating in a delegation to mark the end of the UN Decade on Women. The Ministry was fully staffed by July 1986.[49]

Two reports were published as a result of the forums and the consultation process. One was on the Ministry's policy priorities and the other on what women wanted of the Ministry. It was noted that a "substantial consensus" was reached.[50] However, Marilyn Pryor of the Society for the Protection of the Unborn Child published an alternative report claiming victory for the conservatives. "The 1984 Women's Forums became an arena where motherhood was lined up against feminism – and the feminists went down."[51]

The Ministry's first term report published in 1987 listed priorities under three headings: economic equality, social and cultural equality, and legal and political equality. Among a long list of achievements which the Ministry had influenced were: a programme of public service childcare centres, 400 women appointed to boards, permanent part-time work in the state sector, new rape and domestic violence legislation, EEO and employee assistance programmes, early childhood education transferred from the Department of Social Welfare to Education, and research into equal pay for work of equal value. The report included initiatives from each government department.[52]

What then to make of the forums? The consultation process itself was a reaction to the perceived anti-democratic Muldoon administration and subsequent social severance. But this brave exercise in participatory democracy allowed ugly divisions to surface both within the Labour Party and in society as a whole. Maryan Street, the chair of the Auckland forum and later President of the Labour Party, said in the feminist magazine *Broadsheet*: "We knew from other forums, that the right-wing women were mobilising and organising themselves to oppose every change that would increase women's chances of equality. But to see them in such force, demonstrating their profound racism and hatred, was something I don't think even the most hardened of us was prepared for."[53] In the same issue Sandra Coney wrote: "The Far Right's superb organisation contrasted sharply with feminists' lack of it. Many feminists didn't even bother to come [because] it was Labour Party middle-of-the-road, reformist stuff.... We had no strategy, no tactics."[54] It was also reported that after the Auckland forum a local abortion clinic was set on fire.[55]

As a participant in the Lower Hutt forum I agree with the *Broadsheet* assessments. I was a young mother at the time and although long active in the women's movement and abortion politics, coming face to face with the rigid thinking of the conservative women in the workshops was quite a surprise. Their determination (as I perceived it) to deny other people choice or control of their lives was incomprehensible. In researching this chapter I have talked to many women who attended the forums and most who attended remember them vividly 20 years later. A frequent comment has been that the public battles over social and moral issues detracted from the more subtle changes happening through Rogernomics and hints at the forums of the future force of the New Right went unnoticed. The Labour Women's Council issued alternative policy statements in 1988 in response to Rogernomics, but by then women's energy had dissipated in many other directions. And, of course, some women were happy to join the new Rogernomics revolution.

Many of the same moral debates of the forums surfaced a couple of years later over homosexual law reform. Another great distraction was the Royal Commission on Social Policy (appointed in 1986) which published its magnificent five-volume vision for an equitable and inclusive society in April 1988.[56] Some were still naïve enough to hope that the Labour Party's 1987 election slogan "Let's finish the job" had meant its implementation.

Helen Clark, elected in 1981 and the speaker at several forums, analysed the era in a 1993 interview:

> What went wrong was it [the fourth Labour Government] didn't have a clear economic agenda when it took up power. Douglas supplied one.[57] ... There were quite sharp divisions, and the Women's Caucus didn't really talk about those issues. It talked about the things it could influence like childcare and domestic violence.[58] I suppose the thing that really bugs me ... was that most of the cheer group for Rogernomics left Parliament and the rest of us had to pick up all the odium of things that we never wanted to do in the first place.[59]

In January 2005 Helen Clark recalled:

> I have only a sketchy recollection of these forums. Certainly fundamentalists endeavoured to stack them, making a number of the forums quite difficult. These groups have come into public view time and time again over a range of issues and events, but in the end fail because they do not reflect public opinion. The forum process showed that the anti-feminist goups were well organised. These days it's unlikely that a round of forums prior to setting up a ministry would be held, but the Minister, Ann Hercus, was genuine in her desire to consult women about the ministry's work. I [do not] think that nuclear issues and women's policy were distractions. Rogernomics developed in a vacuum—there had been little economic debate within the Labour Party and in New Zealand at large prior to 1984. The focus was on getting rid of Muldoon—not on what replaced him.

The Ministry of Women's Affairs meanwhile, at times struggling for survival under unfriendly administrations, now has a feminist minister in Lianne Dalziel. Its recent *Action Plan for New Zealand Women* has three priority areas: economic sustainability, work–life balance, and well-being. Getting women on boards and statutory bodies is still a priority continued from the 1970s. Many of the Labour women who organised and spoke at the forums are now in positions of power. Significant initiatives such as pay equity legislation, passed and repealed in 1990, are again on the agenda. And recent battles over legalising prostitution and civil unions have brought out the moral outrage divisions and many of the same arguments as in 1984.

The forum process was a great attempt at partipatory democracy after years of an administration perceived by many as autocratic and opposed to consultation. The idealism of those anticipating a new era of inclusion and equal rights met the opposition of those who were for various reasons fearful of such change. Yet the fact that at least 12,000 women throughout New Zealand cared enough to become involved in discussion on women's rights and social policy is very impressive. The Ministry of Women's Affairs was established as intended in the 1984 Labour election policy and still survives.

GERALD HENSLEY
The bureaucracy and advisors

The changeover of power in 1984 was a difficult one. It was complicated by the currency crisis and consequent devaluation, but the adjustment between the new government and the bureaucracy was also more sensitive than usual. Incoming governments of course always look with suspicion on the bureaucracy they have inherited. They have, after all, been at the side of the rejected government and, who knows, may have shared the responsibility for many of its sins. Labour Governments have been especially mistrustful. Mike Moore claimed that Labour has a tribal instinct of wariness about public servants even though the majority have probably voted for them. Certainly Norman Kirk had it. Even after some months in office he complained that he felt that as Prime Minister he had been presented with a mahogany box with impressive brass handles for him to pull, but when he looked underneath his desk there were no wires connected to them.

In the case of the fourth Labour Government, though, the distrust was especially marked. It was partly inexperience. With the normal swing of the electoral pendulum incoming ministers usually know and in the past have worked with some of their civil servants, but in 1984 few of the new ministers had sat in a Cabinet before. Most of them, including the Prime Minister and Deputy Prime Minister, were not familiar with the uses and limitations of civil servants. They were an exceptionally intelligent group—the brightest that I can recall—and felt less need of advice from others. For nine years, after all, these bureaucrats had been advising on the failed policies of the previous government. There was a widespread sense, almost a 1935 feeling, that the former things had been swept away and that this was the start of a new era.

The adjustment between the new Ministers and their senior civil servants was uneven—much more rapid on the economic than on the international side—but on the whole it was more awkward than with other governments, both before and since. I believe that this awkwardness, which showed itself in a persisting reluctance to place full trust in the public service, had an important influence on the achievements of the fourth Labour Government. It is worth examining four major issues to look at the evidence: the ANZUS quarrel; economic reform; the reform of the public service; and crisis management of the unexpected—for example, the *Rainbow Warrior* affair or the Fiji coup.

ANZUS
Perhaps the clearest mandate given to the new government was its anti-nuclear policy. It was also clear that both the Government and the public wished to continue

in the ANZUS alliance with the United States and Australia. Reconciling the two was difficult but not impossible given patience and the necessary will on both sides. It had been managed, when the issue was admittedly less sharply defined, by the Rowling Government. And this is precisely why governments have experienced public service advisers: to help them weigh the risks, explore the choices and look for ways of achieving two conflicting but not necessarily incompatible aims.

The first requirement was time. In July just before the Government took office, David Lange had apparently told George Shultz, the American Secretary of State, that no action would be taken in the coming months. There has subsequently been much dispute about what he meant by this, but his officials were under the impression that his intention was to secure a breathing space during which possible solutions would be examined. The Americans agreed not to request any early ship visits.

The new Prime Minister, who was also Foreign Minister, established a small informal group consisting of the Chief of Defence Staff, the Secretaries of Foreign Affairs and Defence and the Head of the Prime Minister's Department to meet with him from time to time to discuss the way forward. The strategy settled on, with the Prime Minister's assent, was to quarantine the most difficult issue as long as possible. The best course was to arrange a visit by an American warship which was plainly neither nuclear powered nor armed. Thereafter, with American understanding as in the past, the question of further visits could be postponed for two years or more. The anti-nuclear policy and the American alliance would both remain intact in the meantime.

In November, therefore, the Prime Minister despatched the Chief of Defence Staff, Ewan Jamieson, to Honolulu to discuss an acceptable ship. The CINCPAC there, Admiral Crowe, understood the delicacy and offered a visit by the USS *Buchanan*. Given the Americans' worldwide 'neither confirm nor deny' policy he was not prepared to give any undertakings, but by offering an ageing oil-fired destroyer for a specially arranged visit, rather than returning from a patrol, he was making it clear that the vessel was most unlikely to be nuclear armed.

By now time was pressing. There was to be a three-nation ANZUS naval exercise in the Tasman Sea the following February and it would look odd if an American ship were not to visit at this time. So in December it was suggested to the Americans that in place of their annual request for ship visits they should request a visit by an individual ship, privately naming the *Buchanan*. A Cabinet paper was prepared and the four members of the Prime Minister's informal group wrestled with the wording. We were not in a position to give a flat assurance as to the ship's non-nuclear status—that would have required a detailed personal search of every part of the vessel—but the nature of the ship and the circumstances of its visit made it highly 'unlikely' that it was nuclear armed. None of us had the least doubt about the ship's non-nuclear status.

Events drifted on past the Christmas recess and the Cabinet paper was not considered until the end of January. By then David Lange was incommunicado in the Tokelaus, the fact of the impending *Buchanan* visit had become public and Labour backbenchers had begun a noisy anti-ANZUS agitation. Labour Party policy was changed to exclude, not just nuclear-armed and -powered ships but any ships which were nuclear *capable*. This shut off the possibility of an American naval visit—any vessel could be regarded as nuclear capable. It also, as it was presumably intended to do, shut off any chance that New Zealand could remain within the alliance. Although efforts to heal the breach meandered on until the legislation was introduced, the rejection of the *Buchanan* ended the trust between the allies. Despite David Lange's earlier reiterated assurances to the American and other governments that New Zealand would remain in ANZUS, the alliance was broken.

The Americans, who had tried to be helpful, felt deceived by the New Zealand Government and the resentment of some of their officials persists to this day. Were the Government's advisers deceived too? A senior State Department official, Morton Abramovitz, said to me the following February, "We thought you guys must have been smoking pot, you were in some dreamland". While New Zealand officials were working on the *Buchanan* visit the American Embassy was reporting to Washington that David Lange was saying nothing to inform the public and indeed did not seem to have discussed it with any of his colleagues. There was clearly a lack of frankness in the Prime Minister's dealings with his advisers, but I doubt there was deliberate deception; rather that he disliked showdowns and was content to go with the tide. The tide carried us into a major crisis in our relations with both the United States and Australia, with consequences that are with us yet, and the basic cause was over-confidence and inexperience. A Minister commented to me a few years after, "You know, if we had taken the *Buchanan* decision eighteen months later, it would have been different".

ECONOMIC REFORM

This revealed a very different relationship between ministers and their economic advisers. The two fitted together immediately as a hand into a glove. This was a case where the new government did not have to learn by experience. Treasury had done its homework and had sorted out its ideas. Roger Douglas, who had at times walked a rather lonely path in the Opposition Labour Party, found a machine ready and waiting to do his bidding. The foreign exchange crisis was the immediate trigger or, if you like, excuse. The sixteen carpet factories went out the window and New Zealand embarked on its most sweeping period of economic change since the late 1930s, ironically to undo many of those earlier policies.

The speed and extent of the reforms would not have been possible by ministerial fiat alone; they depended heavily for their implementation on the thinking which Treasury had already done in the last years of the Muldoon administration. It raises the question whether reform had to be so fast and so sweeping. Certainly the social costs were high and we are perhaps still paying them. Some, like Paul Keating, were privately critical of the pain being caused by our refusal to take a more deliberate approach. Others thought that in our haste we did not carry through the reforms in the optimal sequence, and failed entirely to tackle labour market reform.

These charges have some force. On the other hand the reform process in the eighties was not an academic exercise. By 1984 we were drifting dangerously close to the economic reefs; much longer and we would have had to be towed off by the IMF. That might have been more acceptable, and the social consensus might have been better preserved if we had had reform forced upon us by an outside body. I am sceptical—Argentina does not look any happier because its reforms came from the IMF. What is clear is that if the task was to be carried through by New Zealanders it had to be done quickly. New Zealanders are a conservative lot and tend to agree with Lord Eldon: "Why all this talk of reform?" he said, "Things are bad enough already." A stately and well-signalled pace of change—desirable though it is—would have called up such a weight of angry interests as to block any further progress. A small indication is the row which followed a speech in 1988 by John Fernyhough (one of the architects of the SOE model) in Sydney in which he said that the reforms had had to be done by stealth.

What did help the economic reforms, I believe, was the ANZUS crisis. There is no evidence of any conscious trade-off between the two, and a moment's thought tells you that public affairs do not work in that way. But it is a reasonable supposition that, but for the nuclear agitation, discontent with the economic changes would have been much greater in the Government Caucus and the extent of change in, say, import licensing and tariffs, much less likely. Or, to put it another way, if the *Buchanan* had been accepted, the full weight of the Left would probably have been brought to bear on the Government's domestic policies.

REFORM OF THE PUBLIC SERVICE

This was largely a consequence of the urge for economic reform. The trading activities of the Government clearly needed to be put on a self-funding basis and the SOE model was an ingenious solution. Applying this to the core or non-trading government departments was a less happy fit. If reform were needed here (and I am rather with Lord Eldon on this), it would have been better to devise a separate regime. But the commercial model was the only one which the reformers knew or admired, and so the Government was compared to a holding company; departments subsidiary enterprises and their heads were renamed CEOs.

The reforms of the core public service had some major benefits. The introduction of accrual accounting enabled the cost of departmental activities to be accurately measured for the first time. Departments received greater freedom in their employment policies and greater incentives to manage more thriftily. A vast number of niggling rules in the Public Service Handbook were swept away, even, regrettably, the provision (discovered too late by me) that department heads were entitled to half a bottle of wine a day when travelling.

There was, however, a price paid for these good things. The unified Public Service was abolished. The new structure which kept agencies in their own silos made co-ordination across government more difficult, to the detriment of public business. It is hard not to see in the Government's willingness to go along with this a lingering distrust of the old public service. Business school thinking was fashionable but it was never made clear why commercial concepts had to be applied to non-commercial departments. There is in fact no business like public business. It is messy and untidy but that is politics. Governments have to broker and reconcile so many interests that manufacturing or marketing models have, apart from financial management, only limited relevance. Harold Macmillan, asked the most important thing in public affairs, said, "Events, dear boy, events".

A framework of purchase and performance agreements is not much help in coping with events, the unforeseeable, which is the nub of the relationship between ministers and their advisers.

The rearrangement started with the Prime Minister's Department. In 1985 the Prime Minister's Office and Advisory Group were separated under John Henderson, leaving the department with its intelligence and crisis management functions. In March 1987 the department itself was abolished and its duties transferred to a Domestic and External Security Secretariat. Two years later, like some vanishing island, the department reappeared in its original form, when Geoffrey Palmer became Prime Minister.

By then the momentum of change had spread to most of the public service. Doctrines requiring the separation of policy from delivery and funding from providers were applied with what now seems uncritical enthusiasm. The number of departments and CEOs doubled and effective establishments like Agriculture and Justice dissolved into a profusion of smaller agencies. New Zealand became the only country in the world with two Defence Departments—one to reflect and one to fight.

All this was done in the name of management. Repeated statements stressed that management not advice was the job of the public service. Indeed the State Sector Act went through several drafts with management defined as the sole duty of the CEO. Only at the last minute was policy advice included. The relationship between a minister and CEO which the act envisaged was a curiously stilted affair. It was to be at arms-length, governed and defined by formal arrangements like purchase agreements. It bore little resemblance to the informal ways in which successful minister–department head relationships worked. I suspect that in fact things went on in much the old way, not so much from conservatism as from the inner logic of the parliamentary system. The confidence and therefore the quality of the public service was, however, damaged, and the transaction costs of all the changes were never included in the final reckoning.

CRISIS MANAGEMENT

The major responsibility for crisis management rested with the Prime Minister's Department. In 1983 the machinery was revised to make it more flexible. The Terrorist Emergency Group, or TEG, chaired by the Prime Minister, was established to bring ministers and senior officials together in a single body with a floating membership which could be adjusted to suit the nature of each crisis. Regular exercises and briefing of the TEG were carried out as realistically as possible. One was vivid enough for Frank O'Flynn to worry about the fate of supposedly hijacked passengers at Wellington airport, and he was aggrieved when enlightened by his colleagues.

How arrangements work in practice, of course, depends on the inclination of the Prime Minister who directs them. David Lange had all the concern with organisation, all the interest in systems and flow-charts which marks any one-man law office. His sharp intelligence enabled him to grasp situations quickly and with a minimum of paperwork. His restlessness made him impatient of formality and of lengthy sittings. He preferred the personal to the procedural approach; to rely on his empathy for people rather than on consultation with his colleagues.

In the *Rainbow Warrior* affair his disinclination to use the TEG machinery did not greatly matter. Co-ordination of the investigation was left in the hands of departmental heads sitting as the old Officials Terrorism Committee which met seventeen times as the mystery was unravelled. The Prime Minister liked to drop in and be briefed but never stayed for a full sitting. Co-ordination was not a problem: he directed and authorised the enquiries and other ministers were presumably kept informed by their departments.

When an Air New Zealand aircraft was hijacked at Nadi two years later, the speed of events made co-ordination important and the Prime Minister's decision not to convene the TEG left key colleagues and departments in the dark. Without the dedicated communications facilities we had set up for emergencies, I struggled to man the phones in the Prime Minister's outer office, helped by the Minister of Police, Ann Hercus, who happened to be passing by. Between talking to the Police, Air New Zealand, the control tower at Nadi and the pilot, it was simply not possible to brief Foreign Affairs and Defence who, understandably, became concerned. Perhaps fortunately, the crisis was resolved not by official action but by the flight engineer with a whisky bottle.

With the crisis over Cyclone Bola, though, the Prime Minister was in his element. Speed and flexible thinking were needed to restart the East Coast after it had been hit in March 1988 by New Zealand's worst weather disaster. Fortunately we had completed a general plan for disaster recovery just as the rain began to fall, but plans give no more than general guidance in a particular crisis. What determined the pace of the operation was the Prime Minister's close interest, his ability to give quick decisions and then, if necessary, get them retrospectively validated by Cabinet the following week.

As soon as the rain stopped he toured the whole region by helicopter. That gave him a framework in which to visualise our proposals. When we wanted to use unemployed labour to dig silt from houses and horticultural crops the following Saturday, the Prime Minister was about to attend a Samoan Church in Auckland. He listened to the idea over the phone and told us to put it out in his name. Two hours later the rather grandly-named Disaster Recovery Employment Scheme had been announced and the workforce was being assembled. A Sunday later it was the turn of the agricultural compensation plan, a radically new concept which calculated compensation, not on the land or buildings destroyed, but on the loss of income from them. This gave farmers the flexibility to rebuild in different ways or even to take the compensation and sell up. It was an ingenious but untried plan which relied on Landsat photos to carry out a random verification of claims. Again the Prime Minister unhesitatingly agreed to sponsor it (the cost turned out to be around $60 million) and to get it through Cabinet. In this sort of situation, where afflicted people were looking for action, the Prime Minister's energy and readiness to act quickly were the keys to reviving the region's economy.

CONCLUSION

The adjustment in 1984 between the new government and the bureaucracy it inherited was unusually prolonged. Unfamiliarity cannot have been the only reason, nor that progressive governments often find it more difficult to distinguish between the personal and the political. The transition proved easier for the British Labour Government in 1997, though it had been out of power twice as long, and its civil service saw no upheavals. In New Zealand's case it may have been influenced by the relatively shallow roots of institutions like our public service. Perhaps also by a generation gap in outlook and sympathies. The Government passed overnight from the RSA generation to the baby-boomers, and ministers were in many cases younger than their departmental heads. As time passed the Government inevitably came to see its public service advisers in more individual and congenial terms, but it could never quite shake off a lingering distrust of the institution. The shadow of Sir Humphrey was a long one in New Zealand.

JOHN HENDERSON

The warrior peacenik: setting the record straight on ANZUS and the Fiji coup

My objective here is to explode two myths regarding the foreign policy of the first term of the Lange-led Labour Government (1984–1987). The two issues examined are the rupture of the ANZUS alliance and the New Zealand response to the first Fiji military coup in May 1987. They present starkly different portraits of Prime Minister David Lange—as a 'peacenik' in the case of ANZUS, and a 'militarist' over Fiji. Michael Bassett in his *National Business Review* articles of August 2003 attributes New Zealand's exclusion from ANZUS to Lange becoming the captive of a small radical group of left-wing activists within the Labour Party. Richard Harman, writing in the Spring, 1998 *Defence Quarterly* and drawing on Air Vice Marshal David Crooks' recollections, portrays Lange as recklessly militaristic and willing to invade Fiji to reverse Rabuka's 1987 coup.

It is important to set the record straight. New Zealand's departure from ANZUS marked the most significant change to date in New Zealand's post-World War II foreign policy. New Zealand's anti-nuclear legislation remains 'unfinished business' in NZ–US relations. While not of the same order of importance, the issue of military intervention by Australia and New Zealand in the affairs of Pacific Island states to protect democracy remains a highly contentious issue. Sections of the Fiji and New Zealand military believed New Zealand seriously considered the invasion option in response to the 1987 coup. It is a myth which is still perpetuated in important circles in Fiji, and remains harmful to New Zealand's image in the Pacific Island region.

Foreign policy was the area of government that Lange revelled in. He held the Foreign Affairs Cabinet portfolio during the first term (but not—mistakenly in my view—the second) because in this area he could largely set his own path. This contrasted with his growing unease with the direction of his government's economic policy, and the many routine chores of office which bored him. He actually read, and often annotated, Ministry of Foreign Affairs cables, which was in stark contrast to the other trays of papers which his principal private secretary, Ken Richardson, placed on his desk. He paid particular attention to intelligence briefings. Indeed, a way to ensure that a paper was read was to classify it 'top secret'. He delighted in foreign travel (as most PMs seem to), partly because of the flattering attention paid to him by foreign governments and the media, and also because it meant that he could relax and leave the heavy reins of office with another Minister—usually Deputy Prime Minister Geoffrey Palmer.

BASSETT THESIS ON THE ANZUS RUPTURE

Michael Bassett, who served in the Lange Cabinet, offers an unflattering portrait of Lange's management of the ANZUS issue. He attributes Lange's hard line on the nuclear issue to his capture by a small but influential group of left-wing and predominantly female Labour Party figures. He presents domestic Labour Party politics as the "missing piece" of the ANZUS rupture jigsaw: "David Lange used the nuclear-ship issue to try to heal the rift in the Labour Party but was outplayed by the opposing faction." Caucus and Cabinet "went along" because they too hoped to heal the rift.[1] For Lange, according to Bassett, it was the way to place his stamp on the Party and its policy.

While there will always be aspects of domestic politics in foreign policy, I totally reject the Bassett thesis. The reverse is closer to the truth. It was not a small group of Labour officials who held Lange to ransom. Lange was constrained not by a few key Labour left figures, but by the strength of public opinion which makes up the centre ground of New Zealand politics. The anti-nuclear stance had the strong support of mainstream New Zealand. (It still does.) The reasons relate as much to environment as defence concerns. It became part of a growing sense of nationalism. Lange's position contrasted markedly with that of his Australian counterpart, Bob Hawke, who inherited a similar anti-nuclear ALP policy. But in Australia support was confined largely to the left faction of the Labour Party. Bassett notes Hawke's "resolute stand" in 1993 and implies Lange should have followed this example. US officials also had Hawke in mind when they urged Lange to "show leadership" on the issue. But the situation was very different in New Zealand where support extended beyond left-wing activists in the Labour Party to mainstream public opinion. Lange had little room to move. While strongly anti-nuclear, public opinion—and official Labour policy— nevertheless favoured continued membership of ANZUS.

This is a point which was never appreciated by the US and Australian governments. The best evidence came during the 1990 election. National Party leader Jim Bolger promised not to change the anti-nuclear legislation during the next term, or the terms after that, or after that. Bolger remained true to his word after Labour's defeat, despite the US removal of nuclear weapons from its surface ships in 1991, and a New Zealand Government Commission giving clearance to safety issues relating to nuclear propulsion. Bassett mentions these developments at the conclusion of his *NBR* article, but fails to question why the policy did not change following National's election. It certainly had nothing to do with key figures in the Labour Party's National Executive! Rather Bolger, like Lange before him, read the public opinion polls. So too can the current National Party Leader, Don Brash. Labour would love National to return to a pro-ANZUS policy, as this would transform the next election into a referendum on the nuclear issue.

LABOUR'S ANTI-NUCLEARISM

Lange's involvement in the ANZUS issue started early in his leadership term, and highlights the point that he was a moderate, rather than a zealot, on the nuclear issue. It was a policy which he inherited rather than initiated. Just two weeks after he took over the leadership of the party in 1981 he became embroiled in a bitter internal party squabble over the nuclear-ships issue. In a speech he suggested that there might be room for compromise over the issue of nuclear propulsion and nuclear weaponry. He expressed his own confidence in the safety record of the US Navy, while remaining firm in his view that nuclear weapons should be kept out of New Zealand.

His speech created a very strong negative reaction from the Labour Party. At that time I was working on a short-term basis for Lange and clearly recall the outrage expressed about Lange's remarks by the former leader, Bill Rowling, and the future leader, Helen Clark. I received a blunt telephone call from Rowling—who remained the Party's foreign affairs spokesperson—with the directive: "tell him [Lange] what the policy is." Rowling went on to point out what he considered to be obvious: if a US ship was nuclear powered, it was likely to be nuclear armed.

Lange needed little convincing. He quickly realised the Party was in no mood for change and backed off his position on the propulsion issue. The incident was important because it taught Lange a lesson he never forgot. The nuclear issue lay at the core of Labour values, and was not to be messed with. If Lange wished to remain Leader he must toe the party line on the anti-nuclear policy.

A further reason why the incident was important was that it confirmed the suspicions of the Party left that Lange was not a strong adherent of the nuclear policy. Despite Bassett's claims to the contrary, Lange was not the prisoner of the Labour left on the nuclear issue. Helen Clark for one, never really trusted him to remain true to the anti-nuclear policy. She remained vigilant for any wavering on Lange's part. During the first term of the Labour Government Clark, as Chair of the Select Committee on Foreign Affairs and Defence, was in a powerful position to carry out this watching brief. I well recall close questioning from her on Lange's position, particularly regarding the anti-nuclear legislation. Had Lange been "captive" to her view there would have been no need for this concern.

SHULTZ AND LANGE

Lange had three meetings with US Secretary of State George Shultz in an effort to resolve the nuclear-ships issue—in July (two days after the election), in September 1984 (at the UN), and at the ASEAN talks in Manila in June 1986.

At the first two meetings in 1984 Michael Bassett claims Lange "promised" Shultz he would negotiate a means for some ship visits to take place. As I did not join Lange's staff until April the following year I can offer no first-hand view. But perceptions are important in politics. Shultz believed he had been given an assurance by Lange and concluded from his failure to deliver that Lange could not be trusted. He never changed this harsh, and in my view unjust, assessment. Lange is adamant he gave no commitment: "If Shultz had it in mind at that meeting that New Zealand would eventually change its nuclear-free policy, the thought hung in the air unspoken" (Lange, 1990: 58).

How can the misunderstanding be explained? Shultz can be forgiven for not understanding 'Lange speak'. Lange seldom made definitive statements. Lange no doubt did agree to work for a solution—but this is not the same as promising a successful outcome. Lange also agreed that the US should follow established procedures and put forward their December request for ship visits. He later admitted that he was "naïve" not to appreciate that the US would regard this as a signal that the visits would be approved. Nevertheless, the fact remains: Lange gave no such commitment.

This is the background to the ill-fated request for a visit by the USS *Buchanan*. Lange was visiting Tokelau at the time and returned to receive a recommendation from Deputy Leader Geoffrey Palmer, readily agreed by Cabinet, that the visit request be declined. As I was not involved in this decision I will leave it to others who were to give their recollections of what took place. But it is noteworthy that as the assessment and decision was made by Palmer, Bassett's assertion that the ANZUS breakdown was solely the fault of Lange does not stand up to scrutiny.

Furthermore, I wish to contest Michael Bassett's conclusion that efforts to resolve the NZ–US impasse were all over with the *Buchanan* refusal. I spent much of the next three years working for a solution to the stand-off. I did this at Lange's direction. The objective was to find an outcome that preserved ANZUS but kept New Zealand's anti-nuclear policy intact. I would not have been party to a sham. Of course there were those in the Party who wanted these efforts to fail, but Lange was not amongst them.

THE NUCLEAR-CAPABLE ISSUE
Michael Bassett makes much of Lange's capture by the hard-line left over the 'nuclear-capable' issue at the time of the *Buchanan* visit, claiming that he "capitulated" to those who wanted all nuclear-capable ships excluded. My recollection is that Lange had no objections to visits by nuclear-capable ships. Nuclear weapons and propulsion were the issues, not capability. He once joked that even the Cook Strait ferry could be regarded as nuclear capable. Conventionally armed ships were "welcome" even if they were nuclear capable.

The 'nuclear capable' issue did not feature in official negotiations—where nuclear weapons remained the issue. This was the case in the September 1985 talks led by Deputy Prime Minister Geoffrey Palmer on a visit he made to Washington DC. Palmer's fondness for the US, where he had pursued his early academic career, was well known—indeed there was concern in the Lange office that he might be prepared to give too much away to the US. But Lange thought if anyone could succeed it would be Palmer. His mission was evidence of Lange's serious intent to find a solution to the stand-off.

In Washington Palmer's formal negotiations with an inter-agency group (chaired by the current Assistant Secretary of State Paul Wolfowitz) proved to be fruitless. The US side spelt out what they considered to be the obligations of an ally. Palmer pointed to the contribution New Zealand made to Western interests, and reiterated the New Zealand view that ANZUS was not a nuclear alliance.

I accompanied Palmer on a meeting with Shultz. It was a coldly formal occasion. Shultz made it clear that over a period of time New Zealand would have to assume that some of the US visiting warships would be nuclear armed. To his credit Palmer stuck to his brief and responded that if New Zealand made a judgement that a US ship was nuclear armed it would be denied entry. Shultz responded that even making such a determination was a breach of the 'neither confirm nor deny' policy—even if the conclusion reached was that the ship was not nuclear.

Palmer also had a short meeting with US Defence Secretary Casper Weinberger. He took an even tougher position than Shultz and showed no desire to understand the New Zealand position. Palmer gave nothing away, making it clear the New Zealand policy would be firmly implemented, and that New Zealand could not overlook or "wink" at infractions of the policy.

Two months later a further effort to find a resolution was made by a senior Cabinet minister, David Caygill. He held inconclusive secret talks in the US with senior State Department officials on the proposed anti-nuclear legislation, and whether a programme of visits might be possible that was in accord with the policy of both countries.

The Palmer and Caygill visits are important because they refute Michael Bassett's insistence that the problem lay with one man—David Lange. Other senior Cabinet ministers were also involved in finding a solution to the impasse. But the US sought a reversal of policy by New Zealand and was not interested in a negotiated solution. This was despite New Zealand assurances that it would not be seeking any declarations or information from the captain of a visiting US ship. Nuclear propulsion was obvious and New Zealand experts would make their own assessment and advise the PM of the likelihood of nuclear weapons. Australian Prime Minister Bob Hawke's assessment—"if you don't ask them you will probably be alright", although logical, proved not to be the case.

THE PARTING OF FRIENDS

A further opportunity to break the impasse arose at the ASEAN meeting in Manila in late June 1986. Schultz and Lange were both attending the talks and Schultz reluctantly agreed to a meeting with Lange. New Zealand Ambassador Bill Rowling phoned me from Washington to warn that Shultz was "still sour" over his earlier meetings with Lange and that "no miracles could be expected".

At the meeting Schultz quickly made it clear that he was there to deliver a message, not to negotiate. He repeated the fifteen-minute lecture he had given Palmer the previous year on the responsibilities of being a US ally. He also repeated his blunt message that 'neither confirm nor deny' meant that from time to time nuclear-armed ships would visit New Zealand ports.

Lange raised the possibility of resolving differences by following the precedent established for British naval visits to China under what was referred to as the "China formula". Each government would state that the visit was taking place in accordance with established policies. Neither state would comment on the policy of the other. This would allow the US to restate its 'neither confirm nor deny' policy (which the UK also follows) and New Zealand to reaffirm its nuclear-free policy. New Zealand would have to accept nuclear-capable ships, but would make its own assessment of whether the US ships were nuclear armed. This would not involve questioning of US ships crew or searches, or the issuing of any declarations. Nor would there be any public rejection of a US-requested visit.

Schultz responded with the observation that Washington "leaked like a sieve". He also restated the US position that any New Zealand assessment of the nuclear status of a visiting US ship was a violation of 'neither confirm nor deny'. Schultz had clearly made up his mind; Nothing Lange could say would make any difference.

Shultz left the room and declared to the waiting media: "We part friends. But we part." It was a good line, no doubt well rehearsed. With this New Zealand moved from ally to friend.

In terms of New Zealand domestic politics it was a lucky escape for Lange. Had Schultz not made up his mind before the meeting, he could have put Lange on the spot by agreeing to give the "China formula" a try. It was an important concession, which Lange did not have clearance from Cabinet or Caucus to make. It would have landed him in hot water with the Labour left group Bassett claimed he had been captured by. Instead, he could return home and portray himself as the tough leader who had remained true to his principles and withstood the pressure of the world's superpower.

The Manila talks marked an important turning point. Lange felt a great sense of relief. Schultz's firm stand showed there was no room for compromise. Planned talks with the UK about a possible compromise over the nuclear-propulsion issue were called off. Lange concluded that Schultz had shut the door.

FIJI COUP

The *Dominion* put it this way:

> The first they [the Fiji military forces] might have known would have been the appearance on Nadi's airport radar of a lumbering New Zealand troop plane. The aircraft could easily have been fired on in the air by Fiji troops. If it had not been shot down, its tyres would have been shot out on landing. And troops emerging carrying weapons were likely to have been shot .... The incident could have escalated into a military disaster with New Zealand troops pinned at the airport with scant hope of rescue.[2]

New Zealand going to war against Fiji! This extraordinary scenario has been painted by Air Vice Marshal David Crooks, who was Chief of Defence Staff at the time of the May 1987 coup. It featured in a series of *Dominion* articles in 1992 and in the official publication of the Ministry of Defence's, *The Defence Quarterly* (Spring, 1998).

Claims that New Zealand planned to invade Fiji following the 1987 coup have been made by significant figures. Ratu Sir Kamisese Mara, Fijis' recently deceased founding father, who was effectively returned to power by the May 1987 coup, gave the threat posed by Australia and New Zealand military forces as one of the reasons for his controversial decision to head the post-coup administration. "Had they had the means they would have taken over …. We were not going to allow that".[3] In 1992, in response to the *Dominion* articles, which included Crooks' assertions, the New Zealand Prime Minister of the day, Jim Bolger, described this invasion scenario as "appalling" and ordered an enquiry. He later declared that it was "not in New Zealand's interests" to release the report.[4] I wish to use this occasion to set the record straight.

I worked closely with Lange during the Fiji crisis and have no recollection of advice being sought from the military on the invasion option. The only military response contemplated related to ending the hijacking of the Air New Zealand aircraft, the possible evacuation of New Zealand nationals, and the protection of New Zealand diplomats. Such actions were only contemplated in co-operation, not in conflict, with Fiji authorities. Military action to reverse the coup was never contemplated by the Lange administration.

Lange knew Fiji well. He developed many personal contacts while a law student at Auckland University and had visited Fiji many times. At the time of the 1985 Forum in Suva, Lange took lengthy breaks from formal sessions to visit friends from both the Fijian and Indian communities. His knowledge of Fiji led him to accept the view of the New Zealand High Commissioner to Fiji, Rod Gates, given within a week of the coup, that the military takeover had succeeded and that there was no prospect of an early return to constitutional government.

Lange never considered military intervention to restore the deposed government. His reasons related to a rejection of 'neo-colonialism' and to an acceptance of military realities. The strength and professional capacity of Rabuka's 5,000-strong army was well known. Many Fijian soldiers were New Zealand trained. As Lange recalled: "There was no political advice or military intelligence which indicated that we would be in any way positioned to invade Fiji and control it. It just never entered our remote consciousness".[5]

The invasion scenario was initially fostered by reports of the willingness of the New Zealand and Australian forces to facilitate the return of Fiji peace-keeping forces from the Middle East. When asked about this at a press conference, Lange responded that, if requested, "logistic support is a matter which New Zealand could consider".[6] However, the idea had not been thought through and was quickly dropped when the opposition of the Fiji Governor General, Ratu Penaia Ganilau, the only constitutional authority recognised by New Zealand, and the resentment of other island states, became known.

The hijacking of an Air New Zealand 747 aircraft took place on the morning of 19 May—five days after the coup. Lange ordered the preparation of a C130 aircraft to fly an SAS and police anti-terrorist squad to relieve the hijacking. As will be detailed below, clearance for the operation was obtained by the New Zealand High Commissioner, Rod Gates, from the Fiji Governor General, Ganilau. Furthermore, key figures in the Fiji army were informed.

Crooks apparently was under the mistaken belief that there had been no communications with Fijian authorities. He later mistakenly recalled: "The whole climate appeared to be: 'Those dreadful people: they have done something absolutely unforgivable. There is no question of talking to them'."[7]

In fact the opposite was the case. I have, with the assistance of Rod Gates, pieced together the nature of the consultations with Fiji authorities. These have not been previously disclosed. While there were no intelligence warnings about a coup or hijacking, it was a scenario which Gates had previously discussed with Ratu Mara when he was still Prime Minister. It was agreed that the Fiji military did not have the expertise and specialist training to relieve a hijacking and rescue hostages. Mara agreed that if it was an Air New Zealand aircraft which had been hijacked, New Zealand forces should be used. The conversation was reported back to Wellington.

When the hijacking actually took place, Gates recalled this discussion and recommended to Wellington that necessary military preparations be undertaken. He also informed Ganilau (the only constitutional authority recognised by New

Zealand) of his discussion with Mara. He sought and received Ganilau's approval for the despatch of a New Zealand SAS force. Ganilau turned out to be a "fan" of the SAS from his experience of serving with New Zealand forces in Malaya during the Emergency. He had met with the New Zealand SAS when they exercised in Fiji. He agreed that Gates should liaise with his son, Epeli Ganilau, who was the district commander for the RFMF in the Nadi area, about details such as rules of engagement. No one else was brought into the discussion 'loop'.

This placed Gates in a difficult situation, as he was under instructions from Wellington not to talk with the Fiji military. He nevertheless phoned Epeli Ganilau and made the necessary arrangements. He informed Wellington that the Governor General had given his verbal approval and the necessary clearances for the despatch of the C130 aircraft. However, Gates made no mention of his other communications with the Fiji military field commander, Epeli Ganilau.

The Chief of Defence Staff, Crooks, could not have known about Gates' activities. But even the obtaining of the necessary clearances did not resolve Crooks' concerns. "That could have made it worse. That could have simply meant that everyone was pre-warned."[8] However, any ambush of an aircraft following formal clearances would have been a certain recipe for triggering a major ANZAC operation against the Fiji forces—something all sides were determined to avoid.

Rabuka later confirmed that he supported the planned New Zealand operation to end the hijacking. It was one less thing that he had to worry about. Furthermore, if action was required, it was better that it be carried out by a fully trained anti-terrorist squad unit. The Fiji armed forces who arrived on the scene were territorials with no assault training. Some were armed with just 303 rifles.

In the end no military action was required; the co-pilot felled the hijacker by striking him on the head with a bottle of whisky! Lange cancelled the order to despatch the C130.

CONCLUSION

In the end Lange was neither 'peacenik' nor 'warrior'. I believe that in his own flamboyant way, he handled both issues well. Over Fiji he struck the right balance between being outspoken in public but cautious in private. The nuclear issue marked a watershed in New Zealand foreign policy. It completed the process begun by Norman Kirk for New Zealand to pursue a more independent foreign policy.

DENIS MCLEAN
A serious non-meeting of minds

I was Secretary of Defence from 1979 to 1988. It is almost axiomatic that New Zealand governments in peacetime give Defence very short shrift. This was surely the case with the Muldoon administrations of the late 70s and early 80s. For the fourth Labour Government defence was, as we all know, also caught up in new thinking about foreign and strategic policies. Thus the high policy issues were at the eye of the storm. The administrative and financial questions to do with managing a large and complex department, however, were relegated to the very bottom of the policy totem pole and became subject to sad suspicions and nit-picking criticism. It made for a rocky ride.

For 35 years the Cold War had been a dominating feature of the international landscape. For New Zealanders the issues generally seemed remote and the military problems away beyond any likely capability of ours to make a difference. The ANZUS Pact became, nevertheless, a sort of talisman. Successive governments rubbed it from time to time but few in politics seemed actually to have read the treaty. There was little or no sense of a commitment to, or even understanding of, the explicit undertakings it contains with regard to military preparedness and military interaction with our partners. ANZUS was stage centre in New Zealand international policies for thirty years. The emphasis, however, was on the political relationship with the United States which the treaty brought with it, rather than on the associated commitments to the maintenance of effective interactive defence forces.

The Muldoon administration, it will be remembered, pushed ANZUS for all it was worth. The rationale, however, had more to do with confronting the Left in New Zealand politics than any sudden conversion to the importance of defence in the New Zealand scheme of things. The Muldoon thrust was the allegation that fundamental political ties with the United States would be undermined by a Labour Government carrying anti-nuclear baggage. The Labour Opposition believed in having it both ways. With even more cavalier disregard of the issues embedded in the treaty, Labour pressed forward on the anti-nuclear front while professing support for ANZUS and the relationship with the United States. When negotiations towards the conclusion of the ANZUS Pact were being conducted in 1951, the then Minister of External Affairs, Doidge, wrote that he would regard an American guarantee of New Zealand security as the richest prize in New Zealand politics. By the time Mr Muldoon called his snap election in mid-1984, the richest prize had become a mere domestic political football.

It is all too easy in such circumstances for bureaucrats to get caught in the middle. A month or so before the snap election in 1984 a major conference on ANZUS was scheduled at Pennsylvania State University. The Australian Minister of Defence was to attend; for some reason, now forgotten, David Thomson, the New Zealand Minister, could not go and nominated me. When the election was called I suggested to Mr Thomson that it would make sense for me to withdraw, since the conference would now happen in the middle of an election campaign in which ANZUS was bound to be an issue. No, I was told, we (the then Muldoon administration) want you to attend. Unsurprisingly, an academic talk-fest in the wilds of Pennsylvania then caught the attention of the New Zealand media. My speech, which of course stuck to the policy line of the government of the day, was widely reported in the middle of an election campaign. That then served to put me off-side—probably permanently—with the Lange administration which was elected about two weeks later.

The new government obviously carried a high head of steam as far ANZUS and broadly related matters to do with defence and the US relationship went, so I was unprepared for what I think must have been my first meeting with David Lange. He remarked that it was just as well New Zealand was not Norway or some other country beginning with N. I wasn't used to the style at that point and remained puzzled. "Well," he said, "just think what ANZUS would spell without the Z."

Adjustment to the fourth Labour Government was undoubtedly difficult for Defence. There was, in my experience, absolutely no justification for the accusations of disloyalty which were darkly bandied about. There was, however, undoubtedly a serious non-meeting of minds. Like any professional body would be, the New Zealand military were protective of the reputation and standards of effectiveness of their forces—as they should be. They would have assumed that the Government, whatever its political stripes, would regard it as mandatory to maintain the highest professional standards possible in our small military establishment. It was self-evident to them that the military exchange programmes and opportunities for training with larger and better-equipped forces which ANZUS had made possible were the key element in this equation. Those interactions, founded in war-time associations, had sustained the small New Zealand military for forty years. Senior military officers accordingly took time to come to terms with the realisation that what was happening would carry them away from this past. The character and intensity of a military career in the New Zealand setting would never be the same. Air Marshal Ewan Jamieson, the CDS for the first two years of the Lange administration, was a man of the utmost integrity. He offered forceful advice as to the consequences of what was happening, but never wavered in his adherence to the policies of the government of the day.

A similar non-meeting of minds was at the root of a temporary showdown between the Prime Minister and his military advisors at the time of the Fiji coup in 1987. When an Air New Zealand aircraft was hijacked in Nandi, Prime Minister Lange wanted to mount an immediate military demonstration by despatching troops in a C130 aircraft. The Chiefs of Staff felt obliged to seek clarification on what they regarded as essential military questions. What was the mission? Were they to be authorised to use force? Answers to these questions called down planning issues for them—the units to be deployed; the instructions to be given; the logistics of keeping the forces supplied; their specific military roles; how to get them in and out, and so on. The Prime Minister was both baffled and infuriated and believed that the chiefs were out to thwart him. Fortunately the crisis was over before these issues had to be worked through. The incident was, however, another illustration of the problems associated with policy-making on the hoof and the difficult and fraught issues which are at the heart of the civil–military relationship.

The make-up of the new administration, the high energy levels and strong convictions—especially in the area of international relations—would obviously also impact on Defence, as on a number of other departments, in other ways. There was unquestionably a strong strain of suspicion of senior advisors. In one sense such attitudes are to be expected when administrations change after one party has been in power for a number of years. In another sense, of course, deep suspicions that advice is driven by political motivation as opposed to experience or a rational appreciation of the facts is simply churlish and obsessional. It was certainly tedious and a roadblock in the way of effective working relationships.

The fundamental principle that advisors are loyal to the government of the day, rather than to a political party may seem unbelievable to a team which has been long out of office. To public-service advisors of my generation, however, it was the basic law, the rule from which all else stemmed. If that is not accepted by ministers—and it has to be said that more than a few in the Lange administration found it hard to swallow—then the path can be quite hazardous.

There were at that time no employment contracts. Public servants were not in a good position to challenge preconceived notions about their personalities and politics. Indeed, I have to confess that the idea that ministers should be bothered by such preoccupations simply never occurred to me. I believed myself to be apolitical and that I was being paid to offer advice on the basis of experience and judgement. No doubt the position has changed for the better in determining the relationship between the modern CEO and his or her minister. In those long-gone times, however, suspicions on such matters undoubtedly stymied the conduct of business.

The calibre of the Minister and his position in the Cabinet pecking order is the key. David Lange himself was fully able to lighten the atmosphere with a little wit and mutual understanding. It was another story altogether to have to deal with a minister who found himself saddled with a portfolio for which he had little sympathy and which he believed put him out of the main stream of policy-making in a radical administration. It was no doubt frustrating to have waited for a long time to become a minister and then to be put in charge of a department which had little or no standing in the eyes of one's colleagues. But the reverse also applies; it is disheartening for a department of state responsible for expenditure of substantial resources and for carrying out important national roles to have a minister with neither commitment nor sympathy for its purposes.

The late Frank O'Flynn was a charming and engaging man. He had served in the Air Force in the Pacific during the war. If this experience had left him with a distaste for the military and all it stood for, he would not have been alone. Indeed, Rob Muldoon once confided to me when we were looking at British army establishments in Northern Ireland, that he had gladly put down his musket at the end of the war and had determined then and there to have nothing more to do with the military. For Frank O'Flynn, however, the issues were different and conditioned by politics. As well as being deeply mortified to be allocated the Defence portfolio, he found that the Prime Minister seemed not to want to bring him in on the policy discussions. The upshot was a preoccupation with micro-management, which had a devastating effect on morale in the armed services. Decisions were delayed, postings had to be put off, training programmes were disrupted. A smooth-running command system in which it was accepted that regular programmes and established administrative arrangements for training and operations would be maintained was thrown into disarray.

The organisation of the Ministry of Defence at the time put the emphasis on a close co-ordinating relationship between the Secretary and the Chief of Defence Staff. The Defence Act under which we operated established what became known as a diarchy; a relationship between equals. Crudely put, CDS commanded the armed forces, the Secretary of Defence commanded the resources. It soon became apparent that the new government did not like this arrangement, which presented them with a sort of combined front on defence and military issues. Nevertheless, this was the framework within which we had to operate both in dealings with other departments and with the government of the day.

Labour policy before the elections had crystallised around a determination to ban from New Zealand ports not only nuclear-armed but nuclear-propelled ships. The former stipulation, as is well known, ran up against the traditional 'neither confirm nor deny' (NCND) doctrine adopted by the nuclear weapons powers. In other words, we would never be given an explicit assurance as to whether any one ship had nuclear weapons aboard or not. The nuclear propulsion question, by contrast, posed no problems as to verification. It was common knowledge which ships in the British and American fleets were nuclear-powered. Nevertheless, this element in New Zealand's new policies would become a major impediment to resolution of the looming confrontation with the United States. At the time there were still a few US nuclear-propelled surface ships other than the aircraft carriers. USS *Truxton* was one which had visited New Zealand—giving rise to a famous slogan—'Truck the Fuxston'. Within a few years there would be only the aircraft carriers, which are never likely to visit New Zealand; apart from there being no strategic reason to send them our way, they are too big to get into our harbours. The Americans were, nevertheless, deeply concerned at the time that anti-nuclearism could prove contagious. Any concession to New Zealand on the issue of nuclear propulsion could be taken up by other countries and might in effect tie their hands as to their capacity to deploy these major capital ships.

All this was in the future when David Lange as the Prime Minister-designate met the US Secretary of State, George Schultz, in July 1984. It will be remembered that a bizarre ANZUS Council meeting was being held in Wellington at the time. Thanks to the Muldoon Administration's determination to demonstrate their own ANZUS credentials it had been decided to persevere with the meeting, even though it would take place after the elections. The weather was appalling. New Zealand was represented by the outgoing administration, which added an element of farce to proceedings.

David Lange and George Schultz could hardly have been more of a contrast. The one relatively young, jovial and inexperienced in world affairs, the other an austere ex-Marine, veteran of the War in the Pacific, highly conscious of America's global role and the challenges it faced. What in fact happened between them at that first meeting has been raked over many times. I was not there, but I can say with confidence—from subsequent experience in Washington—that the Americans were convinced that Mr Lange had asked for a delay of six months before ship visits could be resumed. He would need that time to resolve the domestic political challenges he faced over ANZUS and related nuclear issues. Paul Wolfowitz, then the Assistant Secretary of State for East Asia and the Pacific and now known around the world as a leading member of the so-called 'neo-cons' in Washington, took the notes, which have never, as far as I know, seen the light of day. He believes, however, that Mr Lange undertook to clear up the ship visits problem within the six-month period.

Whatever the interpretation of the proceedings, it is indisputable that a train of events was set in motion which ended by profoundly altering the New Zealand political landscape. David Lange's operational style was a contributing factor. He set up a group of advisors to attempt to work through the ANZUS issues and agreed that CDS Jamieson should visit London and the US Commander in Chief Pacific in Hawaii to discuss the parameters for a possible ship visit. From the point of view of an operational public sector, however, it is plainly of the essence that the relationship between a minister and his advisors be a two-way street. The minister must obviously have confidence that his advisors will do what has been agreed. Equally, the advisors can only proceed on the assumption that the political way has been cleared by the minister. When asked to pursue a particular objective, public servants must assume that the minister has the necessary political clout or support to carry through what is proposed.

The CDS did what he was asked to do in negotiation with the CINCPAC in Hawaii to secure a compromise arrangement for a port visit. The Americans co-operated, within the limits of their central doctrine of NCND and their need to head off any restriction on deployment of nuclear-capable or nuclear-powered ships. A suitable ship was produced which they would have been entitled to expect would be acceptable to New Zealand. (I recall saying to colleagues that the ancient *Buchanan* seemed such an ideal candidate to break the deadlock that it should visit a couple of ports. There would have been few warships less likely to be equipped for Armageddon than the *Buchanan*; her outdated anti-submarine rockets were of such limited range that if tipped with nuclear weapons they could have sunk the ship.) But there was no political constituency in Wellington for a deal. While the officials had been trying—on instructions—to find a way forward, the Prime Minister had failed to garner the necessary political support. The rest, as they say, is history.

It was a critical time in Washington; a trial of will was taking place between the US and the Soviet Union. The immediate issue was the deployment by both sides of intermediate-range missiles in Europe, which had provoked massive opposition and peace demonstrations in several European countries. Eventually this showdown would help precipitate the end of the Cold War and the collapse of the Soviet Union. The New Zealand 'problem' was a part of a much more potent equation. In such circumstances, Paul Wolfowitz, for one, clearly resented having spent his own political capital in Washington on the search for a compromise with New Zealand based on his understanding that the political will existed to reach for a solution. As for Secretary Schultz, I once went up to him in a crowded hotel lobby in Little Rock, Arkansas. I said I was the New Zealand Ambassador and would like the opportunity to talk to him some time about the ANZUS imbroglio. He flushed, glared at me and said only "Your Prime Minister could not keep his word". With that he turned on his heel and walked away.

MERWYN NORRISH

The Lange Government's foreign policy

The first question to ask when thinking about the Lange Government's foreign policy, is: was it faithful to the intentions expressed in the Labour Party's manifesto?

Any government assuming office after a period in opposition, will find some of its manifesto's good intentions unrealistic or perhaps impossible to implement in the real world. There are many examples of governments pulling back from a manifesto on aspects of foreign policy—few more striking perhaps than on the topic of nuclear-ship visits to the ports of several Western countries. In our own country a previous Labour Government stopped short of banning such visits.

There were heavy pressures on the Lange Government not to carry out, or at least to tone down, some of the manifesto policies. One major plank, the renegotiation of the terms of the ANZUS treaty, was unrealistic as it was expressed and anyway it was overtaken by events. But, with very few other exceptions, the relationship between the manifesto and the policies carried out by the Government was close. What was remarkable was not the extent to which the Government moved in response to pressure, but the extent to which it did not.

This is a point that should not be overlooked or treated as of little importance: on foreign policy, if not elsewhere, the Government could justly claim that it was carrying out the wishes of the people who voted for it.

Immediately after the 1984 election, events moved swiftly in foreign policy, just as they did in financial and economic policy. Two days after the election the ANZUS Council was due to meet in Wellington. When the snap election had been called, the Ministry of Foreign Affairs had drawn its minister's attention to the decidedly awkward timing of the meeting and proposed that it should either be postponed or switched to Canberra. The Minister, Mr Cooper, had declined those suggestions, feeling, presumably, that any change could be interpreted as a lack of confidence in the outcome of the election.

This meant that on the day immediately following the election, Sunday, the United States Secretary of State, George Shultz, and the Australian Minister of Foreign Affairs, Bill Hayden, were to fly in to Wellington. The Prime Minister-elect, David Lange, decided to come down from Auckland to meet them.

Mr Lange asked me to come to the airport with the Foreign Affairs brief prepared for a new minister and to talk about it in the hour or so between his arrival and that of the ANZUS visitors. I thus watched something of a surreal spectacle.

Mr Shultz and Mr Hayden were met at the steps of their aircraft, in atrocious weather, by the outgoing Minister of Foreign Affairs, Warren Cooper. Mr Lange waited inside for a somewhat bedraggled Mr Cooper to present the visitors to him and, of course, all eyes and all cameras were on the Prime Minister-elect. The officiating Minister found himself relegated to the fringes, which he seemed to accept with good humour.

The ANZUS Council meeting itself also had an air of unreality. Ministers and officials from the three ANZUS governments spent the next couple of days talking as though nothing had changed. The New Zealand Ministers solemnly endorsed passages in the communiqué of the meeting, including one on naval ship visits, which they knew would be unacceptable to those who would take office as their replacements in just a few days' time.

Before leaving for home, the Secretary of State paid an informal call on Mr Lange. He was accompanied by a young man whose name, for better or for worse, later became well-known, Paul Wolfowitz.

This meeting became controversial. The Secretary of State convinced himself that Mr Lange had intimated that over the following six months he would bring about some change in his party's policy on nuclear ship visits. I was the only other person there and I did not interpret Mr Lange's comments that way. He did indeed say that he would be talking to party members about the issue at Labour branch conferences over the six months ahead. Perhaps there was ambiguity there, but he did not say that he would bring about a changed outcome.

It seems to me that Mr Shultz heard what he wanted to hear—a not uncommon eventuality. Unfortunately, this misunderstanding subsequently coloured Mr Shultz's attitude to Mr Lange, and also unfortunately Prime Minister Hawke of Australia appeared to accept Mr Shultz's version and to factor that into his own assessment of Mr Lange, to the latter's obvious disadvantage.

Things moved quickly on other aspects of foreign policy also, but in the short compass of this article it is not feasible to try and deal with them all. Suffice it to say at this point that the generality of the Government's policies seemed to me to be positive. A few, however, including the most important, were controversial at the time and are probably still regarded negatively by a section of public opinion.

Attention came to focus quickly on the nuclear-ships issue. The New Zealand Government's position was that ships of the United States Navy were welcome, provided they were not nuclear powered and did not have nuclear weapons on board. The United States Government had a quite unshakeable policy of neither confirming nor denying the presence of nuclear weapons. This meant that no assurances could be given, when seeking the normal clearances for ship visits, that the ships in question would be carrying no nuclear weapons.

That position of stand-off had been arrived at earlier in a number of other Western countries. In those cases it had been resolved by some such formula as the countries concerned stating their policy of not accepting ships with nuclear weapons and then expressing their confidence that the United States fully understood that policy. On that basis of trust, some ship visits were able to continue.

Formulas of this sort were brought about by strong leaders who valued their countries' relationships with the United States and were prepared to face down continuing opposition by sections of their public which were sceptical that the understandings reached were watertight.

The New Zealand Government was not willing to follow a similar course. In the early stages, however, it did wish—or so it seemed to me—to preserve the couuntry's good relations with the United States and the advantages given by its participation in the ANZUS Council (though perhaps later on with modifications to the Council's terms of reference).

So what could be done? The Ministry of Foreign Affairs suggested to the Prime Minister that it might still be possible to find some way of reconciling the apparently irreconcilable. The Prime Minister agreed that officials should try.

A person essential to this search was the Chief of Defence Staff. It was he, and perhaps he alone, who could talk personally and purposefully with the United States military authorities directly concerned. Air Marshal Sir Ewan Jamieson was, and is, a man of considerable distinction, possessing not only the military virtues, but capable of approaching tangled political issues with a high degree of subtlety and inventiveness.

The Government, in accordance with the Party manifesto, wished to "legislate to make New Zealand and its territorial waters nuclear free". If it did this without reaching some workable arrangement with the United States, then no United States naval ships would be able to visit. The Americans made it clear that they would interpret that eventuality as New Zealand having placed a ban on all of the naval ships of its principal ally, its partner in ANZUS. That was not something that an ally was likely to be permitted to do with impunity.

The only avenue open to avoid this situation was for the New Zealand Government to make its own assessments of whether vessels proposing to visit New Zealand would be carrying nuclear weapons or not. If not, under the legislation, clearances for such visits could be granted.

The Americans disliked the whole idea of legislation. And they were adamant that the New Zealand Government would never be able to, and must not, cite American evidence as to the nuclear status of any vessel. To do so, would be to suggest that the Americans had departed from their sacrosanct policy of neither confirming nor denying. The New Zealand Government would have to act on the basis of whatever evidence it could itself muster.

There were, of course, some categories of United States naval vessels that never carried nuclear weapons. They were very much at the bottom end of the scale, however, and the Americans wished to be able to send a larger vessel occasionally—in connection, for example, with ANZUS naval exercises in the Tasman or the South Pacific—which although nuclear capable, would not be carrying nuclear weapons. It was natural enough that they should feel this to be a minimum requirement.

Air Marshal Jamieson had private discussions with the United States officer who had carriage of the issue, Admiral Crowe, Commander-in-Chief, Pacific. He found that Crowe was also seeking a way through rather than a confrontation. There would from time to time be a nuclear-capable ship in the area which it might be apparent was not nuclear armed. The New Zealand Government should be able confidently to make such a judgement on the basis of the type and condition of the ship, the nature of the mission it was on and the evidence available from intelligence and other sources.

The Prime Minister was of course fully informed of these developments. Papers were prepared informing Cabinet in general terms as matters progressed. The Prime Minister decided not to send these papers forward to Cabinet, saying instead that he would handle the issue orally with ministers.

The next major step was when the Prime Minister himself suggested to the American Ambassador that they should test the waters by putting in a request for a ship visit in the usual way. The ship nominated by the Americans was the *Buchanan*.

The *Buchanan* was described by someone knowledgeable as a clapped-out old destroyer on which no one in his right mind would put nuclear weapons. She would first be making a visit to Japan, another country with a policy opposed to nuclear-ship visits, and would come on to New Zealand from there. These factors, combined with a good deal of other information, enabled a Cabinet paper to be prepared stating that the Prime Minister would be justified in issuing a determination under the legislation that the *Buchanan* would be nuclear free and that a clearance could therefore be granted.

The Prime Minister was out of the country at this stage. How matters would have developed had he been in Wellington one can only guess. As it was, the recommendation was received in Cabinet by ministers who appear to have known little or nothing of the background. Both Michael Bassett and Kerry Burke, in newspaper articles, have confirmed this. Bassett went further and wrote: "It slowly dawned on the rest of us"—at the Cabinet meeting, that is—"that our lack of information over such a long period meant that we had lost the initiative." That sentence seems to mean that those ministers who would have wished to find a way through the nuclear-ships issue and avoid prejudicing New Zealand's relationship with the United States found themselves outflanked by those who did not. And so clearance for the *Buchanan* was declined.

The Deputy Prime Minister at the time, Sir Geoffrey Palmer, said much later that he had not found the evidence put forward in the Cabinet paper conclusive. That statement seems to confirm that ministers were not sufficiently aware of the significance of parts of the evidence cited. There is no question but that an impartial observer, aware of the background, would have found the case proven beyond reasonable doubt. New Zealand was still a participating member of the ANZUS alliance. The sanctions which the Americans applied, however, made it clear that, as far as they were concerned, New Zealand had forfeited at least some of the advantages which ANZUS membership conferred. Again, there appears to have been a split in the New Zealand Cabinet between those ministers who wished to maintain ANZUS links as far as possible and those who felt that New Zealand would be better off out of ANZUS altogether.

This was to some extent an unreal division, since the treaty setting up ANZUS has no provision for withdrawal: while the treaty remains, the members remain members. In practical terms, the issue was should New Zealand try to preserve what it could of the ANZUS links remaining or should it let them slide?

Throughout all this, the Prime Minister had appeared—to me at least—to accept the desirability of maintaining as positive a relationship with the United States as the strains imposed by the anti-nuclear policies permitted. It was a complete surprise to me—and, I believe, to many members of the Cabinet—when, in a speech delivered at Yale University, he took the opposite tack and in effect turned New Zealand's back on ANZUS.

I imagine that in time the judgements made by historians on the Lange Government's foreign policies will come to focus on this bracket of the anti-nuclear policy, ship visits and the ANZUS relationship. Were these policies good ones?

My own conclusions are mixed. I agree that the continued piling up of nuclear weapons in the world was more than could easily be borne. I can readily accept that a ban on port visits by nuclear-armed ships was a not unreasonable way to demonstrate the Government's opposition. Where I disagree is with the Government's missing the chance, while making its stand effectively on nuclear ships, to preserve the advantages of New Zealand's relationship with the United States. It had the opportunity to square the circle by accepting the *Buchanan* visit. Good policy, in my view, would have meant taking that opportunity. The kind of fundamentalism involved in turning it down is seldom a profitable basis for foreign relationships.

A fair question about the Government's foreign policies, too, is not only were the policies themselves good, but were they well carried out? I will make no claims in respect of the performance of the Ministry of Foreign Affairs: that is for others to assess.

It is not the purpose of this article to give a full account of the Lange Government's foreign policies. Briefly, however, many things were done very well. The restoration of New Zealand's international reputation after it had been damaged by rugby relationships with South Africa is a case in point. The final chapter of the *Rainbow Warrior* affair is another: much as it hurt, the Government duly recognised that a settlement with France was in New Zealand's best interests and the outcome gave just recompense for Prime Minister Chirac's action in dishonouring the agreement that the two prisoners should see out their 10-year sentences on Hao atoll. A full list would be quite lengthy.

Where doubts creep in over the Government's conduct of foreign policy issues is once again in respect of the nuclear ships and ANZUS policies. To an impartial observer it must have seemed that New Zealand implemented these policies in a muddled rather than a coherent way. And unfortunately, some of that muddling was judged by New Zealand's interlocutors to be deviousness or a deliberate intention to mislead. It was neither of those things, but the perception was damaging. Prime Minister Lange more than once paid tribute to the US Secretary of State, George Shultz, as a man of his word, but, to my great regret personally, the Secretary of State felt he could not return the compliment.

The most obvious example of difficulty was the *Buchanan* affair. The steps leading up to the American request for the *Buchanan* to visit led the Americans to expect, not unreasonably, that clearance would be granted. That it was brusquely turned down they found hard to understand. Had they then been led up the garden path by a Government that never intended to let a United States Navy ship of any sort visit? No, not that. The situation appears to have been that the Government was divided within itself, that there was insufficient consultation among ministers and that, as a consequence, there was no line of approach which all agreed should be followed. This could be called a failure of process, perhaps, but such failures can have significant consequences, as this one did.

During the discussions about these issues, too, it had become clear that a major anxiety felt by the Americans was that a ban on nuclear-ship visits by New Zealand could encourage similar action by other Western countries much more important strategically to the United States Navy. The Prime Minister recognised that it would do New Zealand no good to be seen to be trying to bring about such a result so he adopted a formula suggested to him that the New Zealand policy was 'not for export' and he used that formula publicly on a number of occasions.

The Prime Minister also, however, accepted an invitation to debate nuclear issues with an American nominee at the Oxford Union. This debate is regarded by many as a great triumph and the high-water mark of New Zealand's campaign against nuclear weapons. Perhaps it was, but it was bound also to sit uncomfortably with the Americans, and it certainly did with the 'not for export' assurance over nuclear ships.

Again, consider the Prime Minister's speech at Yale. As far as I am aware, the portion of the speech in which he turned New Zealand's back on ANZUS was not the subject of any formal discussion in Cabinet before it was delivered. This major change of policy came as a complete surprise to several senior ministers, who had understood that the issue would be a subject for later policy discussion in Cabinet. Again, a serious failure of process.

So what overall assessment might one reasonably arrive at? Definitive judgements on the core issues of the Lange Government's foreign policies may not be reached for years to come. There is still a great deal of emotion surrounding the nuclear issue on the one hand and the issue of New Zealand's defence and security posture on the other.

Many people held and still hold the view that the price New Zealand had to pay for its nuclear-ships stand was well worth it. They do not, it seems, feel any less secure in defence terms now than they did before the problems arose. And, many feel that little New Zealand sent an influential message to the world. This is an instance among many where New Zealanders overestimate their country's influence. But people's perception is often what matters most, and that particular one appears to be unshakeable.

On the other side, a smaller number of people no doubt, but people with much experience or interest in defence and security matters, believe that New Zealand forfeited a priceless advantage, a close and beneficial relationship with the only world power in a position not only to guarantee its security, but also to look benignly on requests it might make for economic and financial support or advantage. They wonder how New Zealand's attitude could have come to differ so markedly from that of Australia, noting perhaps the Australian Government's simple statement in a defence paper not long ago that "our relationship with the United States is a national asset". Some of these people, it seems, and not just the "geriatric generals" to whom Mr Lange once memorably if a little unkindly referred, would be content with nothing less than turning the clock all the way back to the defence and foreign affairs posture pertaining before the 1984 election.

Some people came to believe, or at any rate to assert in public, that the Lange

Government was moving New Zealand to an isolationist posture in international relations; that New Zealand was turning inwards on itself and pulling back from its links with the Western world. The proponents of this view cited evidence additional to the nuclear-ships and ANZUS issue—for example, that the Government seemed likely not to proceed with the purchase of new frigates for the navy and would thus, they said, deprive the navy of a "blue water" capacity and limit its role to fisheries protection and similar close-to-shore activities.

It was true that the Government was to embark on a process leading later to major changes in New Zealand's defence posture. Combine that with the Government's turning away from ANZUS, and the notion of isolationism could gain some credence. Particularly was this so since, in the early stages of the period under discussion, the Cold War was still in progress.

Was New Zealand in fact pulling back from the 'Western camp? The answer to that question is emphatically, no. The Party manifesto stated that Labour would pursue "an independent foreign policy", but there is not a word or phrase in the manifesto to suggest that such a policy meant moving towards isolationism or withdrawing support for Western causes. A Soviet Deputy Foreign Minister came to Wellington with the apparent intention of gauging whether and how far New Zealand would be likely to move. He was given short shrift by Prime Minister Lange himself and, in that and other ways, left in no doubt that New Zealand remained actively committed to the Western camp and to Western principles and ideals.

That particular aspect of the matter faded from contention with the collapse of the Soviet Union and so of the Cold War. But the isolationist charge continued to be heard. Experience and the passage of time were to show that there was little or nothing in it. New Zealand continued to act vigorously and constructively internationally in United Nations bodies, in peacekeeping, development aid, trade negotiations, on human rights issues, environmental issues and in many other ways.

Looking back, it seems to me that the proponents of the isolationist charge felt so strongly about the Government's activities on nuclear ships and ANZUS that for them it followed that the whole direction of New Zealand's foreign policies was changing for the worse—that New Zealand was turning away from the world as they knew it. This was not all that surprising given that New Zealand's alliance membership had been a symbol of active engagement with the Western world for more than thirty years. These people noted also that in some quarters in the Government and the Party there was a strong element of anti-Americanism.

But what was happening in fact was that New Zealand was remaining internationalist but was down-playing some aspects of that posture and putting more emphasis on other aspects. We were moving away from a set of positions that may have just about run their course and into a set of positions that, while different, are quite natural for a small country. This was a very significant shift in foreign policy. The real issue it raised, however, was not whether we were going isolationist, but whether the shift was a positive one or a negative one.

A classic definition of good foreign policy is that it should advance or at least preserve a country's national interest. Although that definition seems too stark to people who desire internationalism to prevail over nationalism, it is still to a major degree the way the world works.

So where did New Zealand's national interest lie in all of this? Not necessarily in backing off its anti-nuclear policies. Not necessarily in maintaining intact its pre-1984 defence and foreign policies. But not either, it seems to me, in taking an all-or nothing stand either way. Foreign relations disputes are usually best handled by means of careful negotiation and some willingness to compromise. It may not be possible to get the best of both worlds, but it is sometimes possible, particularly for small countries, to end up not too far away from that desirable outcome.

This is where, in my view, the decision to turn down the *Buchanan* must cloud one's assessment of otherwise good foreign policies. It would have taken careful preparation and strong leadership—not just within the Cabinet but with the Party activists as well—to have had the visit accepted. If these conditions had been met, few if any harmful consequences need have followed. As it was, politics won the day.

It is not unusual in foreign affairs for politics to win out over statesmanship. It is, however, sometimes a pity when it does.

BRUCE BROWN

The great debate at the Oxford Union

On my return to New Zealand in 1992, after eleven years abroad, I found that there was a widespread assumption—fostered further by the TVNZ 'docudrama' *Fallout,* screened in July and still extant—that the debate at the Oxford Union on the nuclear deterrent, which took place on 1 March 1985 between the Prime Minister, the Right Honourable David Lange, and the American Methodist minister and TV evangelist the Reverend Jerry Falwell, was a famous victory for Lange.

In my judgement it proved a soft victory for a speaker and debater of David Lange's calibre. Falwell, a poor choice of opponent to debate what was a central issue of international defence and foreign policy, would probably have been well beaten anyway. But in fact he was beaten before he started because the subject was switched on his understanding of it at the last moment. Nor, considering Falwell's less than convincing performance, was the margin of the final vote of the audience a sweeping one. At 298 votes to 250[1] it was clear enough, but a change of only 20 or so votes in a house of over 500 would have made it, in the famous words of Wellington about Waterloo, "A damned fine-run-run thing".

Mr Lange says in his book *Nuclear Free – the New Zealand Way* that when he received the Oxford Union invitation he was "entranced".[2] In both Wellington and London, New Zealand officials were not, nor was the British Government. In the High Commission in London we saw it as potentially a cavalier exercise which risked worsening the differences over nuclear questions between the two governments at a time when the continued and active support of the British Government was of great importance in negotiations for New Zealand's continued trading access in butter and sheep meat to Britain and the European Community (EC, as it then was).

As Deputy High Commissioner (from 1981–1985) I was present at the debate. The New Zealand team of seven was Prime Minister Lange; the then High Commissioner, the Hon. Joe Walding (who sat with Lange in the front row); I myself, who sat immediately behind Mr Lange in the second row in order that I might field questions from him or offer him points in rebuttal;[3] Ken Richardson, the Principal Private Secretary to the Prime Minister; Margaret Pope, who wrote Mr Lange's opening speech; Trish Green, Assistant Press Officer in the Prime Minister's Office; and Derek Leask, Counsellor in the High Commission.

In fact the debate was arranged directly by the Prime Minister's Office and the Oxford Union, where the principal person involved was the senior vice-president of the Union (and later president) Jeya Wilson, a young New Zealander of Sri Lankan descent. In the debate she herself proved to be an excellent speaker. According to *Fallout*, the initiator of the idea on the New Zealand side was Simon Walker, then a public relations advisor to the Labour Party. (That may well be, although it was news to me. I recollect, however, that as an Oxford debater he first came to New Zealand in 1974 as a member of a combined Oxford-Cambridge University debating team.[4])

No one in Wellington seems to have thought to advise the High Commission in London or the Ministry of Foreign Affairs in any formal way of what was being planned. We first learned of it through the back door from Jeremy Pope, a New Zealander, then in the Legal Division of the Commonwealth Secretariat. He, in turn, learned about it from his good mate Chris Laidlaw, formerly his colleague in Marlborough House in the office of the Commonwealth Secretary-General, Sonny Ramphal, and then (from 1984) for a time an advisor in the Prime Minister's Office in Wellington. Laidlaw provided information to Jeremy Pope (no relation to Margaret) from time to time and Pope similarly advised me. I, in turn, advised Merv Norrish, Secretary of Foreign Affairs in Wellington, by telephone, of what was afoot and brought him up to date. I think Merv first heard of the proposal through me.

This planning on what might be described as an informal net—the Prime Minister's Chief Press Secretary, Ross Vintiner, to the Oxford Union, presumably Jeya Wilson—apparently began in the late months of 1984 when a solution to the conflicting views of the newly elected New Zealand Labour Government and the Reagan Administration in Washington, initially over the visits of so-called "nuclear ships" but in reality over ANZUS, was still being discussed and, I believe, negotiated. It was a decidedly delicate time.

Through Jeremy Pope we at the High Commission heard two versions as to what was to be the subject of the debate:

"That the *Western* nuclear alliance is morally indefensible" (emphasis added);
and
"That nuclear weapons are morally indefensible" (the version the Prime Minister accepted).

One does not need to be an experienced debater to see how much easier it would be for Falwell to negate the first version of the motion. What about the Soviet nuclear alliance? Was Soviet nuclear fallout good for you? Worse, one could all too readily see that for the New Zealand Prime Minister to affirm the first version, that the *Western* nuclear alliance is morally indefensible (emphasis added) would be politically disastrous. It would have placed Mr Lange in the damaging position of blatantly appearing to side with the Soviet Union against the United States, Britain and the whole Western alliance, represented by NATO and ANZUS.

I conveyed these concerns to Merv Norrish in Wellington, who shared them. Even the politically more neutral version we both thought would be likely to offend the Americans and the British. As Mr Lange himself expressed it in his book, "My official advisers counselled against my taking part. I would upset the United States, I would give offence to Mrs Thatcher's Government. (In both those claims they were perfectly correct.)"[5] The prospect of a prime-ministerial visit to Britain for a speech at the Oxford Union took on a sharper focus following the Labour Government's refusal, on 4 February 1985, to accept the visit of the *Buchanan*.

At this point I should turn to the arrival in London of Joe Walding, newly appointed as High Commissioner by the Lange Government, on 21 February 1985, some two weeks after the *Buchanan* decision. I did not know Joe at that stage but we soon got to know each other well in his sadly brief term in London before his sudden death on 4 June 1985. I quickly came to like him immensely and to admire his political acumen. Joe had been a merchant seaman (seaboy, really) in the Second World War and was fond of recalling that at the ripe old age of 18 he had been in London on VJ day in August 1945. From those wartime experiences he remained very pro-British and pro-Royal Navy in attitude. The breakdown of negotiations about naval visits from both the United States and Britain after the refusal of the *Buchanan* greatly disturbed him.

His appointment to present his letter of credence as High Commissioner from Mr Lange to Mrs Thatcher was set for Friday evening, 22 February. She had been in the course of an official visit to the United States in the week in which the *Buchanan* decision had been announced and had assailed the New Zealand Government's decision at her final press conference in Washington and made it clear that it posed problems for Britain too. There was a snide suggestion, I recollect, from some New Zealand sources that she was simply parroting the Reagan line. She was not. She held those views very firmly herself and blasted the retiring High Commissioner, the Hon. Bill Young, virtually out of his socks when, all unsuspecting, he made his farewell call upon her on 11 February. She made clear her displeasure at the New Zealand Government's decision.[6]

Well aware of this immediate history (I had given him a graphic description of the shell-shocked state in which it had left Bill Young) Joe Walding was understandably apprehensive about the reception he was likely to get when presenting himself and his letter of credence at 10 Downing Street the day after he arrived. A bit pale about the gills ("Wish me luck", he said) he went down to Whitehall on Friday night at 5 pm. He returned about 6 pm, all smiles. Mrs Thatcher had sat him down, said she had had a very hard day and a hard week, and asked would he like a whisky? Joe said he most certainly would. They had several, and a good frank talk. Joe soon established a rapport with Mrs Thatcher and senior British ministers. His sudden death was a loss to New Zealand.

After this call he set to work to try to find a formula—pretty much the "trust me" approach which Mr Lange also tried, unsuccessfully, on his party—which might point a way out of the stalemate. In this search he had several lengthy brainstorming sessions with me and Air Commodore Pat Neville, then senior Defence Adviser at the High Commission, and later Chief of Air Staff. Joe became particularly focused on Mr Lange's announced plans for a visit to London and for the debate at the Oxford Union.

Strange as it may seem, Mr Lange initially made no request to call on Mrs Thatcher or indeed on any British minister, a normal courtesy for a visiting Prime Minister. That bothered the British and it certainly bothered us in the High Commission.

I was not aware until I read Mr Lange's book[7] that the British High Commissioner,

Terence O'Leary, had presented a diplomatic note in Wellington which said, inter-alia: "The Prime Minister and Ministers are looking forward to seeing Mr Lange early next month", delicate Foreign Office drafting which might perhaps be freely translated as "when he has requested to see them".

In the note, according to Mr Lange's own account, British ministers asked him not to announce his forthcoming visit and the debate (unless he had already done so) until he had considered their views as set out in it, in which they sought to dissuade him from accepting the invitation. The subject as British ministers understood it was to be "That nuclear weapons are morally indefensible" (Mr Lange's preferred version.) Nuclear deterrence, the note continued, was the basis of British defence policy. Further, nuclear weapons were a major point of dispute between the British Government and the (Labour) Opposition. The clear implication was that if Mr Lange were to affirm that topic he would be intervening in British domestic politics and British ministers might feel obliged to respond. The note stressed that no other party (obviously the Americans) had been consulted. British ministers were concerned solely with the damage that could arise from "this action" (the debate) for British and alliance interests.

In London we got the message clearly from the Foreign and Commonwealth Office (FCO) and reported it. I took the Assistant Under-Secretary of the FCO for our region, David Wilson[8] to a working lunch on 13 February the day Bill Young left London. He was accompanied by John Chick, head of the FCO Australia–New Zealand–South Pacific Division, and I by Derek Leask, Counsellor at the High Commission (and later New Zealand Ambassador to the European Union). Wilson, very able and well-disposed towards New Zealand, complained at once of the perceived discourtesy of the New Zealand Prime Minister: "It's a bit rum, Bruce, it's a bit rum" (he said in his very English way) for a Commonwealth Prime Minister to pay a visit to Britain, make a highly publicised speech (the planned debate at the Oxford Union) attacking the very basis of British defence policy (which rested on the doctrine of nuclear deterrence) and then to depart without bothering to pay even a courtesy call on British ministers. We conveyed the gist of this meeting to Wellington. It occurred to me that a New Zealand parallel of the time might have been for Prime Minister Bob Hawke of Australia to fly to New Zealand, say to Auckland or Wellington, make a highly publicised speech attacking the very basis of New Zealand's defence policy (i.e. the anti-nuclear stance) and then fly out without so much as saying "Good-day" to his New Zealand counterpart, or any New Zealand minister. That would have outraged the New Zealand Government. But that seemed to be what Mr Lange was contemplating doing in Britain. Fortunately, wiser advice finally prevailed and the High Commission was authorised to seek a call for Mr Lange on Mrs Thatcher.

In case there are still those who may wonder why any robustly anti-nuclear New Zealander should have had the slightest worry about offending Mrs Thatcher, perhaps a recital of some basic facts of political and economic life at that time might be salutary. The week before the Labour Government was elected, on 14 July 1984, the agreement for continued New Zealand butter access to the British market at preferential rates of duty, post-1983, and the contemporaneous bargain over the "voluntary" restraint agreement (VRA) for our lamb access to the whole of the EC, had at last been approved by the EC Council of Ministers. For butter, each EC member had a veto. They did not have to vote 'no', but simply to refrain from voting 'yes'—and France and especially Ireland held out for months. The negotiations had therefore taken well over a year and in 1984 New Zealand had been placed on a month-to-month rollover of 1983 quantities for butter, without any formal agreement, for over six months—a precarious situation. Further, while the butter agreement for the period from January 1984 had been proposed by the European Commission to be for five years, the EC Council of Ministers had agreed to the set quantities only for three years, 1984–85–86. That meant, in consequence, that negotiations to settle agreed quantities for 1987 and 1988 would have to be tackled before the end of the Lange Government's first term—preferably, to allow for another lengthy negotiation, in 1985 but certainly by early 1986.[9]

That meant, in turn, that the Lange Government would need to retain the strong support of the British Government in negotiation with the European Commission and the other member states of the European Community. It was the British butter market. If Britain did not support us—and they claimed it cost them negotiating coin on issues of their own national interest to do so—why should any other EC member? Mrs Thatcher personally, British officials frequently reminded us, was New Zealand's strongest supporter on this issue in the British Cabinet. It did not make any political sense to risk irritating, still less offending, New Zealand's strongest supporter. That was the basis for New Zealand officials' concern, both in London and in Wellington.

In his book David Lange contends that New Zealand butter got into Britain "because people in Britain who bought butter liked New Zealand butter and always looked for the little anchor on the packet. It was British consumers who put pressure on the British Government to keep taking our agricultural products."[10] It was true that there was a long-established consumer market in Britain for New Zealand butter, in part (unlike its Danish and Irish rivals) because it was salty and kept well. But consumer preference is one thing—market *access* is quite another. Once Britain entered the European Community, in January 1973, Protocol 18 to the Treaty of Rome, negotiated in 1971, which governed the quantities of butter New Zealand could export to Britain at favourable duty rates, took legal effect. We could have had housewives and consumer groups demonstrating in the streets by the thousands and crying out for New Zealand butter, but we could not have marketed one tonne without the unanimous consent of the EEC Council of Ministers—unless at a penal rate of duty which would have priced it off the market. It might be added that the British butter market was even more important to the viability of the New Zealand dairy industry in those years than it is to the more diversified industry today.[11]

When I conveyed our concerns about the Oxford debate and the prime-ministerial visit to Merv Norrish, he gloomily concluded that he could provide nothing more by way of advice to the Prime Minister but said that he regarded the coming debate with "great foreboding". I recollect that a telegram from the Ministry in Wellington about Mr Lange's forthcoming visit described the trip as being "a damage limitation exercise". Our concern was that it might well become a damage exacerbation exercise.

Mr Lange duly set forth for Britain travelling via the United States, where in Los Angeles he was given the terms of the United States Administration's response to the *Buchanan's* rejection by Deputy Assistant Secretary of State Bill Brown (later my colleague in Bangkok where he was US Ambassador to Thailand). Mr Lange then shed the senior official who had accompanied him, Tim Francis, Deputy Secretary of Foreign Affairs, and travelled on to London with Ken Richardson, Margaret Pope and Trish Green, arriving on Wednesday, 27 February.

The Minister of State at the FCO, Baroness Elizabeth Young, called on him at New Zealand House on Thursday afternoon, 28 February, an obvious British reconnaissance mission for his call on Mrs Thatcher which had at last been arranged for Friday morning, 1 March, the day of the debate. In the course of this discussion, which did not contribute noticeably to any meeting of minds, Mr Lange rehearsed some of the phrases he used the next day at Oxford, saying that when the British High Commissioner, Terence O'Leary, came to see him in Wellington "I could smell the uranium on his breath" and the like. Baroness Young was not amused.

The following morning (Friday, 1 March) Mr Lange, accompanied by Joe Walding and me, called, as arranged, at 10 Downing Street. When we got there Mrs Thatcher made it clear that she would receive only the Prime Minister and the High Commissioner. It was obvious that she thought she might get a franker discussion with them, as politicians, if no New Zealand official was present taking notes. (But, of course, she had at least one of her own officials present, Charles Powell, her influential FCO Private Secretary.) The consequence of this was that, so far as I know, the New Zealand side had and has no official record in any detail of that discussion. Joe Walding, who dealt with most matters orally—and certainly did not attempt to write a report—told me that Mrs Thatcher had asked and Mr Lange had agreed (very much to Joe's approval) to give further consideration on his return to Wellington as to how a solution might be found which would permit Royal Navy ships to visit New Zealand, without compromising the British policy to "neither confirm nor deny" the presence of nuclear weapons, and to discuss the problem further with the British High Commissioner, Terence O'Leary.[12] I wrote a telegram to Wellington conveying the gist of Joe's oral account of the Downing Street discussion.[13]

It is worth interpolating that some months later, after Joe Walding's death and while I was Acting High Commissioner, Merv Norrish telephoned me to say that O'Leary had called on the Prime Minister to enquire what progress he had made in this further consideration. Mr Lange, I recollect Merv saying, had apparently developed "political amnesia" and no one in Wellington, including Merv himself, recollected details about it. He asked me to get what more I could about it from the British. I therefore got in touch with David Wilson at the FCO. He asked rather sharply "Haven't you got a record?" "Not here," I responded. I had no means of knowing whether Mr Lange had made one and had no wish to have Wilson explore that aspect. Wilson, helpfully, then read to me at high speed the key parts of the detailed British record of what Mr Lange had apparently agreed to do and I cabled the substance of it, with direct quotations wherever I could, in a telegram directed to Merv Norrish. As far as I know, nothing more ever came of this.

Returning to the debate. I asked Margaret Pope, who was given the use of an office in the Foreign Affairs suite in the High Commission, if I could see a copy of the Oxford speech. She gave it to me, rather reluctantly I thought, and I returned to my office and called in the Counsellor, Derek Leask, in order that we might go through it. This took time. It seemed to me that not only did the speech make the expected argument against the doctrine of nuclear deterrence, but it also contained some observations about both British and American defence policy which were unnecessary to the substance of the argument and were highly likely to be regarded by those governments, were they to see or hear them, as unnecessarily offensive. I therefore set to work to make a number of suggested deletions and drafting changes. When Margaret Pope returned from lunch she came into my office—where, with Derek Leask sitting beside me, I was still beavering away, amending the text in pencil—and asked to have the speech text back. I responded that I had not yet worked right through it but in any case I would have a number of changes to recommend. She flushed red, stamped her foot, exclaimed "Oh!", turned and marched out of my office.

There followed a lunch for three in the High Commissioner's dining room, David Lange, Joe Walding and me. We went through the speech draft and I described the changes that I recommended and why. My recollection is that all of those which removed or amended comments likely to cause unnecessary offence to the British Government, Joe Walding supported and the Prime Minister agreed to. Those similarly designed to remove or amend comments likely to be unnecessarily offensive to the United States, Joe did not support and the Prime Minister did not agree to. (I had not had time to brief Joe beforehand and we had yet to get to know each other well. I believe that had the issue arisen even a week or so later, he would have supported me right through.)

It was plain that Margaret Pope had resented my actions in asking to see the text and recommending changes, as I suspect she resented all advice from officials to the Prime Minister which did not accord with her own personal political agenda. The direction of that agenda became clear in the course of that visit. "Time we got out of ANZUS, Bruce", she told me at Heathrow, shortly before the Prime Minister's party left for Geneva on Monday, 4 March. I demurred. She did not seem to understand that New Zealand's anti-nuclear policy in general, and what the Prime Minister of New Zealand said about it publicly, in Britain in particular, was a matter of great interest and considerable concern to the British government. This was the time at which US Pershing missiles were being deployed in Western Europe in response to the Soviet Union's deployment of SS-20 missiles, a Soviet action which the former Soviet Ambassador to New Zealand, Yuri Sokolov, later publicly commented was entirely "unnecessary".[14] There was considerable public unease in the European Community over the Pershing deployment, in the Netherlands particularly—the "Dutch qualm" disease, as it was labelled at the time—and in Britain there was the mass protest of the Greenham Common women. The British and European Community governments were therefore particularly sensitive to the whole question of the nuclear deterrent. The High Commissioner had the responsibility to advise the New Zealand Government on all matters likely to affect New Zealand's relations with Britain. As his Deputy and senior official, it was my responsibility to advise him, which I did.

The most dramatic developments, however, as Mr Lange himself has described,[15] concerned the wording of the subject of the Oxford debate. At a very late stage we learned that the Oxford Union had agreed or decided that the wording of the motion would be as first put to Mr Lange, "That the *Western* nuclear alliance is morally indefensible" (emphasis added). I do not know how this confusion came about. Mr Lange reports that he had rejected this first version and insisted that the motion should be the politically more neutral one, "That nuclear weapons are morally indefensible".[16] It may be that the Oxford Union officers allowed the New Zealand side to think that this version had been accepted, while allowing Falwell who, Mr Lange reports, had objected to the change, to continue to think that the subject would be as first proposed, referring to the *Western* nuclear alliance only. In any case, Joe Walding and I urged the Prime Minister, who needed no urging, that he could not agree to debate the motion which focused only on the *Western* alliance. Mr Lange agreed that the Oxford Union President should be so advised and asked us to give urgent consideration as to how we could arrange a platform and audience—for example in New Zealand House, if need be—so that he might deliver his planned speech before he left London.

The President of the Oxford Union, Roland Rudd, a tall lugubrious young man, was summoned down to London by train that Thursday evening (the night before the debate) and at a meeting in Mr Lange's suite at the Howard Hotel was given the prime-ministerial ultimatum. Either the motion reverted to the form the New Zealand side had understood it to be or there would be no debate. He agreed and returned to Oxford.

Falwell, however, had already left the United States to fly to Britain and could not be contacted. I think he arrived in Britain some time on Friday. I don't know when the Oxford Union officers told him what was obviously, for him, a critical change of subject but I doubt that it was much, if anything, before he arrived in Oxford for the debate itself. Certainly, the text of his speech, which he followed pretty closely, made it clear that he had expected to be able to argue on the basis that the *Western* nuclear alliance was necessary because of the threat of the *Soviet* nuclear alliance.

In any case, why the Oxford Union chose Falwell, a highly conservative American Methodist evangelist minister, to debate such a key foreign and defence policy issue, God only knows. He was clearly not at ease with the subject and I suspect had virtually no background knowledge of it. Further, the Oxford Union milieu—a mock parliament with interjections and points of order—was clearly not suited to his experience of the shelter of the pulpit or the television studio. To a brilliant parliamentarian like David Lange, however, it was an ideal setting. Falwell was, therefore, despite his high profile in the American media, a less than formidable opponent. It may not have helped him that he had met Mr Lange at the pre-debate dinner and seemed to have acquired considerable respect for the Prime Minister, who may well have mentioned his own Methodist background. In the event, better arguments were advanced on Falwell's side of the debate from others, including notably the Conservative MP, Julian Amery, who was his seconder. Kevin MacNamara MP, the British Labour Party's associate spokesperson on defence policy, also made a particularly good speech in support of Mr Lange.

David Lange himself was in fine form and showed his well-known ability to embellish his speech notes with off-the-cuff wit, often barbed. To my concern, after all my labours, he ad-libbed some cracks about Mrs Thatcher, which just about brought the house down. I wondered silently how they would play in Downing Street. In fact, while the media, British and international, were thick on the ground in Oxford (a Japanese television team was roaming around there, for example), as far as we could establish, the debate was not televised live in Britain. I am unsure whether it, or parts of it, were ever broadcast there.

It seemed probable, therefore, that Mrs Thatcher and British ministers did not see or hear it. However, the FCO (in the person of John Chick) had asked me for a copy of the speech, for the Foreign Office and Downing Street, before we left London for Oxford on Friday afternoon. I declined, on the grounds that the draft was still being amended (which it was) and in any case would need to be checked against delivery. I told Chick I would get the final text to him on Monday morning. We drove back to London after the debate, on Saturday morning, and Laurine Ford, senior Foreign Affairs Personal Assistant at the High Commission, set to work that afternoon in her office adjoining mine to type up the text from the tape recording we had made. Having regard to the speed at which Mr Lange spoke, and the doubtful quality of the recording, it was not an easy task.

To my surprise, the commissionaire on duty at New Zealand House rang me in the course of the afternoon to say that 'A Mr Chick from the Foreign Office" was on his way up to the third floor to see me. John duly arrived, casually dressed and with two young children in tow. He asked if he would uplift a copy of the final, definitive version of the speech. Told it wasn't yet ready, he settled down in the foyer to wait. In my office I read the emerging text page by page. As I did so, particularly on the later pages where Mr Lange's ad-libs at Mrs Thatcher's expense thickened the text, it made "each particular hair to stand on end", as the Ghost said to Hamlet. My God, I thought, if she reads this either she won't receive him again, or it will be so frostily that it might be better if she didn't. I told John Chick, now pacing around impatiently, that we were having terrible trouble with the tape and would have to work on it over the remainder of the weekend. I promised to have clean copies of the text delivered to him on Monday morning. He departed. I then amended the text once more, going through it to delete some of the more potentially offensive witticisms without damaging the argument. The edited copies were duly delivered to Chick at the FCO on Monday morning. I have no doubt that they were read by appropriate officials there and by Mrs Thatcher herself in Downing Street. So ended the great debate at the Oxford Union.

It is a commentary on both media attitudes and public opinion that two of Mr Lange's overseas visits were perceived and received so differently. His visit to Britain and the Oxford debate in February—March 1985 risked worsening the defence policy differences between New Zealand and Britain and certainly did nothing to lessen them. Even more important, it also risked weakening the British Government's support for the level of continued New Zealand access for butter and lamb to the British and EC markets which we were seeking. As far as we were concerned in London, we could have done without any political grandstanding. After the *Buchanan,* the less said publicly the better. But it seems to have won

Mr Lange popular acclaim in New Zealand, even from his opponents. His visit to Africa, in April 1985, on the contrary, was criticised in much of the New Zealand media's reporting and on balance was probably a minus not a plus for him in his domestic political standing. Yet his gesture in making the African visit did much to restore New Zealand's relations with the numerous African states after the bitterness left there by Sir Robert Muldoon. The great success of the Commonwealth Games in Auckland in 1990 and New Zealand's election to the UN Security Council in 1992 both owed much to his visit and to the approach it represented. For that he—and Russell Marshall, who succeeded him as Minister of Foreign Affairs and also made an African visit—have never been given any credit. Such is the way of the political world.

TED WOODFIELD
International trade relations

I want to comment on the effects of the economic reform programme on the pursuit of our external trade policies in the first term of the fourth Labour Government.

In 1984 there were three main sets of trade policy objectives. The first was to establish a basis for a new GATT Round of multilateral trade negotiations that would encompass issues central to our external trade. These were the need for increased and secure access to markets for our agricultural exports, and the establishment of limits on agricultural price supports and export subsidies. The second was to hold the line, in the meantime, on access arrangements in place in our major markets; find new market opportunities; and try and limit damage to our diversification efforts from subsidised exports from competitors. The third was to 'bed in' the CER Agreement with Australia, and work towards the review due in 1988.

On the multilateral front, institutional machinery had been established within GATT to examine agricultural trade policy issues. In OECD a study of the implications of national farm policies on international trade was under way. This report would provide the intellectual underpinning of the arguments being mounted for reform. New Zealand was making significant contributions in both institutions, but much remained to be done to achieve the political commitment of all GATT Contracting Parties to engage in negotiations on terms likely to meet our concerns.

In 1984 the external market outlook for our vital dairy trade was deteriorating rapidly. In June, just before the election here, European Community ministers, following the usual lengthy and frustrating process, approved access for our butter to the United Kingdom market, under Protocol 18, for the five years 1984 to 1988, although specific quantities were agreed for the first three years only.

While this decision was welcomed, the EC at the same time was intensifying aggressive export programmes for heavily subsidised farm products, including dairy products. These programmes were driving down international prices and threatening access to markets where we were seeking to diversify. Earlier understandings between New Zealand and the EC on co-operation on dairy marketing were being disregarded. There was a major risk too that the US could enter dairy markets to compete with the EC.

With the advent of the new government our efforts to advance the cause of a new multilateral trade negotiations round, to hold the line against threats to our existing export trade, and to seek new markets, were aided significantly by our ability to demonstrate that New Zealand was putting into practice trade liberalisation and agricultural support policies that we had long advocated should be the policies of others.

The Hon. Mike Moore, the new Minister for Overseas Trade and Marketing, and Tourism, mapped out an energetic programme of visits to the main existing markets and target markets, taking with him business and union leaders. In all the countries visited there was considerable interest in the content, direction and timing of New Zealand's economic reforms. Trade and investment opportunities developed. I recommend Mike's book *Hard Labour* to those interested in his own views on the period.

In September 1984 the Minister travelled to Rio de Janeiro for the second in a series of informal meetings of Trade Ministers consulting on the issues relating to the launch of a new round of multilateral trade negotiations. He attended similar meetings in the following two years—in Stockholm (1985) and Seoul (1986)—and New Zealand hosted a meeting in Taupo in 1987.

New Zealand's participation in these select meetings reflected our longstanding strong involvement in, commitment to, and support for the GATT process, as well as our special interest in issues relating to trade in agricultural products. But our participation could never be taken for granted. The Minister readily accepted that it was necessary for New Zealand to make solid contributions to the discussions as well as using the opportunity to develop personal relationships with other ministers. Mr Moore was quickly recognised as a contributor on the substance and to the process. He was able to illustrate from the policy changes already announced that New Zealand was "putting its money where its mouth was". His personal input, his ability to communicate with insight and wit, was widely appreciated by his fellow trade ministers. At times when discussions bogged down and a circuit-breaker was required, Mike could be depended on to provide it—to break down tensions and get the discussion back on the rails.

New Zealand's contributions in these meetings, together with those of Mike's Australian counterparts, John Dawkins and later Michael Duffy, were significant factors in the realisation of our long-sought objective of the inclusion of agricultural trade reforms in the agenda for the next GATT Round of multilateral trade negotiations (the Uruguay Round launched in 1986) and the eventual successful outcome several years later.

It was in discussions between Mike Moore and John Dawkins—first in Christchurch in February 1985 and then in Stockholm in June—that the idea emerged of forming a group of agricultural exporting countries to lobby on agricultural trade issues in the preparatory work on a new multilateral trade negotiation. Out of these discussions came the Cairns Group, which played a vital role in achieving our objectives in the Uruguay Round. Various claims have been made as to the originator of the idea. Much of the credit is due to Mike Moore and his grasp of the realities of international trade negotiation and talent at persuasion.

As in the Minister's talks with other trade ministers, our bilateral negotiations with the European Community on export programmes also bore fruit. In September

1985 the EC made an important decision to resume consultations with us on dairy export issues, and work to achieve improved returns from the international markets. This decision followed representations in Brussels by the Minister and delegations from the New Zealand Dairy Board and Federated Farmers. A crucial factor was a visit to New Zealand by the EC Commissioner for Agriculture (Frans Andriessen) who saw at first-hand the way New Zealand farmers were being affected by, and how they were responding to, the Government's reform measures. The personal impact on the Commissioner of his discussions with farmers—their support for the Government's policies, the case they made for better understanding of their situation, and their perspectives on agricultural trade policies—was apparent to all present. Outcomes were that our developing trade in the USSR and other markets was preserved and international prices firmed.

In addition, in August 1986, EC ministers finally approved access for New Zealand butter for 1987 and 1988 at the levels proposed by the Commission two years earlier. There had been considerable concern that the French Government would oppose this outcome as part of a suite of measures affecting our exports to put pressure on New Zealand in the aftermath of the *Rainbow Warrior* incident. In the event, after skilful work by colleagues in Foreign Affairs, these issues were included in the adjudication process involving the UN Secretary General in which the French Government undertook not to oppose the EC Commission proposal on butter access.

Our ability to move forward on major issues in our trade relationship with Australia was influenced also, in significant degree, by the economic reform programme. The CER Agreement, that came into effect in 1983, was rightly hailed as the most comprehensive, and GATT-compatible, Free Trade Agreement ever negotiated. Nonetheless, there were several elements in the Agreement—access conditions for a number of products, and policy issues which were not specifically detailed—which could have been the cause of significant difficulty if not handled with acumen and sensitivity to the balance of interests achieved in the final rounds of the negotiation. It was also less than certain what the outcome of the review of CER to be conducted in 1988 might be.

Two key factors contributed to moving the relationship forward. One was the commitment to CER of the new Minister, and Cabinet colleagues such as Roger Douglas and David Caygill, coupled with a strong sense of the desirability of establishing and strengthening a close working rapport with the Labour Government in Australia on trade issues, understanding and respecting their interests as well as pursuing our own. The second factor was the new dynamic arising from the economic reforms in New Zealand, and those in Australia also. New Zealand business developed greater confidence in competing with Australian firms in both markets, and Australian business responded in looking for trade and investment opportunities in New Zealand. Commercial chemistry operated to overcome earlier uncertainties and hesitations. Business on both sides of the Tasman petitioned governments to accelerate the trade liberalisation programme and widen the scope of the Agreement.

The outcomes were the ready resolution of issues that arose in 1984 and 1985, and a willingness to consider in the 1988 review, moving to full free trade in all goods and most services by 1990. It may be considered remarkable that these achievements were realised despite the difficulties that existed in respect of other elements in the bilateral relationship.

The one area where our representations based on the economic reform programme fell short of success was in relation to the action of the United States in April 1985 withdrawing the protection afforded to New Zealand exports to that market of an "injury test" when allegations were made that the goods were subsidised. The existence of the "injury test" had precluded on an earlier occasion an initiative to impose additional and punitive import duties on New Zealand lamb.

I will not detail the lengthy and complicated history that led to the situation in 1985. What is relevant here is that in February 1985 we were seeking to persuade the US Administration not to act against us but to take into account the major economic changes initiated by the Labour Government and give us more time (two years) to implement those relating to the export tax incentives that were the chief cause of concern to the US. We knew that the US Trade Representative (Ambassador Bill Brock) was under heavy pressure from senior Congressional figures to act against New Zealand and several other countries on the injury test issue. This was part of a wider argument about protecting US industries. Our case, based on the New Zealand reform programme, was designed to provide a basis for an Administration decision that would be defensible in economic terms before the Congress and other interested parties. We offered the US a transition that was substantively better than what they were obtaining from other countries with which they were negotiating.

As it happened, the same day that we were presenting our case in Washington, the Prime Minister was being informed in Los Angeles of the planned actions to be taken by the United States to terminate military and intelligence co-operation following the decision to deny port access to the *Buchanan*. Two days later we were advised that our case on export incentives was not accepted. Mr Moore travelled to Washington to see Ambassador Brock, who confirmed the decision.

Almost immediately the US sheep industry petitioned for countervailing duties to be imposed on New Zealand lamb. This was granted and remained in force until 1990, at considerable cost to the New Zealand industry. Duties were also imposed in 1985 on certain metal products exported to the US by McKechnie Bros.

Both the US Administration and our ministers were at pains to present the decision solely in terms of a longstanding US trade policy position, and unrelated to the ANZUS issues. US Secretary of State George Schultz and others were quoted as stating that the United States was not in the business of taking economic sanctions and would not target New Zealand on trade issues.

Personally I don't think that was the whole story. I believe that there was considerable appreciation in Washington of the major changes being made in our economy, and the potential benefits for the US as the major world economy and a leading trading partner. On the specific issue of our export tax incentives there had been earlier signals that a way might be found to resolve the problem. It was against this background that we mounted our case. The timing, however, was not propitious. A discretionary judgement in our favour was sought, but the prevailing mood was against any such response.

The New Zealand decision on nuclear-ship visits had highlighted our profile in the trade debate as well as on national security issues. We became the target of attacks in Congress and elsewhere that might not otherwise have occurred. By denying our request the Administration was able to meet congressional objections in both import protection and defence areas without compromising the public statements by Administration officials that New Zealand would not be targeted for retaliatory trade actions.

This was, in fact, the only incident in the United States at this time of a discretionary decision on a trade issue going against us. Over the following two years the Embassy and New Zealand trade officials in the US monitored closely any suggestions of discriminatory actions against New Zealand products in the US market place. In mid-1986, the Senior Trade Commissioner in Washington was able to report that: all specific instances of trade retaliation at the commercial level had been checked out and all had been eventually resolved. What scares there were related to the general US trading environment, the Farm Bill, and congressional pressures for protectionist trade legislation.

At the level of the Minister and his officials, contact with US counterparts was not disrupted. We continued dialogue in meetings leading up to and during the launch of the GATT Uruguay Round, and thereafter. Brock's successor as Special Trade Representative (Clayton Yeutter) attended the Trade Ministers meeting in Taupo in 1987.

It might be a fair conclusion that the countervailing duties on lamb and certain metal products were a small price to pay compared with the adverse consequences of other potential actions that might have been taken by the US.

I venture to suggest that the outcomes over this period in the United States, as well as those realised in Australia and the EC as discussed in these comments, were in large part due to recognition of the contributions being made by New Zealand in the areas of national economic and international trade policies, offsetting the concerns of those whose attitudes were influenced primarily by defence and security considerations. Some credit might be due also to the personal relationships established by the Minister and others working in the trade policy field.

Finally, I might add that apart from the *Rainbow Warrior* incident and its aftermath, I am unaware of any other actions elsewhere in the world affecting our trade—negatively or positively—as a direct consequence of our anti-nuclear policies.

ROSS VINTINER
Dark ink

The purpose of any review, especially 20 years after the event, is to add to the understanding of that event. It would be heroic to attempt to establish new truths about possibly the most analysed government in living memory. It is, however, useful to address and challenge some myths and opinions now perpetrated as fact. The value of an insider's observations on the first term of the Lange Labour Government is that they may assist in greater understanding of that administration and its leader.

The context for my observations is the most poignant political achievement of the fourth Labour Government. Labour came to power in 1984 in a landslide victory, ostensibly to rid the country of Muldoonism. The July 1984 snap election did not affirm a well-understood Labour Party or a populist David Lange. On election, Labour and Lange were political light ink.

Three years on, after the most far-reaching and tumultuous economic, social and foreign policy reform since the first Labour Government of the mid to late 1930s, Labour was re-elected with an increased majority—and an increased share of the popular vote—both unprecedented results in the post-war period. In 1987, an electorate changed in both thread and fabric affirmed the Labour Government. On re-election, Labour and Lange had become political dark ink.

Politics can be thought of as an expression of how the world ought to be. As such, how did Labour manage its affairs and its perceptions between 1984 and 1987 to persuade an increased majority of the electorate that New Zealand was heading in the right direction? What were the factors that gave Labour public opinion leadership for most of its first term, unchallenged preferred leadership status for all that term, and the electoral outcome of 1987? What made the Lange Labour Government the political dark ink that has, by and large, scribed the economic, social and foreign policy direction of successive National and Labour administrations since?

I want to suggest that David Lange played a hugely significant part in these achievements—far more than critics, including some former colleagues, give him credit for. Five touchstone observations help explain the first term of what was the Lange Labour Government:

- Resolving real politic issues
- The value of new leadership and defining events
- The birth of modern government

- Managing politics
- Managing communications.

RESOLVING REAL POLITIC ISSUES

In early 1981 when I began working for the Labour Caucus as a half-time publicist, the major political issues in public opinion surveys were stated to be unemployment and the state of the economy. There were two far more powerful real politic issues that dominated the electorate and election year.

The first issue was Prime Minister and Finance Minister Robert Muldoon. The rampant political and economic authority he had exercised since 1975 allowed him to steer an agenda designed to shore up provincial seats (the Springbok tour), and to inspire economic confidence by leaping across widening economic fissures to a netherworld of state-funded energy and industrial self-reliance (Think Big).

Think Big was part of Muldoon's response to the larger issue of New Zealand's economic determinism. Britain's intention to join Europe critically severed New Zealand's main trading artery and two oil price shocks during the 1970s exposed the balance-of-payment ledger. Muldoon's instincts were interventionist. The ending of traditional markets and an economy dependent on cheap energy would be served by increased state smoothing of trading cycles for farming and industry—and with it increased economic privilege—and a programme to generate greater energy self-reliance.

Muldoon's clever myth projected during 1981 was greater economic independence for New Zealand. The opposite was the case in reality, with an economy at the mercy of higher overseas' debt to pay for subsidised production and living standards. In foreign policy, New Zealand followed the Western alliance and had little independent interest in the emerging nations of the Pacific or Asia. To just enough of the electorate, Muldoon's wily and experienced hand was sufficient cover for what lay underneath.

Muldoon's paternalism and protectionism was curiously at odds with his own party's traditional support for free enterprise and an opening world market place, which he later acknowledged in his greatest achievement, Closer Economic Relations with Australia. As an interventionist, Muldoon was out of step with the emerging 'new Tories' of Britain and the United States, although his approach was consistent with National's patronage of privilege for its traditional supporters, and maintaining the status quo.

The second real politic issue involved Labour's political and economic credibility. In 1981 the Labour Party was politically divided. The attempted leadership coup against Bill Rowling in 1980 by supporters of David Lange limited the Party's credibility to govern. Labour's response to economic determinism was also less than convincing to the electorate. The older guard of Rowling supporters, imbued with the Norman Kirk tradition, bought into Muldoon's agenda and offered only a variation of his interventionism. During the 1981 election campaign Bill Rowling was equivocal on reversing Think Big projects and, like Muldoon, promoted state intervention to pick winners to boost the flagging economy, raising Labour's Achilles Heel, credibility to pay for its promises. At odds with this approach were the more pragmatic new voices of younger Labour MPs, not in the Kirk mould and in tune with economic orthodoxy. They wanted change to the status quo within New Zealand and Labour.

On the road with Labour deputy leader David Lange during the 1981 election campaign, I had first-hand experience of Labour's divisions and their lack of political credibility. Bill Rowling planned his leadership campaign in isolation from his deputy. There was a detailed Labour policy manifesto which Geoffrey Palmer had a large part in, but the election was clearly on Muldoon's terms. Lange and I were told which electorates to visit, starting with the highly contentious New Plymouth seat, the home of Think Big.

On his opening night in New Plymouth, David Lange downed his by-now-infamous fish and chips and drank a large bottle of Coke. He made hard work of the small-talk with party rank and file, who hardly disguised Lange's pariah status within Labour Party circles. His speech was in a small hall with paper-topped trestles adorned with more cakes than audience members. Lange mouthed the party mantra of opposing Think Big and offered a lesser version of the same, somewhat unconvincingly. It was a David Lange without enthusiasm or his usual vocal gymnastics. He remarked to me with justified concern that it was hardly politically smart to condemn Think Big in the very province that would benefit most from it. I felt I had failed in the name of message consistency, a victim of a larger policy problem unresolved in Labour. The faithful clapped politely and David left the meeting, slightly disillusioned, driving through the night to be with Naomi and his children.

I was left with the impression that Lange's talent had been wasted, although I had learnt three key political lessons: Lange needed not only the right message but also the right medium to deliver it; he deserved a good audience; he needed the Labour Party. Second, David Lange was a unique politician and theatrical performer; he did not fit the traditional approach to electioneering. To bring out his best, normal rules did not apply. Third, in an understated way, David Lange valued loyalty. I was in Lange's camp.

The leadership 'team' hardly spoke during the rest of the campaign. To Muldoon's delight, Rowling put his own leadership credibility on the line in election debates, and both ignored Lange for their own reasons.

Given Labour's credibility gap, the 1981 result was instructive. By Labour winning more votes than National, and losing the election by just one seat, the scene was set to resolve three real politic issues. Muldoon remained the main issue but was now seen as highly vulnerable; he had to rely on independent MPs to hold onto power. Next, it was clear even to National politicians that the country's economy and lifestyles could not be sustained by policies masking structural problems and worsening overseas debt. Finally, Labour had the opportunity to go beyond Muldoonism. To do so required a choice between the traditional approach of Rowling and a new approach with Lange and a younger generation of politicians. This group was enthusiastic about maturing a more rational economy, celebrating social pluralism and realising a new generation of nationalism in New Zealanders prepared to confidently face outwards to the realities of a competitive world. They looked to a future New Zealand rather than to its past.

To a large extent, the years after the 1981 General Election saw the resolution of these three issues. Muldoon survived the years to 1984 only by assertion of centralised power. He could not maintain lifestyles and froze them instead. His social conservatism suited an aging National electorate but defied the realities of a changing and maturing society, even in his provincial strongholds. Muldoon began to look old and out of time. Increasingly the unchallenged leader called on diminishing political capital from colleagues who were daring to think, and some to say, he was wrong and that there was another way. His great communications skills that simplified issues to their essentials no longer added up to a convincing story, and a tenuous link to past successful performances was fast fading. The dam was threatening to burst.

The political mood of the country was also shifting. A new political approach to end riddled division was sought. There was a desire for positive expressions of opportunity and endeavour, an articulation of desired inter-generational and suppressed change. A new political language was being developed around notions of 'consensus' and 'celebration of talent'. National felt the winds as much as Labour. Strict party identification between Labour and National was beginning to break down. A new educated middle class was emerging. In Labour, in the months after the 1981 General Election, Rowling could not articulate this new mood. As 1982 drifted on, it was not a matter of would Lange lead Labour, but when—with two caveats: did David Lange really want the job? And, if so, was he up to doing it?

THE VALUE OF NEW LEADERSHIP AND DEFINING EVENTS
Between 1981 and 1983 I continued to work as a publicist for the Labour Caucus and also as an energy, environment and transport researcher in Parliament. With Fraser Coleman I helped to expose the Erebus cover-up, with Richard Prebble to "Save Rail", and with David Caygill and David Lange to expose the cracks of the flawed Think Big projects, such as the Aramoana aluminium smelter and the Clyde Dam. Labour was getting its act together in opposing Muldoon, if not in articulating an alternative to him.

During this time I worked with David Lange to write positioning speeches and media statements on social justice, economics, consensus, the 'value' of the environment and the political convenience to National of nuclear-ship visits. David Lange chose his issues carefully. His legal and political judgement melded into a moderate and often conservative, non-dogmatic array of convincing positions. He explored how the economy could be liberalised but, in keeping with his 1977 landmark maiden speech to Parliament as the MP for Mangere and true to his Methodist convictions, how the instrument of the State would foster and protect those in need. In Parliament it became obvious that Lange was the emerging threat to Muldoon. Lange soared when leading parliamentary snap debates for Labour. He articulated the new mood.

Part of the step towards becoming leader involved his health. David telephoned me one day in early 1982 from his home in Auckland to say he would be out of circulation for a while, and when he came back he would be healthier and ready to play a greater role in politics. He explained his desperate need to lose weight or face the inevitable. He was less explicit about the political code, although I understood enough of politics and him by now to get his drift. With a stomach staple in place, new coiffure and apparent bounding energy, it became obvious that David Lange would take over as leader of the Labour Party.

I was in Sri Lanka—a holiday partly paid for by David to compensate for my low pay in Parliament—when David Lange became Labour Leader in 1983. I received a letter to say I should return to New Zealand as Geoffrey Palmer, elected Deputy Leader, was organising David Lange's office. I never had an interview for the job of Lange's press secretary—I was seen to be loyal—and was thus immediately thrown into the maelstrom of opportunities and challenges that lay ahead. David Lange faced a vast expansion of his role as parliamentary debater. He needed to become Labour Leader and a majority voice to oppose and beat Muldoon. No one, including David Lange, was prepared for the enormity of the job.

His sponsors to leadership, Roger Douglas, Mike Moore, Michael Bassett and Richard Prebble, put their faith in him to deliver leadership from a still divided Caucus of MPs coming from a great mix of political viewpoints. For each sponsor, in new roles, Lange's future was their own.

In the early days as Labour Leader, Lange began to assert his pragmatic and sometimes singular exploration of issues. Nuclear-ship visits was the first topic to come to the public's attention. Although Lange had been barred from visiting the United States because of his student protests against the Vietnam War, he was not anti-American. Quite the reverse, he was cosmopolitan, with a love of India and England, and had an admiration for the freedoms and qualities exemplified by Americans. Nor was Lange opposed to the benefits of technology.

One of Lange's first major speeches as Leader was to the American Chamber of Commerce in New Zealand. There was no funding for me to travel with him and I heard through the news media that in answer to a question from the floor, Lange had said nuclear power should be considered apart from nuclear arms. The implication being nuclear-powered vessels could visit New Zealand ports. The left wing of the party exploded in protest. Muldoon pounced on the issue with a short media statement saying Labour had no foreign policy. After much negotiation, including with Labour Party President Jim Anderton, Lange agreed to a media statement written by Dr John Henderson, a former head of the Labour Research Unit, and me that adhered Lange to the Party's policy of banning visits of both nuclear-powered and -armed vessels. It felt like a temporary compromise and the issue was not fully resolved. Lange had shown how he could act independently and pre-emptively. It was hardly an auspicious beginning to his leadership.

There was political and media anticipation that Lange and Labour would successfully challenge Muldoon. However, Muldoon blunted Lange's rise by concentrating on economic matters, including turning the screws on a worsening economy in the pretence that only he could be trusted in such times. It was a smart move: Lange and Douglas had little economic experience. Lange was also showing signs of being uncomfortable in his new leadership role. He could not find the big occasion. He was awkward on television, even though in Parliament he was becoming Muldoon's equal. By late 1983 Lange neither had the right message nor the right audience to get much above a third of Muldoon's preferred Prime Minister public-opinion rating. And the Labour Party was yet to fully warm to him.

Three actions were taken to assist Lange. First, Brian Edwards was used for

Lange's media training, mostly to improve his television performance. His new suits were more corporate, and he began holding regular media conferences. Second, Lange took to the road in what Mike Moore deftly termed the 'Campaign for the Regions', an unashamed attempt to expose Lange's oratory to the people, to win support in marginal provincial seats and, equally important, to forge relationships with the Labour Party. Third, Lange needed to build his confidence to rise to the big occasion to defeat Muldoon in Parliament. He needed a defining event that would show his own Caucus and the news media that he had what it took to beat Muldoon and be seen as the Prime Minister-in-waiting.

David Lange's capacity to respond to these actions and opportunities gave him a latent advantage that he took into 1984, election year. He quickly responded to television training. His message, body and eye line were all steadier and his booming voice more contained on the small screen.

On the road in the provinces for three days a week, for six weeks in late 1983, Lange changed tack from merely berating the Muldoon Government. He painted a picture of a new direction involving opportunity for all New Zealanders. He scorned all decisions coming from Wellington, praised devolution and local endeavour, and spoke glowingly of the value of education and the need to change thinking about jobs from that requiring "a strong back to having a strong knowledge" of new and emerging work areas. Lange's prescient political intuition was sharpening, and he received enough encouragement from local audiences, business, councils and Labour Party members to believe that a new direction was possible—and that he could articulate it.

The response to the regional tour was low-key outside the provincial seats. Being out of Parliament and the national media spotlight for much of the week cost him political support. I could convince only a few Parliamentary Press Gallery journalists to leave Wellington to accompany us and witness the growing nods from local and Labour Party audiences. Those who did bother to spend a day or so with Lange saw not only an orator but also a visual performer. Press and television images of an active and agile David Lange whizzing up a river on a tourist jet boat, praising local enterprise and talking opportunity not doom and gloom, was a very different image to that presented by Wellington-based Muldoon. He characterised Lange as lazy and unable to concentrate. The tour of the regions was a superb preparation for a new personalised style of television-led politics where image was at least as important as substance. The regional tour saw Lange gain more respect from the Labour Party. In a very rudimentary way, it laid the foundation for Lange's General Election campaigns to come.

The Head Office of the Labour Party was less convinced than regional party members of Lange's ability to win against Muldoon. While policy was debated between the centre and left of the party, another debate was also active. Party president Jim Anderton was of the view that Labour should adopt a 'team approach' to the General Election campaign, extolling the virtues of consensus-style campaigning. The suggestion was ignored by Lange and overtaken by events. His political judgement had again proved superior.

By early 1984 Lange was able to debate Muldoon in Parliament with greater authority. Late one night when Muldoon attacked Roger Douglas, Lange responded in a devastating manner that belittled Muldoon in front of his colleagues. Lange's defence of Douglas showed their closeness and mutual respect. But Lange was his own man on many issues. For instance, he did not agree with Douglas that Air New Zealand should be partially privatised, as had been proposed to the Muldoon Government. Douglas accepted Lange's judgement at the time.

Muldoon's freezing of wages and prices and his attempts to stave off politically crippling opposition from his own MPs on industrial and anti-nuclear legislation began to give Lange the critical mass he needed to attack and beat a wearying Muldoon. While not yet prime-ministerial, Lange was making progress.

It is a statement of how jaded Muldoon had become that he bargained on David Lange being unprepared and unable to rise to the occasion in a snap election in July 1984. It would be wrong to say Labour and Lange were well prepared for the early election, but the building blocks of a Lange campaign had been tested. Mostly, Muldoon underestimated Lange's greatest asset—rising to the big occasion, the more theatrical the better. The snap election gifted David Lange the occasion, message and the defining event he so badly needed. Even without firm policy—an advantage given the difficulty of formulating it—Lange could afford to spring to the broad brush. He appeared positive, active and convincing. People forgave the lack of detail. Lange easily exploited Muldoon's inability to govern. He inspired a more unified and happier—a kind of pastoral vision—of a New Zealand to come.

The opening of Labour's 1984 election campaign at the Christchurch Town Hall is still regarded by many political commentators as the finest moment in modern campaigning. Brian Edwards and I scripted David Lange's speech from Lange's own delivery on tape. Simon Walker helped stage manage the event for television. The Labour Party bussed in supporters. Lange's speech was designed for a live audience but also for people watching television at home who knew little of him. Substance and image were at one. The audience, including a still sceptical media, adored what they experienced; viewers got a similar impression. Lange and Labour were on their way to defeating Muldoon.

Joe Walding, a Minister with Kirk and MP for Palmerston North, accompanied Lange and me during the election campaign, acting as mentor. David had enormous respect for Joe who grounded him, especially under attack from Muldoon who tried to scare the electorate into believing Lange and Labour would ruin the economy. Joe's political guardianship of David Lange gave him the confidence not to be unnerved by Muldoon's bluff and desperation—and to beat him. Joe's death a couple of years later was a great loss to David Lange.

Also vital was the final television debate with Muldoon at Avalon Studios, chaired by Ian Johnstone. On the way to the studio David expressed apprehension to me that he needed the king hit to end any authority Muldoon had left to set the political direction of New Zealand. David Lange pulled out the big line on the big occasion, offering Muldoon a place in the rebuilding of New Zealand under a Labour Government. Muldoon appeared to have tears in his eyes at this point, and I made sure the *Dominion* knew. The studio at Avalon was filled with an ironic sense of pathos for a lowered Muldoon leaving the studio with his wife, both knowing he had lost not only the most important debate of the campaign, but also the General Election.

THE BIRTH OF MODERN GOVERNMENT

Mike Moore had set up an optimistically named Committee of Transition in 1984. The committee would enable Labour to make an orderly transfer to government. Moore's plan contained all kinds of roles from Prime Minister to ministers, to the selection of staff. Moore had imported two Australian media specialists during the election campaign, including Mike Rann who would go on to become South Australian Premier. Moore's plan, which was prudent but included the implication of Moore as king-maker, was unlikely to include personnel from Lange's office in the new government. He saw no real role for Margaret Pope as Lange's new speechwriter, nor for me as Chief Press Secretary.

Thankfully for all of us Muldoon was to deliver another defining event that was to help Labour, Lange and his staff become firmly established in government. The constitutional crisis of the first days of the newly elected government saw a Leader of the Opposition—"playing monopoly" as Lange put it—transform into a Prime Minister and assured leader. A modern government was being formed.

Being there is sometimes as exhilarating as participating. One day after the election I watched the inner 'Cabinet' of Lange, Palmer, Douglas, Caygill, Prebble, Moore and Bassett call Muldoon's bluff from a Mangere Hotel room and to order him to act to devalue the dollar to stem the bankrupting flow of currency from New Zealand. The crisis gave Lange and Douglas exactly what they wanted. For Douglas it began the unleashing of shackles that chained the traditional economy, and implemented the necessary devaluation he had mistakenly foreshadowed during the election campaign. For Lange, it was a reinforcing and commanding performance on television and in the media generally that demonstrated he was in charge. Any remaining doubt about Lange was removed in one of the finest political interviews ever, with interviewer Richard Harman wisely facilitating Lange's grasp of the situation and his own economic determinism. A politically beaten Muldoon was now bereft of any moral authority. Lange and Labour, not yet sworn into government, were firmly in control.

The nuclear issue was less clear cut. Secretary of State George Schultz came to Wellington in the middle of the constitutional crisis. The weather was a portent. It was a Wahine-like storm in Wellington on the Sunday after the election. Lange greeted Schultz with dignity after the Secretary of State had travelled from the ANZUS Council. Lange met him again in his office the next day in the midst of a media blackout on the constitutional crisis. The only official present, Foreign Affairs secretary Merv Norrish, recalls that David Lange gave Schultz no impression of changing Labour's anti-nuclear policy, despite the Americans having that view. What was clear was that the nuclear issue would become a further defining moment in darkening the ink of the fourth Labour Government.

A modern government needs to be broad-based and progressive in policy—what Lange called "open government, not vacant government". Traditional Labour was none of these things. It was the Economic Summit held at Parliament soon after the government came to office that led traditional Labour to fully become aware that a modern government was required—and was occurring. Lange again rose to the big occasion, encompassing the 'broad church' of views expressed at the Summit. The only consensus reached at the Summit involved notional reference to a freer, more co-operative and caring society. What was more certain, but not stated, was that deregulation could not be partial, and fixing the appalling state of the economy would dominate the first three years of the Lange Labour Government. Many in Cabinet, excluding Lange, doubted it would be more than a one-term government given the enormity of the task that lay ahead.

A modern government also requires an inclusive approach, utilising talent for task. Lange adopted the 'chairman of the board' style to great effect in Cabinet, Caucus and in his office. To some critics this appeared a loose form of management. The approach relied on trust and loyalty, and a high degree of professional maturity by those asked to perform the requisite tasks. On a number of occasions, including on complex economic, social and military matters, Lange demanded a better explanation for policy. His great ability to speed read and comprehend and retain a good brief, often ahead of the presenter, gave him the benefit of being informed but appearing to be uninterested.

Lange's approach also led to the impression that he was a puppet of Douglas—and even his own staff. Roger Douglas was a very different politician to David Lange. Douglas liked to offer bold solutions and achieve momentum—the 'crash-through' approach. He was personally determined to succeed with structural ideas and did not easily entertain debate on them. Lange was a trusting and open-thinking politician, accepting of the broad outcome, highly intuitive and highly politically attuned. He trusted Douglas. The two could exist side by side as long as there was general agreement on direction, mutual trust and policy was within broadly acceptable parameters—including Lange's often pronounced statement that the first term of the Government was about fixing the economy and the second term was about social delivery. From 1984 to 1986 Lange and Douglas were united.

Lange informed me on several occasions in the first term that some of his other colleagues resented the apparent influence some staff had on him to the exclusion of certain ministers. Ministers such as Bassett and Moore were disdainful of what they saw as the strictures placed on Lange by his speech-writer, Margaret Pope, and by me in his political and media expression. They had a sense of frustration that David Lange was not 'their' David Lange anymore. Instead, he was maturing into a national and world leader, someone who could think and act by himself, and someone who enjoyed unparalleled "preferred Prime Minister" public-opinion ratings. Lange on a number of occasions expressed doubt about the ability of ministers such as Moore to help him in his role as Prime Minister, and Bassett's contribution as he recorded Cabinet discussion rather than contributing to it. As Lange's role matured, so did his needs and the level of his decision-making.

This is an important observation. As the nuclear-ship issue came to its inevitable head with the secret negotiations by US and New Zealand officials to have the USS *Buchanan* visit New Zealand, some in the Cabinet were becoming very uneasy. Before this time Lange had again ventured an opinion in late 1984 that nuclear weapons, not nuclear power, were the issue. This view was in keeping with a desire not to offend the Americans or Australians, although the Australian Prime Minister had earlier provoked Lange by publicly saying that Lange did not support the New

Zealand Labour Party anti-nuclear policy. Hawke's view upset and angered Lange and was the first of several clumsy attempts by Australia, the US and Britain to bully Lange into submission and to compromise Labour's policy and his own firm belief that nuclear weapons were immoral and unjust.

These various tensions within the Cabinet and Caucus and with major allies would need lancing soon. One Saturday morning in January 1985 I received a call from the *Sydney Morning Herald*, a not unusual experience. A very casual journalist informed me that its Washington bureau was reporting that the *Buchanan* was to visit New Zealand. David Lange was in the Tokelau Islands on an official visit to New Zealand's only colony, a visit he had planned for some time. Acting PM Geoffrey Palmer and the Cabinet did not know of the proposed visit.

It was impossible to communicate with Lange in Tokelau apart from via insecure ship-to-shore radio. I sent a cryptic note to Lange on what was being reported in New Zealand media on the *Buchanan*. I was also aware that Helen Clark and others in the Labour Caucus were active in making sure the *Buchanan* visit would not proceed. I talked to peace movement leaders about their plans for marches and publicity to prevent any compromise of Labour's policy. There was no reply from Lange. Palmer consulted Labour Party president Margaret Wilson and others offered their views, including the former party president, Jim Anderton, now an MP. The case presented to Palmer by the Chief of Defence Staff to have the *Buchanan* visit may have been convincing to him and his colleagues, but it was politically unsaleable. Palmer agreed and asked me to fly to Pago Pago in American Samoa to meet Lange and to take the Defence paper, his own view, that of others in the Caucus, and the media reports concerning the proposed visits.

I flew alone on the Airforce Boeing 727 and when I met Lange he was strangely reticent. He knew he faced one of the toughest decisions of this political career. He didn't comment on the Defence case but with a clear head from his Tokelau visit he read the media coverage of the proposed visit and instantly saw the political logic of the situation. Lange went straight into Cabinet where there was no discussion on the issue; he had no Cabinet paper prepared for debate and instead announced his decision to colleagues as the situation demanded, and later to an expectant press conference.

Lange had no choice but to be decisive with Cabinet, the media and the public. Some critics have argued that he gave in to Clark, Labour and peace activists— and worse, Lange "ran away" to Tokelau to avoid making a decision. This is a superficial analysis. The Tokelau trip had been planned long before the request from the *Buchanan* to visit. Second, David Lange had no contact with his so-called "influencers" before announcing his decision to Cabinet. Cabinet's collective responsibility was hardly usurped as Lange made his decision known to Cabinet— without the clutter of lobbyists (including Cabinet ministers) or big power politics. He knew the view of officials and he knew that a Cabinet paper would engender debate that had only one outcome—a political decision was required. Labour Party policy and his own beliefs on nuclear weapons were honoured.

On logic alone, the ambiguity of the American policy of neither confirming nor denying nuclear weapons on board vessels gave Lange no option. The *Buchanan*, which had visited New Zealand in 1979 under Muldoon, was not unambiguously non-nuclear. It was nuclear capable. For Lange to argue its non-nuclear status was impossible and tantamount to political suicide. The electorate was firmly behind Lange's decision not to agree to the visit, even if some of his drier colleagues were privately opposed to the decision—an observation that belies the myth that the anti-nuclear policy was an antidote to economic policy. In retrospect, Lange's decision provided more life to Rogernomics because it exalted Lange's and Labour's political standing. Lange understood better than most that any compromise on the nuclear policy would have undermined the very political authority that he had been elected to exercise responsibly.

Criticism by officials that the *Buchanan* decision was political or wrong can be accepted only insofar as a government is elected to govern. Officials did not get their way on the *Buchanan* or later prevent David Lange speaking at the Oxford Union. It is interesting to note that it was officials who did get their way in repatriating the convicted *Rainbow Warrior* terrorists to eventual freedom after one of the most blatant cases of state-backed terrorism. Lange's principles and popularity were severely compromised as a result, with little apparent diplomatic or trade gain. The political consequences of taking such official advice for a leader of less stature than David Lange would have been disastrous, and proved how right his decision was to reject the *Buchanan* visit request.

It has also been argued that Lange avoided personal confrontation with his colleagues and that is the reason for not having a full discussion at Cabinet. By making his decision Lange was fronting up to considerable personal opprobrium from the most powerful nation on earth, its formidable Secretary of State, Britain's Margaret Thatcher, and the Australian Labor Government and Bob Hawke. Facing his Cabinet colleagues was a walk in the park compared to what was awaiting him on the international front.

POLITICAL MANAGEMENT

In the above discussion is the seed of David Lange becoming far more assertive about his own direction as Prime Minister. The nuclear issue made him a hero with the Labour Party, even though he resented party complaints on economic policy and direction. To Lange simplistic suggestions to address complex and hard economic questions cut little ice. Through the nuclear issue Lange was also to become far more his own political manager, an observation not lost on some of his colleagues.

It is a complementary point that Labour's Cabinet, with an average age of 43 years, was highly adept at political management. The strength of Prebble, Moore and Lange to manage political advantage was unchallenged. National in Opposition with its various leaders of Muldoon, McLay and then Bolger, was lost. It searched in vain for a direction Labour had stolen from under them, and one that many in National agreed with. The Muldoon legacy was too great to hasten change to a more modern party of government-in-waiting. They were in exile, while Labour's real opposition came from the sections of the community who most benefited from Muldoon, farming and protected industry, and from within Labour's own Caucus.

David Lange is credited with running the Cabinet efficiently. Caucus was a more difficult matter and disagreements with the Labour Party and movement started to trouble Lange. The Lange and Palmer relationship with the Party and unions was robust enough to ensure that both remained at arm's length, and both survived. Labour Party president Margaret Wilson was helpful in this regard, meeting with Lange regularly to express the pleasures and pains of the Party and its affiliates.

It was only the Maori loans affair, involving Koro Wetere, that seriously threatened the Cabinet's astute political management. Some commentators have termed Labour "lucky" in having new issues such as nuclear ships, the Fiji coups, and the *Rainbow Warrior* terrorism to deflect attention from mismanagement, and Lange's lack of political micro-management. This view denies the momentum for change that was generally well communicated, although not as thoroughly as many in the community demanded. The political management of the fourth Labour Government was, most significantly, commensurate with the challenge that faced the country and the Government. Despite the enormity of the changes, Lange and Labour mostly took the people with them. In political terms, there was no alternative party of government between 1984 and 1987.

COMMUNICATIONS MANAGEMENT

To assist the Cabinet in its political and communications management, I initiated a Communications Advisory Committee, made up of officials from Lange's, Douglas's and other offices. Its job was to co-ordinate what decisions Ministers were planning to release to the public over the next week and month. A report from the Committee was presented as the first item of Cabinet's discussion. This approach allowed for proper communications management of what and when to release to the media, although it was noticeable as time went on that Douglas's office chose not to be involved with the Committee, often preferring to make their own decisions on when and how economic information was released. The Committee was designed to prevent office 'silos' and to allow Lange to discuss the public agenda of the Cabinet and to avoid clashes and political mistakes. It has been the system of communications management used by all governments since 1984.

What was remarkable about the CAC report, as it was called, was that it never leaked. It had high strategic value to the Cabinet in managing communications. More generally, only occasionally did material leak from the Cabinet, an indication of the Cabinet and Beehive officials generally working professionally and cohesively in the first term.

Systems helped David Lange, although he also needed room to move, particularly as a communicator. If Muldoon was the great communicator, Lange became even greater. In Opposition Lange struggled to convince many senior journalists he had what it took to be the Leader. However, they enjoyed his personal company in comparison to that of the abrasive Muldoon. During the election campaign and constitutional crisis of 1984 that all changed, and in government and on the big occasions, Lange became the darling of local and global media. His personal charm, quick wit and natural performance ability propelled him to stardom. No system or communications manager could do that for him.

There was, however, much more to David Lange's success with the media than his cosiness and verbal dexterity. Lange's television performances, using strong eye contact and his distinctive voice, gave him unstoppable presence. He appeared real, thoughtful and decisive, difficult though it was for some journalists to determine exactly what he always meant. There was a 'Lange speak'. His surreal humour and candid approach, part of Lange speak, sold media. Many New Zealand journalists earned a good income from their 'rats' to overseas media on Lange's utterances. His press conferences were the best show in town. His overseas media appearances on some of the top television news programmes in the world raised New Zealand's profile to unprecedented and usually positive levels. Lange's talent truly came from within, assisted by the earlier media training of Edwards and during government, from confidante and former television presenter Ian Fraser. I saw my role as facilitator of Lange's media talent.

David Lange personalised media communications, just as Muldoon had done, but he took performance to a new and theatrical level. As noted way back in a New Plymouth hall in darkest 1981, Lange needed the best environment and support to perform. As PM he largely got both, and was not bothered by the need to endlessly reassure colleagues or to 'spin' to the media (the term had not been invented in the mid-1980s). Trish Green, my press secretary colleague, and I saw our job as empowering Lange to perform. To do otherwise, just like giving David Lange the greatest speech lines, was to deny his own gigantic talent. His great lines at the Oxford Union and in debates were his, not written for him. Far from restricting his natural talent, it was his staff's job to seamlessly expose his talent and interpret it to the media.

Internally, Lange's communication skills were being sorely tested. Early in 1987, proposals by Douglas to move New Zealand to the next phase of economic reform had been formulated. To Lange and some other ministers, these initiatives undermined the trust and compatibility he had with Douglas and his Cabinet supporters. Douglas also wanted a major say on social policy direction. In response, Lange and Palmer initiated the Royal Commission on Social Policy to report after the election.

During 1987 Lange was struggling to achieve a majority in Cabinet. To get his way would require non-conventional means. Using the electorate was one advantage Lange had over all his colleagues. The 1987 General Election was his opportunity to make his point about social delivery.

I managed David Lange's leadership campaign in the 1987 General Election. In keeping with the times, and the Lange adage that old rules did not apply, Lange wanted a new approach to campaigning. He wanted to come back to Wellington each night to assert Labour's legitimacy in government. Lange's message was simple: Labour was the party of government and the second term was about the social dividend for people who had endured economic restructuring. This was not a popular message with all his Cabinet colleagues, although it was with the electorate and the Labour Party.

Douglas was determined to speak on social policy during the campaign and only a directive from Lange prevented him and his office from openly being at odds with Lange on policy direction at a major speech at Sails Restaurant, Auckland, just before polling day.

David Lange did not perform to great heights during the campaign. His opening speech was flat and too cerebral for television. It lacked the feeling of the 1984 version, but did address social delivery. Jim Bolger performed surprisingly well, although on the most conservative count, Lange won all television encounters with him and also the news coverage during the campaign. Lange was distracted. Policy differences with Douglas were on his mind, and it was apparent his relationship with Naomi was not what it had been. This time, the right message and the right conditions to perform were not enough for Lange. He did not rise to the occasion, and in two incidents, with a farmer in Geraldine and a teacher who opposed his view, he was seen to be testy and non-prime-ministerial. He was frustratingly aware of policy and personal challenges ahead.

Labour had a large lead going into the 1987 election campaign. Just before polling day Lange and I were told by pollsters that Labour would win by a reduced majority. This view got around and spooked a few key ministers. Lange and I knew that was not the likely election outcome. Nor was there any evidence, as Prebble and Bassett claimed post-election, that had the campaign gone another week Labour would have lost the election, and Lange would be to blame. Labour actually increased its parliamentary majority and its share of the popular vote on polling day.

With the election victory a less than joyous celebratory occasion, David Lange set about his struggle to determine his own agenda for the Labour Government, becoming Minister of Education and giving up Foreign Affairs in a portfolio swap with a perturbed Russell Marshall. He altered other Cabinet portfolios trying to weaken the power vested in Douglas and his supporters to reflect the need for social delivery. His reshuffle, which was not carefully enough explained to all ministers, was resented by many. Lange faced his own surprise: Treasury released two tomes on education policy for the incoming Minister. The battle lines were clearly painted for the post-1987 division within the Labour Cabinet and Caucus.

As the sharemarket collapse of September 1987 gave way to the Douglas flat tax proposal, Labour's political and communications management slipped into internal crisis mode. It was at this point that Lange made a strategic error. He agreed to announce with Douglas the flat tax 'proposal'. I recall Douglas asking Lange if he wanted to delay announcing it. Lange hesitated but agreed, and I organised a presidential-style launch in the Beehive theatrette where key ministers stood behind Lange and Douglas to announce the next wave of economic reform. The image was to haunt the Labour Party for many years to come.

Lange saw the announcement of the flat tax as a *proposal* only, but he became alarmed as he realised the proposal was a reality for a majority of Cabinet and the public. With the benefit of advice from Brian Gaynor and others, Lange quickly saw how flawed the flat tax proposal was for those on low or fixed incomes. It greatly disturbed his sense of social justice, and his office was mostly at one on this view.

What ensued was a counter-productive and destructive exchange of letters between Lange and Douglas. I totally disagreed with the way correspondence written by officials from both offices travelled three levels of the Beehive. Lange and Douglas were, in my view, prisoners of their correspondence. I knew this senseless exchange would only make Douglas more determined and he began trying to justify the flat tax to media on the whiteboard. On several occasions I talked to Douglas's office about the impasse and, unable to influence them or Lange on the matter, I decided it was time to move on to other challenges.

Lange overturned the flat tax proposal in early 1988 without talking to Douglas, who was overseas. Lange had taken time to consider his options and had communicated his opposition to the flat tax proposal to Douglas. Overturning the flat tax was a personally fulfilling moment for Lange, but the true end of the fourth Labour Government. I left the Beehive soon after, in February 1988, with bitter-sweet memories. Lange resigned in 1989 as Prime Minister and I worked as a consultant in 1990 to undertake the election advertising for PM Palmer, who resigned and was replaced by PM Moore. Labour had run its course and lost heavily at the polls.

CONCLUSION

Some critics describe David Lange as an enigma. He has been variously accused of being forced by the Left to reject the *Buchanan* and manipulated to take a harder line than he wanted to on nuclear ships and ANZUS. On the other hand, Lange has been called a prisoner of the Right, forced to accept Rogernomics. Some critics have gone as far as calling Lange the "Prime Minister in name only".

These myths can easily be exposed. David Lange was passionate about opposing nuclear weapons, but never became anti-American in spite of the personal abuse he suffered from the US administration—as well as from Australia and Britain. He made a decision not to allow the *Buchanan* into New Zealand waters, to legislate to make New Zealand nuclear free (a decision backed by his Cabinet colleagues), to help the South Pacific go nuclear free (with Australia's support), and to effectively end ANZUS. In doing so, he faced the considerable duress of allies but enjoyed the support of most New Zealanders and many people throughout the world. No one but a political masochist would allow this pressure to be brought on themselves for cheap political or opportunistic reasons. Lange believed in opposing nuclear weapons, and no government since has disagreed with his position.

On Rogernomics, Lange always favoured a more rational approach to the economy—as long as the new economy delivered to the people who contributed to it and to those least able to help themselves. Along with Roger Douglas, Lange wanted to end economic privilege. That was the "head" part of the first term of the Labour Government; because of economic necessity the "heart" would be delivered in the second term in social policy. His position, which is now described as the 'Third Way' was well understood by all the Cabinet, including those who were so opposed to Lange campaigning on a social dividend in 1987.

David Lange's career had never been about political organisation. The coup against Rowling and his elevation to Labour leader was organised largely by others. He took advice and enjoyed loyal support. If this is politically naïve, Lange compensated by being the inspirational leader, the painter of a vision. He was no one's puppet, as he demonstrated with world leaders and eventually his Cabinet colleagues.

David Lange's journey was one of his finding his own way. The principles of his

Maiden Speech were his general guidelines. He was therefore never a revolutionary—even a reluctant one. He was to realise what was most important to him. Nor was he afraid to confront issues or people. When Roger Douglas became too mechanistic and rationalistic, Lange's principles were tested beyond his acceptable boundaries. Lange was proud of his own role in ushering in the floating dollar in 1985. But, after unilaterally ending the flat tax proposal in 1988, Lange commented to me that he felt "clean again". His method of promoting then ending the flat tax was a mistake and non-consultative, yet, as in the case of the *Buchanan*, he felt he was acting in the best interests of the country and the future of the Labour Party. He rightly perceived the political mood of the country as intolerant of more radical economic change. No government or mainstream party has ever proposed a flat tax since. It took enormous courage to oppose a formerly close and loyal colleague such as Roger Douglas, but Lange, as I argued to the media to the annoyance of Douglas, was the Leader. Lange took his actions against the flat tax largely out of principle and political judgement, based on the advice of several of his officials, not just the one or two conveniently named by his embittered opponents.

It is a mark of enormous disrespect for the political calibre of David Lange to claim he was the "Prime Minister in name only" or that while he won the 1984 election, Roger Douglas won the 1987 election. Without Lange's political cache, Labour—with Douglas—would not have won the 1987 election. Douglas could never have led Labour. Lange was the political glue that held Labour and the electorate together during 1984–87 and in political terms, Lange won the 1987 election.

David Lange could be a world-class leader demonstrating enormous courage at home and abroad. He stood ten feet tall at the 1984 election, during the constitutional crisis, at the Economic Summit, during the *Rainbow Warrior* terrorist attack, at the Oxford Union, during the Fiji coups, always in Parliament and mostly in the news media.

He had another, more restive and risky, side—including driving racing cars, playing rock music at his prime-ministerial desk, imperiling his health by smoking cigars and drinking alcohol, and by being seen to be too close to his speech-writer. He could be self-important, as he was on his trip to the frontline African states. His actions could disappoint those who cared for him, but his wit and good nature were supremely disarming and made forgiving him easy.

David Lange is a complex person. He took from his youth the considerable ability to turn adversity and criticism around and beat it with brilliant performance. Lange was supreme in public debate. On a one-to-one level, he was far harder to read. I saw great kindness and humbleness to those he liked, mixed with vitriol to those who opposed him. He spurned great wealth but mixed with it and enjoyed playing the sharemarket. As the youngest Prime Minister in the twentieth century, Lange did some of his growing up in office. As time went on, he confronted his Methodism and staunch social values, and widened his own 'broad church' of ideas, influences, his way of life and those he shared it with.

Lange realised his own basic principles of fairness and 'giving a fair go' were his most valuable assets. He increasingly regretted the hurt imposed by the rationalistic approach during 1984–87, losing support from many colleagues and friends who preferred the Douglas approach over his. By becoming his own person, David Lange brought principles, enriching talents and political instincts to the national and global stage. New Zealand was better for this and for the mana he generated on his long journey.

IAN GRANT

Lange takes the high ground while Douglas burrows deep into the economy

Famous British cartoonist Michael Cummings once said: "You can make a tremendous point in a cartoon that takes five seconds to read that may take an entire leading article to say."[1] According to Murray Ball, creator of 'Footrot Flats': "It is a cartoonist's job to hold up a mirror to the people—a distorting mirror it is true but, if they are any good, the distortion serves to amplify rather than obscure."[2] And David English wrote, when editor of Britain's *Daily Mail*: "The cartoonist, given that special licence granted over the centuries, can say things others only dare whisper."[3]

It has, of course, been said by some, and notably *New York Times* founder Adolph Ochs, who would not allow them on the editorial page, that cartoons cannot say "on the other hand". In response, Thomas Griffith wrote of political cartoonists: "Undoctrinaire iconoclasm is their style. They think more in metaphors than in arguments and don't want to dull a witty simplicity with a weighty qualification."[4]

It can certainly be claimed that cartoons provide a time capsule for historians.

Three Months Without ANZUS, Bob Brockie, *National Business Review,* 1984. (ATL: A-317-008)

We Want to be Your Friends, Trace Hodgson, *NZ Listener*, 1984. (ATL: A-317-3-001)

Yah Gotta Pick a Pocket or Two, Chicane (Mark Winter), *Southland Times*, 1984. (ATL: H-752-001)

As Dr Graham Thomas, founder of the Centre for the Study of Cartoons and Caricature at the University of Kent, put it: "Cartoons are the grotesque anteroom of history in which gather all the moods and prejudices that lie unspoken behind the official record of the time."[5]

It may well be that the cartoons of the 1984–87 period in New Zealand will puzzle future historians but, having looked at many of them, I believe they fairly represent popular sentiment at the time. Future historians might ask how could a government that punished the electorate so savagely, in part and whole, retain its popularity so long? Or, how could there be such preoccupation with the obtuse details of a nuclear-ships policy when seismic shifts in economic policy were soon affecting many New Zealanders, some brutally.

The actual result aside, there was enormous public relief when Muldoon was defeated at the 1984 snap election. The cartoons of the day reflected this but, from a professional point of view, there was genuine regret among cartoonists. As Muldoon had dominated politics, he had dominated cartooning as well. There was little room for other National Cabinet ministers and even less for Opposition politicians—David Lange generally pictured as a blob with accompanying speech balloon. Muldoon might have become something of a monster in the eyes of many New Zealanders, but monsters are much more interesting to draw than earnest, young, clean-cut political tyros. Over the Muldoon era, caricatures of the Prime Minister became more grotesque; even those by as mild-mannered a practitioner as Eric Heath, on the *Dominion*, morphed over the period from a smiley little man

ANZUS, Peter Bromhead, *Auckland Star*, 1984. (ATL: A-331-137)

to a leering, lantern-jawed, eye-popping, foot-stamping tyrant.

But just as cartoonists had attacked Muldoon with relish, he was as likely to have a metaphorical poke at them. Muldoon excluded Tom Scott from press conferences and overseas trips and reviewed at least one of the cartoonist's books with unfeigned glee ("Reading through 150 pages of Scott was just too much of a bad thing.").[6] It was the perfect environment for very good, spleenful cartoons, a veritable golden age of New Zealand cartooning.

Probably not before and certainly not since has there been such an array of cartooning talent on regular display in the daily and weekly press. There was almost an embarrassment of riches in Auckland. Peter Bromhead—at the height of his considerable powers—was at the *Auckland Star* where Tom Scott had been lured to write and draw as well. Minhinnick, long since officially retired, was still producing two or more cartoons a week for the *NZ Herald*. Anthony Ellison was cartoonist at the short-lived *Auckland Sun*, in 1986–87. Nevile Lodge and Eric Heath were nearing the ends of their long careers at Wellington's *Evening Post* and *Dominion* respectively. Al Nisbet's cartoons appeared regularly in Christchurch's *Press* and Hugh Todd had followed Sid Scales at the *Otago Daily Times*.

In the weeklies, Trace Hodgson was gaining a reputation at the *NZ Listener* as one of the country's most formidable cartoonists, Bill Wrathall was at *Truth*, Malcolm Walker at the *Sunday News* and Bob Brockie and Bill Paynter at *National Business Review*. Chris Slane, named Cartoonist of the Year in 1986, was busily freelancing for several dailies and weeklies.

With Muldoon's defeat, not only had the cartoonists lost the richest lode of cartooning gold since Richard John Seddon, but they had to learn to draw a new cast of characters. A new Prime Minister or President has always been a problem

ANZUS, Eric Heath, *Dominion*, 1985 (ATL: B-143-009)

Oops! That's the Rough Draft, Tom Scott, *Auckland Star*, 1986 (ATL: H-752-003)

for cartoonists. Australian Pat Oliphant, who became a leading cartoonist in the United States, once said: "I hate changes of Administrations. It takes six months to 'get' a new man."[7]

Muldoon began as and remained a garden gnome in the cartoons of the *New Zealand Herald's* Sir Gordon Minhinnick, who had mastered the physical characteristics of 11 prime ministers, beginning with Gordon Coates in 1925. Minhinnick officially retired in 1976 but continued to appear regularly on the editorial page of the *Herald* through Labour's 1984–87 term. Although then over 80, he did not welcome the new government with much enthusiasm. As a later *Herald* article put it: "The buttoned-down so-called technocrats of the Lange Administration seemed not to offer such good material for cartooning, although the Prime Minister made a distinctive subject. Offering facetious reason for his retirement, Min said he could not face further years of drawing the 'prime monster'."[8]

There is always a 'honeymoon' period for a new government, particularly if the previous one has grown stale and tired. With Labour, though, it was more of a 'whirlwind romance'. It was whirlwind because of the speed of government action, largely necessitated and endlessly justified by Muldoon's attempt to forestall devaluation following the alarming election campaign run on the NZ dollar. Lange's impressive staring down of Muldoon, and Douglas's decisive 20 percent devaluation, were widely applauded. Then there was the studied building on the palpable countrywide relief that the new government could actually govern with largely symbolic coming-together gestures that were balm for a national psyche rattled by years of divisiveness. The September economic summit threw together the unlikeliest movers and shakers in a talkfest that impressed participants and the country alike with the possibility of reconciliation, consensus and shared goals.

There were other reasons, too, for the Government's popularity with the media and cartoonists: the new ministers seemed absurdly young, they were not hidebound old pros; they had the courage of their convictions but didn't take themselves too seriously; and they were actually doing the things the pundits had for years been saying should be done. Above all, David Lange, stomach-stapled and smartly suited, was an attractive figure, particularly on a compare and contrast basis. As Tom Scott recalled in a 1994 interview: "He's been a terrific politician to cover; he's been accessible, he's been a source of great copy. The press wanted David to do well."[9] Apparently TVNZ's Richard Harman became concerned at the laughter being heard on TV from journalists at Lange's press conferences, and asked his colleagues to desist. The next conference, Scott recalled, they sat stony-faced for one minute, 15 seconds.

Lange's lieutenants had little of his charisma. Roger Douglas and David Caygill were about as colourful as the national balance sheets they studied; from the cartoonists' perspective their saving graces were two suitably different moustaches.

Hi, Remember How You've Been Coming, Nevile Lodge, *Evening Post*, 1986 (ATL: B-136-527)

But What Other Country, Peter Bromhead, *Auckland Star*, 1986 (ATL: A-331-159)

Richard Prebble had yet to earn his 'Mad Dog' reputation as SOEs minister in Labour's second term. Geoffrey Palmer was, in manner, style and role, the tall, gangling school prefect or scoutmaster.

Considering how close New Zealand had come to the economic precipice, it is surprising in retrospect how little time cartoonists devoted to economic issues, particularly during the first months of the Lange Government. But Labour's crucial economic changes happened so quickly, with so little discussion, that they did not provide ongoing cartoon fodder. It was the later instalments of Rogernomics that gave cartoonists the opportunity to sink their collective teeth into Labour's thickening hide.

Although of less immediate or practical importance, New Zealand's anti-nuclear policy was much more interesting to cartoonists—and to much of the public. In part this was because it was so closely identified with David Lange, from the first eyeball-to-eyeball meetings with US Secretary of State George Shultz. While he was far from an anti-nuclear zealot, the nuclear issue was to become the centrepiece of his time as Minister of Foreign Affairs. He was not closely identified, literally or figuratively, with any economic policies; 'Rogernomics' was the preserve of Roger Douglas.

New Zealand's anti-nuclear stand was a David vs Goliath contest in more ways than one. It was a dramatic global issue on which a small country could take the moral high ground; it did our reputation no harm abroad and instilled a sense of pride at home. If it annoyed the hell out of the Americans that was, for many, an added plus. So there was, and the word is particularly apt, a proliferation of cartoons on New Zealand's stance about whether nuclear-armed and/or -powered vessels should/could visit our ports, and about thumbing our nose at the United States.

We've Developed a New Postbox, Trace Hodgson, *NZ Listener*, 1987 (ATL: H-509-037)

On top of the immediate economic crisis Lange and his inner circle had to tackle, chance and fate dictated that there was a meeting of the ANZUS Council in New Zealand immediately after the mid-July 1984 election. While the first economic moves had been made in as much secrecy as possible, the Ruritanian comedy that was played out when US Secretary of State Shultz met formally with ousted government ministers and informally with Lange were much more public and dramatic in a 'good guy versus bad guy' sort of way.

The ANZUS saga was played out over a lengthy period. While the conclusion might have been self-evident, the slow diplomatic foxtrot was danced for months, with Lange having further inconclusive talks with Shultz in New York, the Americans proposing a warship visit early in 1985, and the New Zealand Government declining, with the hope that ANZUS might survive. The United States promptly announced the end of ANZUS as a three-partner pact. The cartoonists, and seemingly the public, found it all riveting stuff.

The nuclear issue remained on the front pages when French secret service agents sank the Greenpeace vessel *Rainbow Warrior* in Auckland harbour in July 1985, killing a crew member. The Government's understandable indignation, masterfully finessed by David Lange, further boosted popular support for the country's anti-nuclear stance, now facing down France's imperious continuation of Mururoa Atoll testing.

If it first made international headlines for nuclear policy reasons, the Labour Government was soon in the spotlight for, in a few short months, transforming New Zealand from one of the most restriction-riddled Western-style economies to one of the least regulated. Roger Douglas's first budget was roundly praised by the unlikeliest people as the silver-tongued Lange poured healing balm on a badly bruised electorate with his broad-brush inspirational style of leadership, capitalising on the ANZUS issue and the *Rainbow Warrior* affair to keep the country and Caucus united and distracted while his finance minister beavered away at restructuring the economy. "Whatever the explanation, the fourth Labour Government has, up until now, enjoyed a charmed life," wrote Tom Scott in November 1984. "The fast lane for most of the journey has been a leafy boulevard, sun-dappled and wide, with green lights at every intersection."[10]

Meanwhile, Douglas continued through his economic reform list, nothing deflecting him from what looked more and more like a messianic crusade: floating the dollar, deregulating the money and foreign-exchange markets, introducing radical tax changes, slashing agricultural subsidies and removing much of the manufacturing sector's protection.

The short-term effects of 'Rogernomics' hitting home were sobering. Inflation was at high levels, with interest rates in pursuit, economic growth plummeted, overseas debt soared, and the number of unemployed doubled as local and international 'market forces' buffeted New Zealand.

Yet it was only later in Labour's first term—when witticisms could no longer paper over the cracks appearing in Labour's initially impressive solidarity, and the consequences of the government's economic actions were being severely felt—that cartoonists shook off the almost hypnotic hold Lange had had on them and much of the public, and began to attack the economic consequences of Rogernomics, the widening gap between promises and performance, and between political rhetoric and economic reality.

It may have been one of the longest honeymoons cartoonists ever gave a New Zealand Government, but it was well and truly over by early 1987.

We Wriggled off the Hook, Tom Scott, *Evening Post*, 1987 (H-733-025)

JON JOHANSSON

The Falstaffian wit of David Lange: rhetorical brilliance in the Beehive

They are to him absurd; and to reduce a thing ad absurdum
is to reduce it to nothing and to walk about free and rejoicing.
                      A.C. BRADLEY, ON SHAKESPEARE'S FALSTAFF

Many of my generation marvelled at David Lange's rare and exotic mastery of language, so now, twenty years on, it gives me particular pleasure to reflect on the quality of Lange's rhetorical performance while he led the fourth Labour Government during its first three years in power. Also, with the focus here on Labour's first term, my examination of Lange's rhetoric represents far more a salutation than any detailed scholarly criticism. The cynicism and bitterness that crept into, and then largely enveloped Lange's public performances after the 1987 election is cast aside in favour of a celebration of some of Lange's peak rhetorical moments during his time atop the 'greasy pole'.

One must also raise one obvious caveat before proceeding further. In 1984, at the same time as the fourth Labour Government launched its revolution, I was only 21. And it would be fair to say that my political interests, such as they were, were more narrowly confined to Jefferson's pursuit of happiness than to absorbing either Roger Douglas's whiteboard wizardry or Lange's loquaciousness. Yet, after talking to many politicians of the era, and absorbing the analyses of the original explainers—those media commentators, informed observers, participants, and scholars who first chronicled the revolution and its leading actors—I would argue that David Lange's most significant legacy, arising wholly from his rhetorical leadership, is that he, more than any of his colleagues, embodied the very freedoms ushered in by his government. After the conflict-ridden oppression of Muldoon's last term, Lange symbolised a liberation of both our politics and our language.

It is in that sense, and from this distance, therefore, that an underlying motivation for this chapter is to free the word 'freedom' itself from the more narrowly confined economic rationalist explanations that have tended to dominate post-Rogernomics discourse. Greater or lesser state involvement, more or less tax, further economic rationalisation, efficiency arguments, the problems of welfare dependency—all these ideas have heavily influenced our post-revolution political language. In many respects they've had another renaissance during the recent Dr Don Brash-led election campaign against Labour's Helen Clark, the 2005 campaign representing one final generational argument about the efficacy and success of the neo-liberal reform era, its effects, and its 'unfinished business'.

Likewise, Lange is largely remembered for his leadership during the currency crisis that surrounded his elevation to the prime-ministership, presiding over the Douglas-led policy revolution, a breathtakingly brilliant articulation of his government's anti-nuclear stance at Oxford, and for that fatal moment, back in January 1988, when Lange publicly defected from his previously close colleagues over his government's flat-tax proposals. His defection guaranteed the spiking of Douglas's next proposed tranche of radical reforms and then, over the ensuing months, it led to the cataclysmic self-destruction of Labour's historically reformist government. Yet, as dramatic as those moments were, Lange's embodiment of a real sense of post-Muldoon liberation represented the most important shift in the nation's psyche as he hammered home the critical message that things simply had to change. Lange's initial eloquence, his sense of fun, and his focused rhetoric were all crucial for what then ensued.

In 1984 David Lange was the right man in the right place at the right time. His great wit, his irreverence and humour, and his fine sense of the absurd, all expressed through his rhetoric—complemented by superb non-verbal skills that served to enhance the power of his oratory—soon projected themselves dramatically onto the public stage. Lange, in short order, freed us from our immediate past. Muldoon's veil of fear and intimidation lifted.

Another important shift that accompanied Lange's elevation was a generational one. Muldoon's Depression/World War II generation gave way to the first of the baby-boomers. In this sense, Lange publicly wresting power off Muldoon during the devaluation crisis represented a crucial forking point, one where New Zealand passed through an 'invisible membrane in time' which divided one era from another.[1] Aside from a passing of the torch to a new generation of New Zealand politicians—or, as actually happened, wrenching the torch from an obstinate Muldoon—Labour's fresh Cabinet contained within it a new, highly educated cohort, one comprised largely of lawyers and academics.

Women were also restored to the Executive, after a nine-year absence, with the elevation of Ann Hercus and Margaret Shields prefacing a truly dramatic change in the participation of women at the apex of governmental decision-making, a process that would reach its zenith when first Jenny Shipley, then Helen Clark ascended to the prime-ministership during the late 1990s.

Looking back, the exciting sea-change that Lange's leadership represented was a genuine break from the bitterness and division that marked the early 1980s, the period of Muldoon's personal rule. Exclusionary and authoritarian leadership gave way to David Lange's call for a 'new politics', a politics Lange characterised as positive and decisive, a politics where he intended to exhibit a more consultative leadership style, and one where his government wouldn't take itself too seriously or react too bitterly to criticism. The idea of politics as fun was certainly something refreshingly new. There wasn't just the devaluation imbroglio, the ANZUS dispute, deregulation of the finance sector, or removal of farm subsidies for reporters to analyse, discuss and report on. The country also observed a Prime Minister who while handling multiple crises, maintained his fine sense of humour, with an ever-vigilant eye for spotting the absurd in any situation. Furthermore, Lange exhibited a cognitive vitality that was unsurpassed among New Zealand Prime Ministers before or since. Here, it is argued, Lange's rhetoric was qualitatively different in kind from the more functional prime-ministerial discourse to which we have become conditioned, and which our political culture has seemed to produce and prefer.

David Lange said during the 1984 campaign that he hoped to breath a measure of joy back into the body politic. During the early months and years of his stewardship Lange effectively achieved this: it wasn't just the new economic freedoms that New Zealanders enjoyed and came to embrace, but a greater sense of psychological freedom was arguably the significant 'gain' of Labour's first term. The public, who had been denied choices for so long, were suddenly freed from the strangulation of Muldoon's heavy interventionist hand and authoritarian rule. So, for me, David Lange was a genuinely charismatic leader, not in the sense of Weber's more confined and constricted sociological definition, but anticipating, rather, Oscar Wilde's thought that *comprehensiveness of consciousness* was the sublime value when personality was at the centre of one's concern.[2]

That is, of course, quite an abstract hypothesis, but one I hope to illustrate over the course of this brief chapter. For, during Labour's first three years in Office, New Zealanders undoubtedly saw the peak of Lange's performance in the theatre of politics that he so loved and preferred to the grind of Cabinet committees and so on. Whether it was, as Tom Scott described, the eloquent wrath that Lange displayed when publicly wresting power from Muldoon,[3] or the brilliant oratory he displayed during the Oxford Union debate, Lange's rhetorical abilities during that first term were breathtakingly unique and refreshing in our domestic context.

LANGE'S LIBERATION OF LANGUAGE: AN ABSURDIST UNLEASHED
Anthony Hubbard aptly described Muldoon's press conferences as a "bear pit".[4] Ugly confrontations, threatened or real media bans, and Muldoon's own vituperative attacks on the nation's newspaper editors and their journalists perpetuated a deepening pall over media relations with the Muldoon Government. Once Lange appeared on the scene, however, press conferences soon became a glittering showcase for his dexterity with language, a sublime verbal acuity that forcefully projected itself onto the national stage. The relief for all must have been palpable. A pact not to laugh so much at Lange's quips was soon struck between press gallery journalists as television images of a contented and laughing audience, consisting of the cream of New Zealand's political media, didn't correspond with their preferred image of themselves.

An example, my favourite in fact, from Lange's first press conference as Leader, anticipated the sea-change in media atmospherics that would follow Muldoon's final defeat. Lange was asked if he thought his lack of economic knowledge could prove a potential future weakness for his leadership—quite a prescient question as it transpired. Lange replied:

> I am not an economist. Am proud to assert I'm not an economist and can use them inasmuch as they can be used, although I remember there was a chap called Stalin once who had them all shot.[5]

It should be duly noted that Geoffrey Palmer sat through this entire exchange, his gaze fixed on one particular spot, looking very statuesque.

Muldoon also provided the perfect foil for Lange. During that final debate in 1984 between Lange and Muldoon—the one where the Prime Minister was reduced to his "I love you too Mr Lange" quip, the momentum of power palpably shifted from Muldoon to Lange and the mantle of succession was created at that moment, before the votes had even been cast. Lange had been forceful, eloquent and conciliatory. His opponent was rendered impotent, defeated, without answers or solutions.

Lange's rhetorical power had been displayed right from when he delivered his maiden speech. In a brilliant exposition of his belief that politics must be underpinned by a sense of community, fraternity and unity, Lange said:

> I believe that our challenge is to create a society where people feel committed to each other, where they have an interdependence which no adversity can force apart, where they realise they have a duty to their brothers, and where the fruits of such a society are seen in the love, the charity, and compassion of people…[6]

Rarely, if ever, has a politician featured, as Lange did, in preferred Prime Minister polls immediately after the delivery of their maiden speech. His humour, so necessary in politics but usually so absent from its discourse, served as a welcome contrast to Muldoon's constant rhetorical strikes against perceived communists, liberal academics, newspaper editors and other opponents not viewed as part of Muldoon's image of 'mainstream' New Zealand.

Lange's brilliant humour was displayed in our cities, our towns, and, of course, in our Parliament. On one occasion Lange asked the Speaker to allow him to address Robert Muldoon in Samoan, as Muldoon had also been conferred an honorary title from our Pacific neighbour. Lange then paid tribute to his fellow noble: "Talofa lava lesapie afio mai lau afioaga." Muldoon shot back a disgusted look before barking at Lange, "Tuck your shirt in."[7]

Another one of my favourite examples—one that showcases the absurdist, and cognitively exquisite quality to Lange's wit—was when he said about National's John Banks, "the day I take legal advice from Mr Banks will be the day that I buy sausages from a petrol pump".[8] With Banks' mayoralty no more, we shall never know whether a public/private partnership between Banks and the Mad Butcher, Peter Leitch, would have seen Lange's vision come to pass. Lange's self-effacement also repeatedly came to the fore while he was Prime Minister. Once, when visiting Germany, Lange was forced to climb to the top of a turret of an ancient castle overlooking the Rhine. One of Lange's staffers asked the local guide how old the ruin was, at which point a gasping Prime Minister interjected, "Forty-two years".[9] When asked by a journalist once for a short word, Lange replied, "it," another time "wombat" was offered. Another time, when asked what he intended doing after he retired from politics, Lange's quicksilver response conjured another vividly absurdist image, "I'm going to be a jockey."[10]

Then, of course, there was Lange's farewell to American Ambassador H. Monroe Browne. Browne owned a racehorse called Lacka Reason, which prompted our Prime Minister to inform Browne that he must be the only Ambassador who owned a horse named after his country's foreign policy.[11] This Lange quip also possessed the added virtue of withstanding the test of time and three more US Presidents, and counting. Finally, when quizzed about how Labour Party defector John Kirk would be greeted if and when he returned from overseas, Lange said, "If he came back we would have a welcome. We would go to the airport and shake him by the throat."

Humour is, of course, disarming, because it serves to divert attention from more uncomfortable avenues of inquiry, which proved a particularly useful technique for Lange until his humour left him. Humour can also act as a defensive shield of sorts, and one thinks that David's one-liners and fabulous story-telling was employed at times in the service of maintaining an emotional distance from his colleagues. Ultimately, however, the absurdist quality of Lange's rhetoric conjures up a different quality altogether, a quality of verbal and cognitive awareness that was in a class all of its own and extremely liberating in a New Zealand Prime Minister.

That is why I am drawn to comparing Lange's cognitive acuity with Shakespeare's Falstaff in the two parts of *Henry IV* (as opposed to Shakespeare's much paler imitation of Falstaff found in *The Merry Wives of Windsor*). Celebrated literary critics such A.C. Bradley, W.H. Auden and, more latterly, Harold Bloom have elevated Falstaff to a pre-eminent position among Shakespeare's many glittering characters, surpassed only by Hamlet as the fullest reach of the bard's powers of language and psychological insight.[12] Just as Falstaff's enforced absence from Henry V is palpable—"one touch of Falstaff in daylight, would have destroyed all touch of Harry in the night"—so too was Lange's cognitive acuity sorely missed when he lost his sense of purpose.

LANGE'S LIBERATION OF POLITICS:
CULTURAL LEADERSHIP IN AOTEAROA

Turning now to the serious, political rhetoric is one of a leader's main strategies, alongside their bargaining, or lobbying, or their ability to structure political situations to their benefit. Rhetoric also plays an important role in providing cultural leadership—by presenting effective and politically appealing remedies for public problems. Cultural leadership provides a way in which leaders may appeal to "the better angels of our nature". But such idealism must be tempered by the realities of the technological and 24/7 mass media age, not to mention the political pragmatism that is often required to win and then maintain power. It is increasingly difficult in the contemporary environment for the harmony of one's message to survive the sheer noise of rival counterstories. In the modern media environment, effective political rhetoric is any message that can get through the filter, penetrate widely, and then resonate with the people. We witnessed, here in New Zealand, one such instance early in 2004 when Dr Brash took to the podium to deliver his Orewa speech on race.

The character of a leader's political rhetoric, however, and in sharp contrast to Brash's Orewa effort, should be properly measured by whether or not it contributes to the overall quality of political discourse in the country. Does it educate rather than seek to manipulate? Does the message simplify, or distort? Does a speech identify scapegoats or stereotypes? Or does it introduce a sharper and more genuine sense of reality?

With these questions in mind, two particular examples of David Lange's cultural leadership stand out during his first term—two examples of Lange exhibiting strong rhetorical and cultural leadership. The first was his publicly wresting control from Muldoon during the height of the currency crisis. Lange waded into the constitutional interregnum with a highly charged and focused repudiation of Muldoon and Muldoonism. Lange told the country:

> The nation is at risk. That is how basic it is. The Prime Minister, outgoing, beaten, has, in the course of one television interview, tried to do more damage to the New Zealand economy than any statement ever made. He has actually alerted the world to a crisis. And like King Canute he stands there and says everyone is wrong but me.[13]

Lange later reflected that the effect of Muldoon's own performance was to convince the country that the former Prime Minister could play no part in any solution and that it was a terrible mess that the country was in. It was David Lange who drove this idea home.

In concert with the Economic Summit—which hinted, at least to some degree, at the possibility of Lange fostering a more inclusive politics—the Prime Minister sheeted home to New Zealanders the message, compelling, as it was, that things simply had to change. We had to take the fork in our nation's journey. That was crucial to carrying the people between '84 and '87 while the Government administered the too-long-delayed pain. Our social cohesion may have faltered badly under the assault of Labour's juggernaut if Lange had not been able to win the electorate's trust. As a result, New Zealanders were ultimately better educated about their economy, and ideas that had been too long suppressed were finally discussed. The significant achievement was that the country's future choices expanded. We have Sir Roger Douglas, David Lange, and their colleagues to thank for that.

Lange's second great rhetorical performance took place at the Oxford Union Debate. By besting the Reverend Jerry Falwell, thereby joining pornographer Larry Flint as an ongoing source of humiliation for America's former Moral Majority leader, Lange locked the anti-nuclear policy into the nation's cultural fabric (with considerable help from the French saboteurs and other Goliaths, one should acknowledge). But it was Lange's Oxford Union performance that was the policy's flagship.

The origins of the anti-nuclear policy, the myriad motivations behind it, David Lange's true convictions and commitments over it, and its ongoing relevance cannot be dismissed from a wider discussion of Lange's rhetorical leadership, but this is not the occasion for that sort of analysis. Ultimately David Lange took the many disparate strands supporting the anti-nuclear policy and broadened them into a much wider groundswell of public support. This was a rare example of cultural leadership—and at its most politically effective and enduring.

At Oxford, Lange used body language, his wit, powerful allegory, and reason to deepen and enlarge the understanding of his audience. His performance approached a high thought—one expressed by Shakespeare in *Henry IV*—of mastering a double spirit, of teaching and learning instantly. Lange saying, "You can't have it both ways"—when focusing on the irrationality of nuclear deterrence—still echoes today.

Lange, after a typically humorous handshake, where he played on Thatcher's bullish disgust at both Lange and our nation's anti-nuke policy, put his case simply:

> I hold that the character of nuclear weapons is such that their very existence corrupts the best of intentions; the means in fact perverts the end. And I hold that their character is such that they have brought us to the greatest of all perversions: the belief that this evil is necessary—as it has been stated tonight—when in fact it is not.[11]

The crux of this aspect of Lange's argument was then unfurled when he said, 'there is … a quality of irrationality which does not sit well with good intentions. A system of defence serves its purpose if it guarantees the security of those it protects. A system of nuclear defence guarantees only insecurity.'[12] As speech-writer Margaret Pope said, this was the vital first step in Lange's logical chain, a debating point he needed to establish immediately with his audience.

Lange then proceeded to differentiate New Zealand's position from other countries that faced far less benign security environments and thus different demands from our own, a point he continued to make *ad nauseum* throughout the entire anti-nuclear backlash. Lange said:

> And the people of New Zealand reached a very straightforward conclusion: that nuclear weapons which would defend them, they believed, caused them more alarm than any which threatened them, and accordingly, they deem it pointless to be defended by them.[13]

Lange further emphasised this point later in the speech by saying that New Zealand was not creating a policy for either imitation or export. This was also a vital aspect of his overall argument as it served to undercut the United States' position that others would follow New Zealand's lead if we were to be let off cost-free. Lange reminded the audience that New Zealanders had a proud tradition of defending the West in conventional conflicts: "they have died in African campaigns, they have their bones bleaching in deserts, they are buried in Italy. They have fought in Vietnam."[14] Yet, Lange argued, New Zealand was to be singled out, not by its enemies, but by its friends. He completed his essential argument by saying forcefully:

> It is a self-defeating logic (nuclear deterrence), just as the weapons themselves are self-defeating: to compel an ally to accept nuclear weapons against the wishes of that ally is to take the moral position of totalitarianism, which allows for no self-determination, and which is exactly the evil we are supposed to be fighting against.[15]

If there is a peak moment in Lange's oratory it is, to me, the eloquent and strong expression of idealism he made in response to an interjector's question about Europe's relative tranquillity, post-World War II, while living under the umbrella of nuclear deterrence. Lange replied:

> Have you considered the proposition for one moment that that war that cost those casualties might have entrenched within people the yearning for peace, the growth of democratic institutions, the accountability of political representatives, so that none wishes to wage in conventional or nuclear terms, any war?[16]

If Lange was a natural orator, he also honed his non-verbal communication into something of an art form. An example was his retort at the Oxford debate when an interjector—one with an American accent—stood up and addressed Lange and the Prime Minister swivelled slightly, in mock surprise ... then delivered his (in)famous line that he could smell the uranium on his breath. The fit between Lange's body language and his chosen response increased the poignancy of that reply. The audience, if not the Americans, loved it.

If the late John Roberts' observation is true—that "a tiny society at the ends of the earth makes no observable ripple on the stream of history"—then Lange's rhetorical leadership at least momentarily disturbed the pond. Oxford was high theatre and in that type of forum Lange was superlative.

CONCLUSION
Rhetoric was undoubtedly David Lange's greatest leadership skill—perhaps the one that history will primarily remember him for—because Lange lacked many of the more mundane, but equally crucial leadership skills one usually finds in political leaders. Thus, Lange's prime importance to his government was in this. He was irreplaceable as its public voice. The greater freedoms that deregulation brought to the country were facilitated by Lange's rhetoric and his own personal embodiment of the idea of freedom, whether it be the break from Muldoon's last divisive and oppressive term of personal rule or, when considered more expansively, economic freedom from Muldoon's tired and failed preference for heavy interventionism. Each, at least to an extent, reinforced the other. In history's final accounting, Lange facilitating a new direction is a not inconsiderable achievement.

Lange's preference for mass audiences over intimate ones was not particularly unusual in a political leader. There is not as much intimacy in a mass audience, but conversely the acclaim is that much greater than found in one-on-one situations. The costs are minimal but the rewards may prove great, especially for someone like Lange who, perhaps more than most, needed to be liked. We witnessed in Lange's second term how onerous it proved to be for him, both physically and psychologically, when the scales tipped in the opposite direction and Lange became conflict adverse, unhappy at the public disgust directed at his fractured government and fatalistic about the impending doom.

Lange's all too brief time as Prime Minister also serves to emphasise that political rhetoric is a grossly underestimated and under-utilised art in the New Zealand context. We do not possess a pantheon of great rhetorical leaders or stirring oratorical performances. Indeed we, as scholars or as a country, cannot even access our best political rhetoric. We do not necessarily know where it lies buried, if it exists at all. Nor does our literature produce anthologies dedicated solely to great speeches—and lofty ideas—expressed by our political leaders, nor can we chart the progress of our nation through prime-ministerial rhetoric as other nations can and do. That, one feels, is to our cost.

Ideas about identity, tolerance and unity, about the successful resolution of past crises or about possible futures serve as vital guides to the present. Instead New Zealand politics lacks such a fundamental nutrient to our democratic discourse. Perhaps we are too self-conscious to talk openly about the ties that bind us together.

Perhaps, too, the type of Prime Minister our indigenous politics has tended to produce has been ill suited to the demands of appealing to our better angels. Maybe our nation has not confronted the manner of crises that have presented leaders elsewhere with the opportunity to place politics on a higher plane.

Yet we have seen the reverse: Muldoon's Dancing Cossacks, Winston Peters' anti-immigration 'Howick' speech in 1996 and Dr Brash's Orewa speech in 2004 all represented the rhetoric of illusion. Brash's speech identified Maori as the scapegoats for what he perceived as our nation's lack of progress. The dramatic, emotionally laden response to Brash's speech revealed there was a ready audience for this type of message, but it was a message conceived in desperation, was ill-informed, and built upon, at the very best, an extremely parsimonious understanding of our nation's past.[17]

When a nation can be exploited by demagogy but remains stubbornly unresponsive to uplifting rhetoric it tells us something about how fragile our sense of unity and bonds of fraternity are. For a brief time Lange brought us together as we embarked on dramatic and traumatic change. He stands out.

Bradley's insight, highlighted at the very beginning of this chapter, gets to the very core of David Lange's contribution to the immediate post-Muldoon era. He did, however briefly, restore some joy back to the country. He did convince the country that change was necessary and that it could be liberating. And in these days and times—where debased political rhetoric is doing a good job of corrupting the country's wider political discourse—what we should be most grateful to David Lange for is this: that he, and through him his government, embodied—albeit too briefly—a sense of renewal, a sense of freedom and a sense of possibility.

STEPHEN LEVINE AND NIGEL S. ROBERTS
Not quite Camelot

> We were a government that changed things for the better.
> ROGER DOUGLAS, INTERVIEW ON
> RADIO NEW ZEALAND, 29 APRIL 2004[1]

> I want to thank those people whose lives were wrecked by us, because we did do that. They had been taught for years, conditioned to believe, that they had the right to an endless treadmill of prosperity and assurance, and we did them ....
> DAVID LANGE, VALEDICTORY SPEECH,
> NEW ZEALAND PARLIAMENT, 22 AUGUST 1996[2]

Has there ever been a farewell address quite like that given by David Lange? In New Zealand we pay relatively little attention to rhetoric and its uses, which, with a speech such as this, is a great pity, for in a society more consumed with the way leaders lead and leave us, these are remarks which would be much studied.

For, in this speech, we have no review of lofty purposes, programmes articulated and achieved. There is no far horizon to be glimpsed, no soaring words designed to inspire. Here we have a leader looking back, grimly, not content with self-justification nor concerned to deliver a sermon to colleagues and countrymen. Instead, we have a once-popular and respected parliamentarian, formerly a force in the land—able to move voters and mobilise votes through words alone—now speaking frankly, and savagely, about his own performance and the damage inflicted by his own government.

This was not only a negative farewell but also a very personal one. We have here no abstract ideas about the national interest—no warnings of "entangling alliances"[3]—nor affirmations about the state of the national mood—"it's morning in America".[4] Nor is there a particularly personal plea, as in Richard Nixon's final speech in the White House, to his staff just before walking out to the waiting helicopter—"always remember, others may hate you, but those who hate you don't win unless you hate them, and then you destroy yourself"[5]—though in Lange's speech there is, as it happens, mention of hatred:

> People over 60 hate me. They hate me because I was the symbol of that which caused that assurance of support and growing security to be shattered. That is something that has always been part of my burden.[6]

This speech was given nine years after David Lange had led the New Zealand Labour Party to re-election—the first time since 1938 a Labour Government had won a second term, a stunning accomplishment that seemed to remove a stigma or curse from Labour Governments. The 1987 election should have been an occasion for much celebration for the Labour Party, its leaders, parliamentarians, rank-and-file, and voters. Labour was no longer doomed to one-term status, with its opponent, National, invariably identified as New Zealand's 'natural party of government'. The Lange-Douglas Government's performance had been vindicated. If it had not had a mandate for much of what it had done from 1984 to 1987, it could now claim to have achieved one, its handiwork retrospectively validated.

David Lange's look-back at his prime-ministership—its effects on ordinary New Zealanders—was, however, harsh rather than celebratory. He could have chosen to speak about other matters or to impose a different perspective over not-so-distant events. But of all the themes to emphasise he chose his own government's culpability, its lack of "justice to those people who cannot foot it".[7]

This summing-up from the former Prime Minister, with its words of criticism and disappointment—a look back in anger and dismay—was yet one more reason to regard David Lange as a political figure not quite cut from the same cloth as other politicians. Normally this would have been a time to be sentimental, yet Lange's sentiments were far from misty. Others have shared Lange's lack of nostalgia for the fourth Labour Government, both its first term and its ultimately self-destructive postscript. At a 2004 reunion of Lange and Douglas, a former minister in that government, Helen Clark, distanced herself from the soft sounds of reconciliation, recalling a time closer to the 'worst of times' than to the best of them, filled with strife, intrigue and reaction.[8]

There is, nevertheless, often a temptation to smooth out the rough patches of the past, allowing emotion to cloud judgement and ease the pain of promises unfulfilled. Nostalgia is part of the appeal of history—an attraction to a bygone era, with its causes and personalities—but it can lead to reassurance born out of misrepresentation of what actually occurred. In 2004, with 20 years having passed since Lange and Labour ousted the Muldoon Government from office, several television documentaries were broadcast focusing on the election, the aftermath, and the rise and fall of the Lange-Douglas Government.[9] It is difficult, still, to produce a judicious appraisal of that government's record, with its impact on the lives of New Zealanders and the New Zealand way of life, an assessment free from ideological preference. What seem blessings to some remain acts of betrayal to others. The tone of much comment parallels Lange's farewell, with its undertone of bitterness and subdued recrimination. Yet despite this the content of what was done during 1984–87 remains largely intact, little affected by reproach. Whereas Robert Muldoon sought to undo as much of the third Labour Government's record as he could—and quickly—the National- and Labour-led administrations that followed built upon (rather than removed) the work carried out by the fourth Labour Government during its first term. This is a legacy more noteworthy and more enduring than that left behind by many New Zealand governments.

THE LEGEND OF LABOUR

A difficulty in looking back at the 1984–87 period is that we know what comes after it. This inevitably affects our judgement of those years, and of that government, and of the people who contributed the most to that very important historical record. One result is that much of the commentary forms a narrative that is not so very far from archetypal themes found in myth and legend. A précis of the arc of the Lange-Douglas regime finds the friends and collaborators striving together at the outset to build a better world—to remake it in a new, fresh way, one both more rational and more caring, protective of the people and their country. They meet weekly to make and implement policy—to form plans and carry them out—taking action on behalf of the public good. The meetings are held in a special room, fitted out with a round table. And all goes well until, as ever, a woman intrudes, disrupting the harmony, destroying the friendship, defeating all hope of working together for a common purpose.

There is in this something of the mystique of charismatic government, the true 'holy grail' of politics: to have a political leadership characterised by intellect and compassion, unified in outlook, energetic and vigorous, genuine in its motives and aspirations. But was the youthful Lange, keen and quick-witted, ever close to leading such a government? Did New Zealand, even briefly, move suddenly out from the Muldoon years to a brief exposure to our own little Camelot?[10] And was it all brought down by a female, one gifted with words and with political principles of her own?[11]

Of course the electorate's 1987 verdict on the Government was delivered with little realisation that the Labour Caucus and Cabinet were deeply divided. That there was such antagonism among Labour Cabinet ministers pledged to support the Party, the Government, and one another was hardly to be imagined. Nor was there any awareness of the influence of a woman—of a romance with political consequences—on these internal divisions. In this respect the 1987 election—the campaign waged by Labour without a manifesto (it was released after the election); the campaign in which David Lange made promises uncleared with the Cabinet or the Party, based on a misreading of his speech notes—was more flawed than most. Voters cast their ballots with expectations about government policy and perceptions about government cohesion and performance altogether at variance with the facts. Labour succeeded in winning a second term at least in part because of the skill of its leader and his colleagues in disguising the true state of affairs within the Cabinet room from the voters and the New Zealand news media.

Even so, voters' perceptions about the quality of the Labour Government were in some ways less deluded than some might suggest. Much is sometimes made of Labour's increased parliamentary majority in 1987, as though the Party had won a resounding nation-wide vote of thanks for what it had done. In fact, a closer look at the 1987 results shows a more complex picture, one that helps to dispel both the exaggeratedly positive reading sometimes given to the first term—a shining vision of idealism wedded to analytical brilliance—and (particularly later on) the excessively negative assessments of a brooding, conscience-stricken leader and the various vengeful voices on the Left.

For what voters saw, from both the Right and the Left, was not quite Camelot.

THE REALITY OF 1987

The myths include the perception that Labour gained a ringing endorsement in the 1987 election and that as a consequence the party increased its majority in Parliament.[12] These perceptions are in part fuelled by the fact that Parliament was enlarged by two seats—from 95 seats in 1984 to 97 seats three years later. The second thing fuelling this perception is that for nearly a year after the election Labour held the Wairarapa seat (won both on election night and again following the counting of special votes by its candidate Reg Boorman) before losing it as a result of an Electoral Court hearing which awarded the seat to National's Wyatt Creech. Thus the glow surrounding Labour's triumphant return to power included a seat which in reality it did not win. A third element influencing the image of the Labour Party's re-election victory is that the Party's share of the vote rose by 5.0 percent—from 43.0 percent to 48.0 percent—an accomplishment seldom achieved by incumbent governments. This result, however, primarily reflected the collapse in the share of the votes won by minor parties in 1987, with the disappearance of the New Zealand Party and the loss of support for the Democrats (formerly Social Credit). In 1984 Labour and National together obtained less than 80 percent of the votes, whereas in 1987 they won 92 percent.

What is often overlooked is that, like Labour, the National Party also increased its share of the vote—and, what is more, did so to a greater degree than Labour. National's share of all the votes cast in the election rose by slightly more than eight percent—from 35.9 percent in 1984, when it was led by Sir Robert Muldoon seeking a fourth successive term as Prime Minister, to 44.0 percent, under the leadership for the first time of former Minister of Labour Jim Bolger.

Much the same can be said about the number of seats in Parliament. Whereas Labour's rose by one (from 56 in 1984 to 57 in the enlarged House of Representatives), the number of National MPs on the Opposition benches for Labour's second term was three more than before (up from 37 to 40). Overall, in 1987, Labour lost three seats—Rangiora, Timaru[13] and Wairarapa—and gained three—Birkenhead, Manawatu and New Plymouth. National lost three seats (the ones gained by Labour) and won five (the three lost by Labour, as well as two lost by the Democrats, namely, East Coast Bays and Pakuranga).[14]

Since the advent of MMP the concept of electoral 'swing' has fallen into disuse.[15] It used to be a crucial tool for measuring not only the relationship between votes cast and the number of seats won in an election, but also for measuring variations in the electoral performance of political parties on an overall and on a seat-by-seat basis. In 1984, when the fourth Labour Government gained power, it did so on the strength of a 4.4 percent swing in its favour. In 1987, in winning a second term, throughout the country as a whole there was an overall 2.4 percent two-party swing away from Labour to the National Party.

Looking more closely at the electorate-by-electorate results[16] in what was still a first-past-the-post system, the average (or mean) swing was 1.4 percent to National. Similarly, the median swing was 1.8 percent in National's favour.[17] What all this shows is that no matter how one looks at the election figures, the net movement of votes was undoubtedly to National, and not Labour, in 1987. This is further borne out by the fact that there were 63 electorates in which there was a two-party swing

Figure 1: The Range of the Swings in the 1987 General Election

to National, compared with only 34 seats in which Labour did proportionately better in 1987 than in 1984 in the competition between the two parties.

Figure 1 provides an even clearer picture of the movements of votes that occurred at the 1987 election. There were some unusual features to Labour's re-election victory that are highlighted by the figure. The strongest move to Labour tended to be, perhaps ironically, in what were National strongholds, while some of Labour's worst-performing seats were in the Party's own heartland. In the 18 electorates that were classified as safe National seats (requiring a swing of 10 percent or more to fall to Labour), there was an average swing of 3.0 percent to Labour. This contrasts not only with the overall average swing (which was to National), but most markedly with the swing in Labour's 37 safe seats (again requiring a swing of at least 10 percent to fall to National)—4.9 percent to National.

The voter movements are underscored by the data in Figure 1. The single greatest swing to Labour was in the blue-chip National seat of Remuera, and the swing against National's deputy leader, George Gair, who was standing in the North Shore electorate, was 7.8 percent. As for Labour, three of the seats which had the largest swings to National were held by high-profile Cabinet ministers—Russell Marshall in Wanganui, Colin Moyle in Otara and Michael Bassett in Te Atatu.

What is clear from the election data is that there was no across-the-board endorsement for the handiwork of the Lange-Douglas Government. There has been a prevailing view, by contrast, that the 1987 election proved the wisdom of the aphorism that 'one good *term* deserves another'. Figure 1 is a clear reminder that in 1987 voters had not, in fact, been all that certain that the first term of the fourth Labour Government had been all that good.

A further measure of voter enthusiasm—or the lack thereof—is to be found in the proportions prepared to take part in the election itself. Turnout at the 1984 election was an astonishing 93.7 percent[18] (higher than any election throughout the 1960s and 1970s). Three years later, by way of contrast, turnout fell to 89.1 percent.[19] Analysis of turnout rates in the different electorates suggests that some of the abstentions came "from Labour voters ... concerned to communicate a message of warning to a party seemingly certain of victory".[20]

SURVEY SOUNDINGS

Survey data from 1987 reinforces the picture of an electorate not altogether convinced of the good intentions or positive outcomes of Labour policy-makers. For example, when it comes to leadership, a country that felt singularly blessed by the quality of its government might have overwhelmingly endorsed David Lange as its Prime Minister. The 1987 surveys incorporated two measures of voter preference with respect to choice of Prime Minister.[21] The first question asked participants: "Of all the politicians in New Zealand of any party, which one would you personally prefer to be Prime Minister right now?" A view that saw the first term of the fourth Labour Government as pioneering, and as exceptionally able, would have generated a crescendo of support for its leader and incumbent Prime Minister. In fact, the response of electors was very different: 71 percent of those polled did not choose David Lange as their "preferred Prime Minister". While Lange had more support than any other politician, the margin separating him from the National Party Leader was only three percent—a smaller advantage for the incumbent Prime Minister than in any of the preceding four elections for which we have survey data using this question.

In a second question, voters' views about political leadership were given a more searching appraisal. This question presented a scenario in which voters would actually have the opportunity to cast a vote for Prime Minister as well as for a parliamentary representative. The question was as follows: "Let us suppose you could cast a vote for Prime Minister separate from your vote for your local MP. Of all the politicians in New Zealand that you know of, who would you vote for as Prime Minister?" This led, in turn, to successive questions, narrowing the choice ultimately to the leaders of the two major parties, Labour and National. In 1984 the result of this process was to reveal that despite an initial disadvantage David Lange actually had a slight edge over the incumbent Prime Minister, Sir Robert Muldoon. Three years later, Lange's narrow advantage after the first question all but dissipated, with 45.0 percent favouring his continuation in office and 43.8 percent of respondents preferring Jim Bolger instead. This is hardly consistent with a picture of a grateful electorate giving a ringing endorsement to the Lange-led Government or for that matter to the Prime Minister personally.

The survey also asked participants to assess the overall record of the Government: "During the last three years, do you think that the Government's overall performance throughout the country as a whole has been very good, reasonable, unsatisfactory or very poor?" Only 15.0 percent thought that the Government's performance had been "very good", a figure significantly less than what would be expected if there was merit (other than simplicity) in an image of a government portrayed as doing very well until the post-election sharemarket crash and consequent policy imbroglio over flat tax proposals and other ideas. Those who thought the Government's performance "unsatisfactory" or "very poor" were 22.7 percent of the sample. The largest group of voters (58.5 percent) considered the Government's performance to have been simply "reasonable".

Another set of questions focused broadly on electors' expectations about the consequences of the 1987 election. Whereas almost 80 percent of participants expected Labour would win the election throughout the country as a whole—that the Lange-Douglas Government would be returned to power for a further three-year term—it is significant that only half that number—40 percent—thought that "once the election [was] over ... things generally will get better".

These figures point towards a cautious endorsement of Labour—with some of the support coming from former National supporters—rather than an enthusiastic surge in the Government's direction based on appreciation of its various 'reforms' and policy innovations. Was this (as Roger Douglas observed) a "government that changed things for the better" or was it (as David Lange concluded) a government that "wrecked" people's lives? In 1987, survey participants had been asked to identify the "single most important problem facing New Zealand right now?" Another way of looking at that question was that, in effect, it asked voters what, after the reforms of the first term, remained to be done?

For most electors the nuclear issue had been resolved. Unemployment and the economy—linked concerns—were still regarded as the country's most important remaining problems. A second survey question, however, asked voters to identify "issues in this election which are particularly important to you personally ... when it comes to voting?" This question saw two further areas still on voters' minds: education—which Lange took as his portfolio of choice in his second term as Prime Minister—and law-and-order. With National not yet offering a credible alternative, Labour was able to gain a second term, but—as subsequent events showed—the Labour Party that had been returned to office "had in some sense lost a good measure of the public's trust along the way".[22] What was remarkable about this, in retrospect, is that among those who had lost trust and confidence in the Government was the Prime Minister himself.

The Lange-Douglas Government had been perceived as a unified, professional administration and there had been little information disseminated to the public to the contrary. Electors expected Members of Parliament in New Zealand's parties to stand shoulder to shoulder, as united as an All Black scrum. Like the Kennedy administration in the 1960s, this government was a young team, energetic and ambitious, filled with zeal and vigour.[23] When it had come to power there was an excitement surrounding its victory, some of it associated with Lange's effervescent personality and flashes of wit, and some of it brought about by a sense of relief at the fall from power of Muldoon.[24] The new government had inherited problems from the Muldoon years but—in stark contrast to Muldoon in the waning years of his tenure—it was committed to tackling them. Three years later, although the Royal Commission appointed by Labour had recommended a new electoral system, the Government still benefited from the old one, with the first-past-the-post electoral system exaggerating its triumph, making it seem as though Labour had been returned unscathed by an appreciative, and in some ways patient, electorate. Despite some misgivings the country had clearly been prepared—given the alternatives, which were, in 1987, an untried and in some ways still tainted (by his association with Muldoon) Bolger—to give Lange and his colleagues a further term.

The country's hopes—derived from the manifold activities of the Lange and Douglas team of ministers—were, in the event, utterly unfulfilled. Having turned to Labour with such excitement in 1984, and having been prepared in 1987 to give it a second chance to govern, the disintegration of the fourth Labour Government following its re-election was a bitter disappointment for many. Lange's sudden departure from the prime-ministership just under two years later was an astonishing development. His government had been seen to be fomenting what had been characterised as a "quiet revolution".[25] But what happens when revolutions fail? Having raised the country's expectations, having encouraged New Zealanders to believe that they were gaining a government of new ideas and fresh ideals, the reality—a twisted politics of ego and invective, of infighting and instability—was itself a betrayal of a dream.

There is little so dangerous in politics as a failed revolution. In this case, the first term of the fourth Labour Government had lifted New Zealanders' sense of what might be possible. It was a "quiet revolution" not only in terms of policy departures, but also with respect to people's hopes for a different, better New Zealand—freer and more prosperous. What were the consequences of failure? Labour lost more than merely the 1990 election, which, with some realism, it recognised it was never going to win. The legacy of the fourth Labour Government includes more than the floating of the exchange rate, the achievement of nuclear-free status, and the offloading of state assets. It also includes another nine years of National rule.

'MILES TO GO'

Yet there had still been 'promises to keep', tasks left undone.[26] What had happened?

Sometimes forgotten now is Lange's erratic 1987 campaign. Among the voters he seemed at times "ill at ease … and easily distracted". On television he looked occasionally "bored and uncomfortable". On election night, when he might have been savouring his triumph, the Prime Minister had been "irritable and grumpy". Back in Wellington Lange lost little time in cancelling the traditional post-Cabinet meeting press conferences. All this projected a prime-ministerial personality at once "moody and somewhat unpredictable", awkward traits in a parliamentary leader.[27]

It was all less glittering than it might have been. In 1984 there had been a magic about the young Lange, 41 years old, younger even than Kennedy when he took office. There was a likeability, a "flair and brilliance" about Lange.[28] When it all began, New Zealanders were proud of his intellect, appreciative of his courage, entertained by his wit and good humour. He restored a certain self-respect to the country's politics, and there was pride in his leadership and respect for his integrity and principles.

At one point there was even some concern that the media might be enjoying him just a bit too much. Reporters were supposed to be critical of politicians. Now, with Lange, they were laughing too readily to be sceptical. They liked him; they wanted him to succeed; they were on his side. He had emerged dramatically, been given a 'make-over', and in his first campaign as leader had swept from power a person who had become for many a figure of menace—not by any means on the world scale a tyrant, but a fearsome character all the same. Suddenly Muldoon was gone, brushed aside by a desire and a need for change. It happened unexpectedly quickly, in a 'snap election' that broke a nine-year spell. What replaced him was new, fresh and captivating.

Lange was playful, good-hearted, appealing; the public enjoyed his company. But after three years, the joy went out of it for him. He had said it in his Maiden Speech—a man could "gain the whole world" yet lose his own soul.[29] This was the sort of person, the sort of leader, he was: too introspective, too vulnerable, too brittle for the long haul. To others he left the details of governing, the minutiae of statutes, the figures in budgets and account books. He was looking, as he might have said, at the peaks of aspiration and the valleys of human suffering and disappointment, seeking to make New Zealand a better place than he found it—a loftier ambition than that of his predecessor. Others were accountable to parties, colleagues and institutions. He was accountable to those he loved and to those who loved him; answerable, in the end, to them and to himself.[30]

When the laughing stopped—when the people stopped laughing with him and when he stopped giving them things to laugh about—it was over. And the country was sadder and poorer for it. Now the Lange years are over, but when he is remembered as he was, at his best—light-hearted and mischievous,[31] yet also eloquent and passionate, a man of purpose and vision—there can still be seen, however briefly, that dream of democratic leadership: an individual, humane and inspired, gifted and distinctive, attractive and compelling enough to be able to move a nation. The years are gone now, but "the cause endures, the hope still lives, and the dream shall never die".[32]

And so, as elsewhere, here too in New Zealand one can still choose to remember the delight at the outset, when all was new and so much seemed possible, and recall, in tribute, that "for one brief shining moment"[33] there was, even here, just a glimpse of Camelot.

Appendix I
Transcript of an interview by Linda Clark with Margaret Pope on Radio New Zealand

WEDNESDAY, 28 APRIL 2004

Linda Clark: In July this year it will be 20 years since David Lange and the fourth Labour Government came to power, 20 years since the end of Muldoonism and the beginning of Rogernomics. All new governments change laws but the Lange-Douglas Government changed a country. The economy was turned on its head, the public sector was either privatised or corporatised. Either way it's never been the same, and this was sacrificed for a popular and independent nuclear-free policy. Job security ended and Saturday shopping began. The other truly memorable thing about that government is that it imploded and the divisions between those who backed Lange till the end and those who backed Douglas, remain to this very day. This weekend the Stout Centre at Victoria University will hold a major conference marking this 20th anniversary. All of the people who played a role in this extraordinary time will be there. Sir Roger Douglas and a whole host of other former Cabinet ministers, the former mandarins from Treasury, trade unionists, lobby group leaders and spin doctors, they'll all pick over what happened and what legacy has been left. The glaring omission is David Lange himself. He was not invited he tells me, and he's too unwell anyway. Well, on the eve of that conference we're going to be talking about this fourth Labour Government. Tomorrow at this time you can hear Sir Roger Douglas's perspective. This morning, though, you can hear from the woman who began as Lange's assistant and speech-writer and ended as his wife. Margaret Pope has never before agreed to be interviewed about this time. I talked to her yesterday and I began by asking for her first impressions of those first days after election victory.

Margaret Pope (David Lange's former speech-writer and now his wife):
They were confused and confusing. I was very busy, everybody was very busy and great events took place around the time of the election.

Clark: Because in the days prior to election day, you must all have known you were going to win? There must have been that sense of inevitability about it?

Pope: Yes, we did expect to win.

Clark: But did that mean you were prepared for what happened immediately afterwards?

Pope: No, no. A lot was left unprepared simply because of the way in which the election was called. All the Party's planning, all the Caucus planning had been directed toward an election in November. All of a sudden the election was in the middle of the year.

Clark: I re-read Bruce Jesson's book on this period *Fragments of Labour* over the weekend. He talks there about the television images and of course as soon as you hear about this you can visualise them, the television images of David Lange striding through the Mangere Airport Hotel and what Jesson said is, that showed a man who looked like he was very much in control but in fact he was anything but. What do you say to that?

Pope: Well, Bruce Jesson was a good man and he and David actually became friends later in Bruce's life, but when he wrote his book *Fragments of Labour* he was a declared political opponent. He was very much involved in setting up the new Labour Party, which left the Labour Party and became part of the Alliance.

Clark: Jim Anderton's lot in other words?

Pope: That's right. So Bruce's book was written to push a particular point of view and his view of those events in Auckland, it's good writing but its bad history.

Clark: Well, he records history as being that the Foreign Exchange crisis which occurred, created this opportunity for Treasury and the Reserve Bank to set the agenda and once they had done that there was no turning back?

Pope: That misses the point that there was a crisis and there was a decision needed to avert the crisis. There was a run on the currency. David and his colleagues formed the view, as did many others, that New Zealand's international reputation was at risk, that the wider economy was at risk. Some response had to be made. David and colleagues met in Auckland with government officials. They decided that the appropriate response was to devalue the dollar. Now, that's one decision and to say that one decision then led on to every other decision, well, it doesn't make sense to me now and it certainly doesn't do justice to the individuals involved.

Clark: So that decision taken in the moment of crisis wasn't as Jesson would paint it, the kind of first stake in the ground and all of the other stakes that Roger Douglas would put in, in the years following, were a natural consequence of that first stake?

Pope: No, no, it was a decision made in response to a very specific crisis.

Clark: See, in a way … I mean you're right about the time when Jesson wrote this book. He wrote it in 1989 and he wrote it with that sense of betrayal that so many in Labour's ranks felt about what happened under this government. Were they betrayed do you think?

Pope: I'm sure they felt betrayed, but I don't think it's accurate or fair or even reasonable to suggest that there were deliberate acts of betrayal.

Clark: So what we now call Rogernomics, that wasn't a deliberate act?

Pope: It was an evolving act. It wasn't done cynically, it wasn't done with a sense of okay, now we're in office let's fix these people. It happened as a result of various incidents, various forces, various crises. It happened. Many people in the Labour Party didn't like it. Many others did approve of what happened, did agree with it. There's certainly a great deal of irony in the election of 1984 when you look back at it, but it's a long, long way from irony to betrayal.

Clark: Where do you see the irony?

Pope: Well, if you remember, the 1984 election was fought largely on a platform of consensus which was a response to the brutality of the Muldoon days but in the end the Labour Government ended up perhaps the very opposite of a consensual government, but that was not how they set out.

Clark: Well, the road to hell is paved with good intentions?

Pope: (laughter) Yes.

Clark: And is that what happened here?

Pope: No. What happened was that there were many competing economic policies in the Labour Party. When the snap election was called they hadn't as yet been able to agree on their economic platform. There were divisions in the Caucus, there were divisions between some in the Caucus and the Party outside Parliament which in those days was a far larger and more powerful organisation than it is now. When the election was called they cobbled together an economic statement which was so broad in its terms that it could have encompassed just about anything. There's no doubt at all that Roger Douglas had a set of views which you could identify with what happened afterwards but they weren't clearly formed in June of 1984.

Clark: Do you think even in the mind of Roger Douglas they weren't clearly formed?

Pope: Well, I certainly can't speak for the mind of Roger Douglas but there was no established agenda that I knew about. I think it's actually fair to say that the intellectual powerhouse of economic policy in the first term of that Government was the Treasury rather than Roger Douglas.

Clark: Yeah, but those two forces became so interwoven it was hard to tell who was driving what. Yes, Treasury certainly had an agenda and we saw this in their briefing documents, but there was such a natural fit at that time between what Treasury wanted and what Sir Roger Douglas wanted and his key supporters like Richard Prebble, can you divide those forces?

Pope: It was a very happy marriage. I think you can divide it because what Treasury proposed in 1984 was … well, in David's view it was mainstream, it was orthodox, it was the correct response to the excesses of the Muldoon years. The 1987 Treasury platform was more extreme.

Clark: Well, that moved from being a document call Economic Management to being a document called Government Management, didn't it?

Pope: I can't remember its title but …

Clark: I mean they wanted control of everything by that stage?

Pope: They did and they had what became called a New Right Agenda very, very clearly formed by the 1987 Election and I think it may be fair to say that before the '87 Election, Roger had even moved ahead of them in his view of the economy.

Clark: So during that time … I mean you're painting a picture here where David Lange and Roger Douglas are in unison when they come into power in '84?

Pope: Oh, there's no doubt about that. I think it's almost impossible to understand David's career in Parliament without considering his relationship with Roger. Roger Douglas was one of the few among his parliamentary colleagues that David actually liked. He was … I don't mean to suggest that they were close because I don't think they were, but he certainly relied on him. He admired his abilities, he trusted his judgement. He saw Roger as the ideal Minister of Finance and he was greatly disappointed in what happened afterwards.

Clark: See, I'm interested you should make the point that he trusted Roger Douglas and he had that affinity with him because I mean in a way how history recalls that relationship now, I think many commentators would think that Roger Douglas was the more forceful of the two individuals and probably manipulated Lange to a certain extent. He used him. He used his affability, his wit, his television appeal?

Pope: No. No, they complemented each other. David needed Roger to be Minister of Finance, Roger needed David because Roger, for all his very great political abilities, could never make it at the very top level of politics. He didn't have the public persona, he didn't have the capacity to inspire, all of which David had. Their views on the economy in the immediate post-Muldoon era were originally very, very similar. They were both identified with that particular section of the Caucus which supported Roger and his ideas in the first term of the Government.

Clark: So do you remember a moment if you like, when the division between these two men became inevitable?

Pope: They had disagreements I think as early as 1986 over the ill-fated Royal Commission on Social Policy.

Clark: Well, Roger Douglas didn't want it, did he?

Pope: No, he didn't, but he agreed to it. And I should make the point that during the first term of the Government there was a great deal of effort made and Roger Douglas was a part of it, to find a synthesis between the demands of the newly liberalised economy and the need to make sure that there weren't too many casualties of it. The GST for instance, was quite carefully calculated along with the tax reforms which came in with it, to make sure that it didn't do any damage to people on low incomes, and Roger Douglas played a great part in that. There were tensions later on as economic policy seemed to want to take over social policy but I think what particularly settled David's mind about Roger was an extraordinary document which he received quite early in 1987 and it wasn't a Treasury document although it had a Treasury commentary. It came from Roger and it proposed I suppose it would be the full-blown Act Party agenda.

Clark: This is the flat tax idea was it?

Pope: It suggested a 15 percent flat tax, GST at 15 percent, the privatisation of almost all of the infrastructure of public services, social services, the creation of quite an elaborate income subsidy and voucher system so that people could purchase their own privatised social services including health and education. David, when he saw it, was quite astonished and that's putting it mildly. He was staggered. I think it's at that point that he stopped trusting Roger.

Clark: So did they ever debate that package?

Pope: Oh yes, very much.

Clark: This is before it went to Cabinet because a version of that went to Cabinet eventually?

Pope: It did eventually but this was early in '87.

Clark: And the package we're talking about became public on December 17.

Pope: That was a later version of it but the 15 percent flat tax, 15 percent GST package went to David I think in March of '87 and it was accompanied by a peculiar proposal that Roger suggested to David that he would prepare two budgets, one the conventional one which Ministers and everyone else were expecting some time later in the year, but if David agreed, he would continue to work secretly on this which really would be a better budget if David would agree to it. But David didn't agree to it, but that really was the end of all trust between him and Roger because the implications of it were quite shattering. I think at that point David realised that Roger had departed from orthodoxy and that their usefulness to each other was really at an end at that stage.

Clark: And yet all through that year the two continued to govern together, to put on a unified front because it wasn't until December of that year, so what, six to seven months later, that the public really became aware of how radical Roger Douglas's thinking had really got?

Pope: That's right. I mean, the election campaign of '87 on the surface was a great triumph for the Labour Party. I mean not only did they win a second term, which had been the goal of the Labour Government since the first one, but they increased their majority. But I think the joy went out of it for David earlier that year. His campaign in '87 was a long, long way from his best. I mean some of his performance at times was quite desultory. After the campaign he reshuffled the Cabinet in an attempt to contain Roger. He moved different people into the social portfolios, he took over the education portfolio himself. That made almost nobody happy. That was followed by the stock market crash of '87. There were disagreements as to the meaning of the election results, there were disagreements about the response to the stock market crash and the economic package of December 17, 1987, which proposed a flat tax among other things, was portrayed by Roger as the response to the stock market crash.

Clark: Through that time though I guess it was dawning on David Lange that he really was in a minority in his own Cabinet?

Pope: Oh, he knew that. He was hugely demoralised that year. He was as low as I've ever seen him.

Clark: So he's in the minority and he feels that he can't do anything about it except that in a way the cards are in his hands because he's the Prime Minister?

Pope: He was but he was in a small minority in Cabinet. I'm not really sure what the voting would have been in the Caucus but he was probably in the minority there as well.

Clark: He had the Party support but they're all on the outside?

Pope: To some extent. That was one of his difficulties because the Party Opposition and those in the Caucus who were most vehement critics of the Government's economic policy were the Anderton faction and there was no love lost at all between David and Jim Anderton. He felt no affinity at all for the old left of the Labour Party. They were not his supporters as you could tell from reading the Jesson book.

Clark: Oh sure. I mean in fact the criticism of Lange by his many critics during this time or those looking back at this time, say really there was an inevitability about this because of the great lack of the Lange political creature was that he couldn't actually pull people behind him, he couldn't win over his own Caucus. He certainly couldn't win over his own Cabinet and we go back to that point I was talking to you about before that you rejected which is, that he'd been used by those in the Douglas camp. When they tired of him they still stuck together and he was the one who was isolated?

Pope: Yes.

Clark: So what do you say to that? Was he weak? Was he too weak during this time?

Pope: No, I think he showed extraordinary strength and resilience. I think it's most unfair to say that he needed Roger Douglas, because if you look back at the first term of the Government and take another issue like the Nuclear Free Policy, which was an extraordinarily complex issue, a really difficult political issue which turned into a substantial political achievement, and David is far and away the most significant figure in that, he did that without Roger Douglas. I mean Roger Douglas was as much in support of it as anybody else but if it's any individual's achievement it's David's achievement. What he couldn't do was achieve the same level with the active opposition of Roger and his faction.

Clark: So tell me about what it was like working in the Beehive during this time because by this point the factions would hardly have been speaking to each other?

Pope: No, it was tense. It was unpleasant. There's very little of the second term of that Government that I remember with any joy at all.

Clark: And then Lange calls for the cup of tea. This is after the announcement of the December 17 package, and then it's open warfare?

Pope: Yes, he suspended the package, but did he call for the cup of tea then?

Clark: I think that was when the cup of tea came in (both laugh).

Pope: Well, if he didn't, that's probably what he meant. He suspended it I think in January or February of '88.

Clark: Yes, he said it was time for a pause, for everyone to catch their breath?

Pope: That's right, that's right.

Clark: And that's when the war really began isn't it?

Pope: Yes, it was open at that point, public.

Clark: So how was David Lange during that time?

Pope: He was under a great deal of pressure. He actually had a heart attack in the middle of '88. I don't know … I wouldn't put that down to stress but it was a measure of how difficult things were, but he soldiered on. He thought that what he was doing was right.

Clark: When he sacked Richard Prebble and that … I mean so many of these were such exaggerated moments if you like, but he sacked Richard Prebble on the back of an interview Richard Prebble did with Lindsay Perrigo all those years ago on late night television where essentially Prebble went on air and … I mean it's unbelievable to think of this now … he went on air and questioned Lange's sanity?

Pope: He did. Look, I tell you, in those days politics were wide-screen and technicolour and none of the audience ever fell asleep.

Clark: So can you remember watching that interview go to air?

Pope: No, no, I can't.

Clark: You must have though, surely? It's just part of a blur now is it?

Pope: It has become just part of life's rich tapestry but I don't particularly remember it.

Clark: So when he sacked Prebble and then not long after Roger Douglas was sacked too, did David Lange expect his government to survive?

Pope: I don't know the answer to that. He hoped it would. He wasn't sure probably if he would survive and if that was what he thought, he was right.

Clark: Well he stepped aside in … ?

Pope: He stepped aside after the Caucus re-elected Roger to Cabinet.

Clark: Which was the final slap in the face?

Pope: Well, it was a clear sign that Caucus thinking was not in line with his and at that point he couldn't continue.

Clark: Did anyone counsel him against it? Did anyone say stick around?

Pope: I don't know.

Clark: You didn't?

Pope: Oh no, no.

Clark: So you wanted him to step down at that point?

Pope: I understood why he had to step down.

Clark: What do you think in the end the legacy of this government will be?

Pope: I think in many ways we're still living in it.

Clark: Well it's interesting isn't it we should be talking on the day that Richard Prebble steps aside. These figures are still in our midst.

Pope: Yes.

Clark: And the divisions and arguments are still being relitigated, just in new ways I suppose?

Pope: Yes.

Clark: But is the real achievement of that government its economic policy?

Pope: No. It was a watershed government in the sense that after it, a great deal was changed. A lot of what it did shifted thinking here. It made the country more outward looking, more resilient. It certainly instituted a model of economic management which hasn't as yet been repudiated although it has been refined and remodelled.

Clark: It's been softened a little?

Pope: It's been softened around the edges but the fundamentals are still as they were in the '80s.

Clark: Well, voters are probably more cynical as a result of that government, do you think?

Pope: Oh yes, certainly.

Clark: So coming back to the irony you identified before about the Government that came in to make us all feel better after years of Muldoon, in a sense that's the final irony isn't it? At the end of that period of Government voters felt more cynical than ever about what to expect from politicians?

Pope: Yes, it is.

Clark: I listened to an interview the other day that David Lange gave on the day that he retired, with Kim Hill, and she asked him then who did he think would be remembered most from that period, him or Roger Douglas, and he said he would be. It's a kind of dreadful question in a way because it smacks of such immodesty, but what do you think he would say now, years later?

Pope: I imagine he would say the same. You know, what does he think about what happened after 1984? David was there and what he said and what he did made a difference. You can't separate the events of the time from his presence and his personality and that is a significant mark to leave on history.

Clark: He has since made his peace with some of these men, Mike Moore, I think. Has he made his peace with Roger Douglas?

Pope: No.

Clark: Is it possible?

Pope: Yes.

Clark: What would it take?

Pope: Probably a meeting in an airport lounge.

Clark: Is that likely though?

Pope: Yes. Sometime.

Clark: Do you think he would like to make his peace with Douglas?

Pope: I'd be guessing. I haven't asked him that. No, no, I don't know.

Clark: Do you wonder if ... I mean, he's been, I was going to say vilified, that's not quite correct but in some quarters vilified in the years since we're talking about, and I wonder whether you ever think has that played a part in his failing health?

Pope: No.

Clark: So they're not connected?

Pope: No.

Clark: In the time you were there, did you have a sense that you were making history?

Pope: Oh yes, yes. Not in the sense that I came to work every morning thinking goodness it's a historical day today, but you had to be aware of the changes which were taking place. There were great events, they were exciting times. Once in a lifetime is enough, but they were great times.

Clark: They must have been very intense?

Pope: They were.

Clark: So nothing could match it?

Pope: No, no.

Clark: And when you reflect on those days, what are you left with?

Pope: For myself, it was the best job I ever had and various things happened which have made me very happy ever since.

Clark: Well, that's nice. You were vilified too of course?

Pope: Oh yes.

Clark: I remember when I first came to Parliament I was a very young reporter in those days and the male reporters around the place would always talk of you as if you were the woman in control. You must have known that's what they said of you?

Pope: (laughter) That is very easy to say and if people want to believe it, they'll believe it.

Clark: Did it ever bother you?

Pope: It did at the time. It doesn't now.

Clark: It's been very nice talking to you, Margaret.

Pope: Thank you.

Clark: That was Margaret Pope who came into power with Labour in 1984. She had been one of David Lange's assistants when he was Leader of the Opposition. She became his speech-writer and later his wife. That was the first time she's ever spoken about those years in public.

Appendix II
Transcript of an interview by Linda Clark with Roger Douglas on Radio New Zealand

THURSDAY, 29 APRIL 2004

Linda Clark: Well, along with David Lange, Sir Roger Douglas is without question one of the pivotal figures of New Zealand's recent history. The Lange-Douglas Government changed this country radically, quickly and painfully. Lange's charisma and Douglas's economic policy were a powerful combination. And then, when the two fell out, their Government imploded. A major conference about those years, the years of the fourth Labour Government, is being held by Victoria University this weekend. Sir Roger will be there, David Lange will not. He was never invited as we found out yesterday, and he's not well enough to travel anyway. I spoke yesterday about that time to David Lange's speechwriter and wife, Margaret Pope. This morning I'm joined by Sir Roger Douglas, good morning.

Sir Roger Douglas (Former Finance Minister): Good morning.

Clark: Well, we heard from Margaret yesterday that the two of you are still not talking. You've never been tempted to simply pick up and the phone and … ?

Douglas: Oh, I have and I haven't done so … David and I have seen one another at airports on occasions and that's probably where it's been. I think I probably should do that. I certainly sent him a copy of my speech that I'm making on Saturday.

Clark: Well, that was a nice touch. I mean you know, he has made peace with some of his other old enemies. Can we call you enemies? Is that too strong?

Douglas: Oh, I think that's too strong. I mean we definitely fell out in '88 but …

Clark: Deeply.

Douglas: Deeply, deeply, but I've never been one to hold grudges so, you know, from my perspective I look back with a certain regret but you have to move forward and what's gone in the past has gone.

Clark: But your names are forever linked in our history?

Douglas: Oh, absolutely and I think we did an enormous amount for this country over the first three or four years.

Clark: So do you feel a personal connection to each other do you think?

Douglas: I think we worked pretty well together. I think we were complementary. I mean David connected with the electorate in a way that no one else has for quite a long time, and I think I was just able to add some grunt at the back end.

Clark: Well, in fact that's what Margaret Pope said yesterday. She described you as the perfect political combination and at the time did you think that too?

Douglas: Oh, absolutely. And I think we worked pretty well together for the first three years. I mean you may want to get to it later, I think Margaret touched on the fallout in 1987. In retrospect I can understand that. At the time, that early fallout, it didn't seem much to me. I mean all we'd had was a discussion of ideas and we'd disagreed.

Clark: Well, let's talk about that. We'll come to the other earlier stages later, we'll do the later stages first. But she said yesterday the moment when Lange realised he couldn't trust you was in March '87.

Douglas: That's right.

Clark: When you came to him with this idea of a second secret budget. Is her recollection your recollection?

Douglas: Well, I'm sure that's true but it wasn't as if I realised that was the case. We were going into the '87 budget and I put on the table a number of options, one being a very radical one of 15 cents tax in the dollar and a whole lot of other …

Clark: And 15 percent GST and …

Douglas: And GST and a whole lot of other issues but that simply didn't fly. It didn't fly with David but it also didn't fly with Caygill or Prebble or Palmer so from my point of view it wasn't a worry. Well I mean, you put a thing on the table—it wasn't the only option there—and we had a discussion about it and by a vast majority they decided that they weren't going to go with the radical option.

Clark: So at that point he made up his mind about you; that you'd gone off the rails?

Douglas: Yes, sure.

Clark: But you didn't realise he'd made up his mind about you?

Douglas: Well, I should have in retrospect because he did say to Bassett that I'd gone mad and in a way I didn't sort of take too much notice of that and it may well be that had we sat like we are this morning, we might have been able to work it through. And I think in the end I pondered about that. It's our different style. I was always … when I made decisions, I like to make it with a whole group of people and I was happy for all issues to be on the table. And what I have now come to realise is that David had boundaries and if one went beyond the boundaries then he closed in.

Clark: And you didn't know at the time where his boundaries were, is that what you're saying?

Douglas: Oh no, no, because he never really communicated that to me, so at the end of the day we were both at fault. When Bassett told me that Lange said I'd gone mad I should have gone and seen him because I should have realised that hey, there was a real problem here. But then David could have these throw-away lines at times and in any case, it seemed to me – what's new? This was just another day in what I'm doing. I had these debates all the time. You win some; you lose some.

Clark: But if history paints Lange as the kind of colourful, witty creature who had these throw-away lines no one took very seriously and as a leader who didn't necessarily follow the detail through, didn't necessarily always concentrate on the detail, that's how history recalls Lange. History recalls Roger Douglas as the dog with the bone. You had the bright idea, you put it forward as early as March, and then even though the others in the team said this is never going to fly Roger, you didn't really give it up because come December when you unveiled the December 17 package, there was enough of that very radical package in December 17 to still scare the bejeebers out of Lange?

Douglas: Well, but it had been modified. But if I can just finish the other thing. I made a mistake, I should have gone to David, but he made a mistake that he should have come and told me of his deep concerns and so history will show that that was a turning point and that we both made, I think, big errors of judgement in a sense. When it came to '88, I had a very strong feeling that we had been re-elected on the basis of finishing the job. It was quite apparent to me that '88 was going to be a difficult year, that some of the measures that we had taken were going to start to bite home, and that my view was that the country needed to know the direction of the Government over the next two or three years. That was important to confidence, that business people in particular went away on holidays and dwelt on and thought about their investment decisions. So we went through a process before that '87 package and that process was no different to any other process that we'd gone through. And it probably might be worthwhile just understanding how I generally worked on the packages. Quite often I'd send Treasury and in this case, in the '87 package, I sent Treasury a four-page letter in August about what I was thinking about and they worked on that. Once it was ready I would have talked to both Caygill and Prebble. Both had probably been involved at various stages in getting it together. At that point I would have taken it to Lange and to Palmer and Lange's team would have seen most of the papers as it went through the process so they always had a chance to put some input in whilst it was going through that process. And we did debate it and it's fair to say that David had a different view, which would have probably been stronger on the labour market and some other changes. But in the end we had something of a compromise package but it probably lent far more heavily towards my package than it had David's. And we had a Cabinet meeting … it was passed … we announced it. David was unhappy. I mean, I had a grapevine into that office. I understood he was unhappy. I went and saw him on the 18th or 19th of December with both Palmer and with Prebble and I said look David, if you can't support it, then we'd better go back to the drawing board and talk about it. And so I gave him the option … I didn't ask him once, I asked three times then, and he said no, that's fair enough. If you make these modifications I can live with it and I can't remember what the modifications were but there were two modifications, more particularly I think with the way family support worked or something of that nature, and there were a couple there that I made readily to the package and he then announced it. Now, I may be wrong on the dates, you know, but he went so far as to say if I made those modifications he'd come back and sell it. Now, what happened, he came back and then I got a letter from him and again I think in hindsight I probably made an error of judgement. I went and saw Trevor de Cleene. I showed Trevor the letter. Trevor said well you know, Lange has had possible problems with one or two other issues but he's never backtracked once they're announced so you know, I don't see a major problem. And so I decided well, David's written to me so I replied and we had a couple of exchange of letters, which are all there for people to see.

Clark: Which have all been published.

Douglas: Which have been published. And then I heard again that he was really uncomfortable and still very unhappy so I was about to go off to England and then to Davos and I went and saw him and I sat down with him. As it were, we eyeballed one another and I said look David, if you're unhappy we're going to have to meet and if changes have got to be made, you know, they have to be made, and let's have a meeting of the Committee on priorities within the Government—we had a Cabinet Committee—I'll be back here … we sat there … we organised the dates. I went back, told my office what was happening and that there would be a Cabinet committee meeting on policy and priorities and that, you know, we were going to, you know, review the package. I was comfortable with that, I was happy with that but David, you know, made the announcement that we weren't going to go ahead …

Clark: Without telling you first?

Douglas: Without telling me first or without telling the Cabinet first, frankly.

Clark: And by this stage, I mean let's give some context to this, not only were you and Lange really only communicating by letter but your two floors of offices were really at war with each other?

Douglas: Oh, I don't know that that's entirely fair. I mean you know, in the process leading up to that December package, I mean we'd gone through the same process as we'd done before … probably from my point of view there wasn't really a problem at all until Lange broke his word to me. I mean the rest was process. I mean these things happen in government. I mean if the Prime Minister wants something reviewed, you're a bit nuts not to sit down and review it. But I think it really does (and I'm going to say this, you know, on Saturday) in the end to some extent … you know, come down to a question of style. And that's not to hide the fact that there was a big philosophical argument about what constituted fairness. I mean that really was at the heart of David's problem.

Clark: He had this idea did he not … I mean you said earlier that the '87 election victory was a vote for you guys to continue the job?

Douglas: Oh yes.

Clark: But in a sense both you and David Lange interpreted that victory in different ways didn't you, because he saw the victory as being about well, we've done the economics and now we're going to deliver on the social policy?

Douglas: Well I think we had, to be fair, a difference about how we would run that election campaign as well. I mean that's fair. David wanted to run—you've had the pain …

Clark: Here's the gain.

Douglas: Here's the gain and I was saying well hey, that's not on. We've got to run on our record, we've got to run on finishing the job because you know, we're not in a position yet to deliver those rewards.

Clark: And the campaign promises, such as they were, were kind of a muddle of those two really?

Douglas: Yeah, well I was not deeply involved in putting that together but certainly …

Clark: And what we heard from Margaret yesterday is that he was very depressed during the election campaign. He didn't like that election campaign. So neither of you really bought into it in a way?

Douglas: Well, we both did our job though, I think. I mean David did the high points and I was constantly on radio and … but sticking pretty much to my area. But there was that deep philosophical difference and in a way you can see it for example in what's happening in the UK to a lesser extent between Blair and Brown. It's very much the same general argument with Brown actually taking the sort of Lange view if you like, and Blair taking more my view. I guess … you see … it really was about you know, what constituted fairness. I don't think there was ever any difference between David and me on the goals. What there was, was a sharp difference about how we might best achieve it—the means.

Clark: The means to an end?

Douglas: The means to the end, and I think … David had boundaries beyond which he wouldn't you know, contemplate thinking. He was more traditional in the sense that he felt that the Government should be delivering education and health and that in essence we should be you know, putting more money in and my view was look, we put billions in and it's not making any darn difference, and so there was that edge …

Clark: But in that sense …

Douglas: From my perspective, that could be worked through just by debate …

Clark: Except … except that in that sense he was more Labour.

Douglas: He was traditional Labour.

Clark: That's right and I wanted to ask you about that because I mean you've got a terrific Labour upbringing and roots in the Party, but when you look back over this time, do you think you were ever truly Labour?

Douglas: Oh, absolutely. I think ... in fact if you look at all the policies that we implemented between say '84 and '87 and even into '88, that you could actually summarise those policies as that we were against privilege. Because what we did was unwind the privileges that previous governments had put in place, not just Muldoon, but previous National and Labour Governments. I mean when we took away subsidies we were removing privilege. When we took away import licensing we were in fact removing privilege.

Clark: Except that your critics will say that further down the track, two years, three years later when you started privatising ... first corporatising the public sector and then privatising it, you created a new class of privilege. These were your mates, these were the guys who were ...

Douglas: No.

Clark: ... first running the SOEs and later on were buying them?

Douglas: Well ... if ... I mean they were always up for the highest bidder. I mean ours was the most robust sales process that you could imagine. Certainly in some cases New Zealanders bought some of the SOEs, but in many cases they didn't. I mean you take Telecom for example, and I wasn't actually in the Government at that point, but you know, Hugh Fletcher wanted it to be sold to Hugh Fletcher at $2.6 billion. In fact it was sold to overseas buyers primarily at $4.3 billion. So you know, we did not discriminate or give an inside edge to anybody in that process.

Clark: But you did buck the Labour tradition and that was why ... I mean Margaret Pope conceded yesterday that voters did feel ... and Labour Party members did feel betrayed by the agenda of this government and she thought they probably had good reason to. Do you accept that?

Douglas: No, I don't accept that. I think that in reality Labour Party people were substantially better off and fairness was a key component, as Margaret said yesterday, in what we did. For example when we did GST we designed it very carefully to ensure that low-income families were better off, and they were as much as $20 per week better off which was a lot of money in those days.

Clark: Except that this Labour Government that's in now, has twiddled with the dials if you like, of your economic changes because when they looked back over 15 years of first Rogernomics and then the bedding in that occurred under Ruth Richardson, what they identified was this widening of the gap between rich and poor in New Zealand?

Douglas: Yes, but look ...

Clark: You can't just say "yes but …"

Douglas: No, no, no, no, I …

Clark: I mean it existed, it happened.

Douglas: I'm quite happy to answer that. I mean it's pathetic really, that comment. It didn't come about as a result of Rogernomics. I mean you take any country in the OECD and there has been that phenomenon that's taken place and it's taken place in every country. What has happened … and this has impacted on males more than females … if you look back 40 years you will see that across all the socio-economic groups, about 80 percent of people who could, you know, be eligible for the workforce, males, were in the workforce. Now, in the bottom socio-economic group, it's dropped way down and it's only when you get up to about five or six that it plateaus off. Women have actually increased across the board. Why is that? It's not because of Rogernomics, it's because of changing technology first of all. It happened right through, and secondly the jobs which are being lost as a result of technology are, you know, blue-collar jobs. They have been replaced by service jobs which that group of males who lost those jobs because of technology, have not in fact been trained to replace. And if there is a problem, it is not acknowledging the real reason why it has happened and blaming a Trojan horse and you know, that's what gets to me. I mean the one thing about the Labour Government between '84 and '87 is that we actually asked ourselves what is the problem and having identified what the problem was, we established goals recognising our Labour tradition, and then we sought the best means possible to achieve reaching those goals and recognising that there would be lags in the programme.

Clark: But in the process of that, in identifying what the problems were and setting goals, you alienated a whole lot of your members and a whole lot of voters.

Douglas: Oh, I don't know … I don't know …

Clark: Margaret Pope talked about that as being the irony of this government. The irony is, you were elected in '84 on a platform really of bringing the country together and at the end of that period not only was the country not unified but your government couldn't hang together?

Douglas: Let's not confuse the issue. We got re-elected as Margaret said, in 1987 with an increased majority. If people were totally unhappy about us we would not have got re-elected with an increased majority. And the interesting thing about that election and I accept that there's a measure of truth in what you say … in the safe seats like David held and I held, our majorities increased substantially. People wanted us to finish the job that we had started and I think that where you know, we fell apart as a Government is essentially probably ... it comes down to simple things. People ... I worked in one way, David worked in another and we probably didn't recognise that ... how the other worked. I didn't care when people came to me, what they put on the table. You know, they could put any idea on the table. I wasn't offended by it, I wasn't fazed by it because I like that and I found that with that sort of debate, you made better decisions. David on the one hand, had a very clear idea about what constituted fairness, just as Brown has in the UK, and on the other hand, I was saying hey David, we agree on the goals but your means aren't going to get us there. Your means are not actually going to help low-income people. My means will actually help low-income people.

Clark: But if that was the argument between the two of you and in a way you're saying ... what you're saying is, it fell apart because you had different ways of dealing with conflict essentially ...

Douglas: Yes, and we therefore didn't talk about it.

Clark: Therefore didn't talk about it.

Douglas: Exactly.

Clark: If you had talked about it, do you think you really could have reconciled that very fundamental difference about fairness?

Douglas: No, probably not because I ... David would have believed what he had and I would have believed ... but had we talked it would have gone through a process and Caucus, or Cabinet and then Caucus would have decided. And frankly, I think on the economic issues, it may well have been that David would have won most of those arguments.

Clark: Although you always carried more sway in Cabinet?

Douglas: Yeah, but I mean ...

Clark: I mean Margaret talked about that ...

Douglas: Of course ... of course ...

Clark: He was way in the minority.

Douglas: Of course.

Clark: That was one of the things that caused him the most depression?

Douglas: Yeah, but you know, we never really got to debating really radical changes in health or education or welfare. I never put really radical options on the table.

Clark: What, so the vouchers idea wasn't radical?

Douglas: Well, where was that?

Clark: Well, according to Margaret that was in …

Douglas: No, no.

Clark: That was in the paper that came through in March … '87?

Douglas: No, no, mainly the paper in '87 was based on a 15 cent tax and the main reason the way we would have got that would have been wholesale privatisation. Now, that wasn't privatisation in the sense that the Government wasn't going to provide the income for the schools, it was just simply that the Government, just like it does … Radio New Zealand say, it used to be owned by Government … they didn't necessarily need to own this office block so the Government didn't necessarily need to own the schools in which the education took place. We never really got down to talking about vouchers and things like that in any fundamental way.

Clark: In the Jesson book, the Bruce Jesson book *Fragments of Labour* which I put to Margaret Pope yesterday when I spoke to her, he paints the portrait of the dynamic between the two of you as being one where really Lange was manipulated in a way, was used by you and Mike Moore and Michael Bassett because he was witty and he was charismatic, but also he was none too schooled up on economics. So he could be the convenient front man if you like?

Douglas: I don't think that's fair to David frankly. I mean, look, through those three years there wasn't any major decision in the economic area that David wasn't involved in. I mean, that was my job. I mean, he was Minister of Foreign Affairs, he was Prime Minister. How could you expect him to spend a huge amount of time? I mean, we would prepare what we felt was the right policy but David was always involved. For example when we floated the dollar, Rod Deane … we put Rod Deane on a plane to go and talk to David personally. It wasn't going ahead until David had actually given it his blessing. To say he wasn't involved I think is wrong and to say he didn't understand was wrong as well. I mean sometimes I'd take him a paper and he'd read it so damn quickly that I, you know, would assume that he couldn't possibly have read it but when you actually talked to him about the issues in the paper you realised he

Clark: Except that when you go forward in time to the '87 package which as you described, you put it in front of him, you had all those meetings, briefings, so forth, he went yes—that's okay.

Douglas: Oh, no, no, no, no. He only went yes to the second part. As I said, he ...

Clark: Yes, I understand that.

Douglas: He had his own proposals and I had mine and we went through the process and we came out with an end package which comprised some of his but the majority of mine.

Clark: But it is still as if after the fact the switch ... he flipped his switch really, didn't he? He'd had enough?

Douglas: Well, yes and in all probability I should have recognised that but you know, my argument would be that there is a process. I went and saw him even late in January of '88 and said hey, if you're really uncomfortable with this, we can go to the policy and priorities committee and work it through. Now, no doubt I would have argued strongly for my point of view and maybe that was what concerned him, that he didn't feel that . . .

Clark: What, that he'd win the argument?

Douglas: That he'd win the argument, but on the other hand I always had an attitude that I had to have David essentially on board and I was always prepared to make compromises because he was so important in talking to the Labour Party, talking to Labour voters. He created . . . saw the climate. He created in many ways, the climate that enabled me to do the 1984 Budget. I mean Muldoon helped in his attitude and his behaviour on the Monday because that made David look prime-ministerial. You know, one day into the job and he was already looking ...

Clark: In charge?

Douglas: In charge. And then came the summit where he was able to create a framework and an understanding that things had to change and I came along with the details.

Clark: So let me put to you the same question that I put to Margaret Pope yesterday. Who will be remembered most?

Douglas: Oh look, I don't know about that. I mean I think in the end that that's hardly important. I think what will be remembered is that we were a government that changed things for the better and that this country's growth rate subsequent to that has been better than it had, and that we changed it for ordinary people. I remember after I was out, 1990 and I was a back-bencher and I was going to retire. Instead of having a ministerial limousine I had to go in a taxi and I had a Samoan taxi driver and I said to him, how's business and I thought he'd say no good because of deregulation, and he said not particularly good. I said why is that, and he said look, a lot of the people who used to come in my taxi now own cars. And that's because we'd opened up the imports, David Caygill had opened up imports, and he came from Otara. So instead of people having to go and get a taxi to take their groceries home, they were able to afford a car, and people just simply don't recognise some of those things and I think that's the achievement of David Lange and that's my achievement, along with our colleagues I might add.

Clark: How do you feel about it personally? How do you feel about those years?

Douglas: Oh, I look back on them feeling that we accomplished a lot. I have regrets that I think the job if you like, was left half done. I believe … I was coming round to the view in '88 that we needed to reform welfare and education and health and really that was where we parted company. What I'd say is that we've tried throwing money at it, so that doesn't work. Whether my sort of general direction would have worked I don't know, but I had never developed my ideas in '88 to the extent I have now. So they were in some ways much milder then.

Clark: How do you feel emotionally about all that time though because I mean coming back to where we started … I mean you and Lange fell out spectacularly; you've hardly spoken. There were a lot of friendships that broke apart in the course of that government—people who still don't talk to each other? Is it that tribal?

Douglas: Look, there were always some people … I mean some of the biggest opposition was from within the New Zealand Council of the Labour Party I guess, and those people were always very unhappy you know, with what we were doing but you know, I have no bitterness about it. I mean, I'm just not one of those people who … and I don't reflect … I mean, it's gone, an opportunity has gone. I will always regret the fact that David and I fell out and that we didn't together go the extra mile but, you know, that's life.

Clark: Well then, you should ring him because he's not a well man.

Douglas: Sure. It will be my intention to do so.

Clark: It's been very nice having you on the programme. I hope you have a good conference.

Sir Roger Douglas there, and as I said at the outset, the Stout Centre at Victoria University have got a major conference that kicks off tomorrow marking the 20th anniversary of the election of that very historic fourth Labour Government.

Notes

MICHAEL BASSETT ~ *Cabinet making: Cabinet breaking*
1. Lange, who had tipped the scales at 27 stone when he entered Parliament on 26 March 1977, had his stomach stapled in April 1982. This resulted in an immediate considerable loss of weight.
2. See Margaret Wilson, *Labour in Government 1984–1987*, Wellington, 1989, Chapter 3.
3. The story of the Cabinet's selection is taken from my notes kept as proceedings unfolded. Bassett Papers, ATL.
4. Michael Bassett, 'George Shultz and David Lange: the Collapse of New Zealand's Military Ties with the United States', Fulbright Lecture at Georgetown University 2 December 2002, and Wellington 5 August 2003. The full text appears at http://www.michaelbassett.co.nz/

DAVID CAYGILL ~ *Industry policy*
1. E.g. "*The Industrial Policy Debate*", edited by Chalmers Johnson, published 1984 by the Institute for Contemporary Studies, San Francisco.
2. Op. cit., p. 7.
3. Man Fed paper to EDC.
4. Paper to Minister of Finance 29 January 1986.
5. Readers interested in this debate are referred to a paper by Douglas F. Greer: 'Contestability in Competition Policy' and the reply by Kerin Vautier in 'The Influence of American Economics on New Zealand Thinking and Policy', published by NZIER 1988. Simply put, around the world, anti-trust authorities do not think contestability alone is enough. In any event, that was the perspective that prevailed.
6. In 1988 this was advanced by five years, when CER was reviewed.

GARY HAWKE ~ *Bliss at dawn*
1. 8 February 1985. Throughout these years I kept a journal. It is cited simply by date. I appreciate that this is not always convenient for those wishing to test an argument. I will respond to genuine scholarly enquiries with information about the nature of the material relied on. I have benefited from discussion at the seminar for which this paper was prepared, and from comments from a number of readers, especially Sir Frank Holmes and Malcolm McKinnon.
2. 14–15 February 1985.
3. Wordsworth Prelude

> *Bliss was it in that Dawn to be alive*
> *But to be young was very heaven.*

As with the French Revolution, the experience of the 1980s was mixed, but the liberation was enduring—notwithstanding Wordsworth's eventual acceptance of official patronage

4   John Gould, *The Muldoon Years* (Auckland, Hodder and Stoughton, 1985). Cf 16 December 1985, 24 December 1985. The EMG had carefully kept clear of general statements on import licensing etc., eschewing what it thought better to leave to historical analysis.
5   14 March 1985 Meeting with Rodger, Burke, Prebble, Caygill looking for central path.
6   Roger Douglas and Louise Callan, *Towards Prosperity*. Ironically, Bryce Harland assures me that this book convinced Margaret Thatcher that the Government was not totally beyond the pale and served us well in getting tolerance when intolerance could have affected our relations with the European Community.
7   10 April 1985. The theory was first advanced (to me) in the context of the Commerce Act. I also recall it explicitly in the context of occupational licensing.
8   24 July 1987.
9   27 July 1987.
10 28 July 1987. It was Avery Jack who first formulated the question in these terms for me.
11 9 May 1987. (Margaret Wilson keeping control of the Wellington division of the Labour Party.)
12 *Oxford History of New Zealand.*
13 17, 18 March 1985; 25, 26, 29 March 1985; 16 June 1985; 31 August 1985. IPS studies showed that GST was not more regressive than other indirect taxes and could be countered, with exemption of food not being a sensible countering mechanism.
14 11 July 1987.
15 1 August 1987.
16 5 August 1987; Cardinal Williams was more moderate than *The Tablet* and also talked about the widening gap between rich and poor; the Planning Council's message about how little we knew about income and wealth distribution was not widely appreciated.
17 5 February, 1985; 15, 22 March 1985; 2 June 1985; 24 September, 1985.
18 7 January 1985.
19 10, 13 February 1985; 27 March 1985; 17 April 1985; 13, 15 July, 1985.
20 3, 18 April 1985.
21 9 January 1985.
22 27 March 1985.
23 26 May 1985; the Labour Department was already thinking of redundancy in terms of property rights, 26 June, 1985.
24 Advice which Howard Fancy recalls as among the best and most difficult with which he was engaged. The Planning Council was aware of Treasury thinking before mid-1985. 17 May 1985.
25 13, 23 July 1985; 2 December 1985; 26 September 1985; 30 September 1985.
26 Enterprise bargaining was expected by all sides in 1987. 23 July 1987.
27 Ken Douglas tried. 31 July 1985.
28 14 February 1985.
29 Between governments and banks.
30 Notably the Ross Committee of 1967.
31 1 February 1985.
32 30 October 1985.
33 2 November 1985.
34 4 November 1985.
35 12 December 1985.
36 14 February 1985.
37 24 February 1985.
38 18 March 1985.

39 And was "more market" a Labour market philosophy as Rob Campbell asked. 26 September 1984.
40 As I argued in an address to the Canberra branch of Economic Society of Australia and New Zealand 11 October 1984.
41 "Efficiency" in the sense of achieving the best available ratio of outputs to inputs implies that desirable objectives have already been defined; only if efficiency is understood as least cost for some unconsidered notion of output does one need to specify effectiveness separately. Roger Kerr surprised some by arguing for a work–leisure choice rather than a simple idea of maximum output. 23 May 1985.
42 4 April 1985.
43 21 May 1985.
44 3 August 1985.
45 22 June 1987.
46 16 September 1985; cf Labour Market Flexibility.
47 *Oxford History of New Zealand.*
48 5 July 1987; Lynn Peck, *Closedown: A Review of New Zealand Literature Pertaining to Industrial Closedowns and Mass Redundancies: 1980–1984* (Town & Country Planning Directorate, Ministry of Works and Development, May 1985, 0-477-07076-0).
49 E.g. 7 March 1985, 12 March 1985, employment conference in Auckland and conference of the Maori Caucus.
50 2 October 1986.
51 4 December 1986 – East Coast survey.
52 29 October 1986 Ngatata Love.
53 17 November 1986.
54 6 May 1987, 24 June 1987—the immediate reaction of the Maori Council was that it had been trumped.
55 6 March 1987; 24 March 1987.
56 4 June 1987.
57 Not least because Graham Butterworth, who had written as a historian about the Ngata experience, was working in the Deparment of Maori Affairs in the mid-1980s.
58 17 December 1986; 18 December 1986; 2 February 1987, 5 February 1987.
59 12 February 1987.
60 29 June 1987.
61 6 May 1986.
62 26 March, 1987 Paul Temm joined Eddie Durie in making statements along these lines. Keith Sorrenson provided an exemplary link between history and current affairs in his study of the Waitangi Tribunal in *The N.Z. Journal of History* 21/1 (April, 1987).
63 11 May 1987.
64 27 August 1987, 28 August 1987.
65 6 August 1987.
66 18 May 1987; 17 July 1987; Ranginui Walker's column in the *Listener* argued that the Maori Council is a genuine Maori organisation and that tribalism would be disastrous.
67 28 October 1986; 31 October 1986, *Project Waitangi.*
68 6 March 1987.
69 E.g. anti-Maori sentiment in Christchurch in mid-1985; 26 June 1985; 27 June 1985.
70 8 February 1986; P. McKinlay, *Corporatisation: The Solution for State Owned Enterprise* (Wellington, Institute of Policy Studies, 1987, revised edition, 1987).
71 4 June 1985.
72 9 November 1985; G.R. Hawke (ed.), *Access to the Airwaves: Issues in Public Sector Broadcasting* (Wellington, Institute of Policy Studies, 1991).
73 4 December 1985.

74 G.R. Hawke 'After the world had changed' *New Zealand Books* 6(1) (March 1996), pp. 19–21.
75 28 May 1986.
76 13 September, 1986, 16 September 1986, 9 November 1986, 5 December 1986.
77 Sir Frank Holmes & Gary Hawke "The Role of the State in New Zealand", in *The Role of the State: Five Perspectives* (Wellington: Royal Commission on Social Policy, 1988, Paper V, pp. 1–39.)
78 P. McKinlay (ed.) *Redistribution of Power? Devolution in New Zealand* (Wellington, Institute of Policy Studies, 1990).
79 J. Roberts *Politicians, Public Servants & Public Enterprise* (Wellington, Institute of Policy Studies, 1987).
80 25 June 1987.
81 6 August 1987; the reference is to debates about Electricorp asset valuations where directors like John Fernyhough suspected Treasury of simply trying to maximise government revenue.
82 *Monitoring* (Wellington: Industries Branch, the Treasury, June, 1987).
83 There were some, such as the Christchurch West Coast railway. 9 April 1986.
84 J. Singleton *et al. History of the Reserve Bank* (forthcoming).
85 13 February 1987 (Beattie Report); 14 May 1987 (RSNZ conference).
86 E.g. *Dominion* editorial, 24 April 1987.
87 3 March 1987.
88 28 May 1987.
89 30 June 1986; 16 July 1986, 28 July 30 July 1986; 11 August 1986; 10 June 1987.
90 Cf appendix 1.
91 20 August 1986; 8 September 1986 (noting Policy Discussion Papers from the Parliamentary Commissioner and Ministry for the Environment Establishment Unit).
92 2 April 1986; 30 April 1986; 12 May 1986.
93 28 July 1986.
94 23 April, 04; 3 September, 1986; 24 October 1986; 30 October 1986 31 October 1986; 21 November 1986; *Dominion* 23 October, 1986, 25 October 1986.
95 10 December 1986, 12 December 1986, 20 July 1987, 27 July 1987, 28 July 1987.
96 By 2004, Geoff Palmer recalled the major battle of the 1980s being to get a GST without exemptions. 30 April 2004. That was a major issue but it flowed out of a technical analysis of tax incidence and an intelligent process of policy analysis; it was not the ultimate objective, whatever one might have thought from the debate among political activists.
97 Vance Catherwood and Don Ferguson. The same idea was present in Australia, with Meredith Edwards as an advocate.
98 7 August 1985; 9 October 1985.
99 14 May 1987.
100 W.L. Renwick, *The Treaty Now.*
101 And which was nevertheless much misunderstood. The settlements depended above all on student numbers and while formally negotiated between Treasury and UGC, Treasury drew on a lot of Department of Education analysis. The UGC might think that it was the prime adviser to government in the area and that Treasury should confine itself to thinking about mere money, but Treasury was far more informed about universities than that acknowledged; Treasury knew more about many aspects of universities than the members and staff of the UGC did. 6 December 1985. One of the major problems of the quinquennial system was the way that Department of Education and Treasury expertise was diverted to specific issues at long intervals.
102 As early as mid-1985, Geoff Palmer was concluding that the UGC was inadequate. 8 August 1985.

103 16 November 1985; 4 March 1986; 5 March 1986; 19 March 1986; 16 April 1986; 19 April 1986 (*NBR* publicises Treasury thinking about middle class capture); 3 June 1986; 13 June 1986; 24 June 1986; 2 July 1986; 16 October 1986.
104 20 February 1986; 8 December 1986; 1 May 1987; 23 June 1987.
105 9 March 1987.
106 The Scott Report on teaching standards, a report of a committee chaired by Hon. Noel Scott, emerged in this context. Noel Scott, who was an Associate Minister of Education, was a former teacher and principal. He was not betraying his former colleagues but looking for ways forward from an unsatisfactory outcome. 10 June 1986.
107 8 December 1986; 11 December 1986; 12 December 1986; 23 June 1987; Minister of Education Russell Marshall specifically noted that his concern was not with the questions Treasury was asking, but with whether their answers were right. 1 May 1986. My observation of the papers from bodies like the Cabinet sub-committee was that the Department of Education was not equipped to debate the questions being posed, whether by Treasury or the Department of Labour. There were important educational points to be made, but they had to be distinguished from attempts to shield existing educational practices from enquiry.
108 11 June 1986; 19 July 1986.
109 24 June 1986.
110 6 July 1987.
111 16 May 1987.
112 I learned the term from Michael Bassett, but he attributes it to Frank Rutter—usually in the form "people will die if you don't do as I wish".
113 As in a radio talk by Henry Lang with Keith Ovenden. Henry wanted more resources for health and he did not share any belief in the desirability of a minimal role for the state, but he ended with an endorsement of more accurate targeting. 6 July 1987.
114 16 August 1987.
115 1 August 1987.
116 13 July 1987.
117 17 December 1987; 18 December 1987; 24 December 1987.
118 Peter Wardley, review on EH.NET of Margaret Ackrill and Leslie Hannah, Barclays: The Business of Banking, 1690–1996 (Cambridge: Cambridge University Press, 2001).
119 14 March 1987.

HILARY STACE - *Labour owes us – the 1984 women's forums*

1 Joanna Beresford quoted in *Broadsheet* December 1984 p. 7 and reported in the *Evening Post* 5 November 1984. She was also a member of the advisory group setting up the Ministry. The Economic Summit was held in September see *Dominion* 23 August 1984.
2 Ibid.
3 Baysting, A., Campbell, D. and Dagg, M. (eds), *Making policy … not tea* (Auckland, OUP, 1993), p. 88.
4 Pryor, Marilyn, *A funny thing happened … : an alternative report on the 1984 women's forums*, Paremata, 1985. p. 3. This is her estimate from media reports.
5 [Signing of CEDAW] Article by Suzanne Pollard 24 November 84.
6 Stace, Hilary, 'Making policy as well as tea', in Clark, M. (ed.), *Peter Fraser: Master Politician* (Palmerston North, Dunmore, 1998). About Peter Fraser's wife Janet Fraser and other Labour women of her generation.
7 Else, Anne, *Women Together* (Wellington Dept. of Internal Affairs, 1993), pp. 102–4.
8 Ibid., p. 103.
9 New Zealand Labour Party Election '84 Official policy release (held at the National Library).

10 'Snap Election Special' *National Business Review* 2 July 1982, p. 15.
11 *Concerned Parents' Association Newsletter* July 1984, p. 1.
12 Archives New Zealand, Wellington Office. Ministry of Women's Affairs, ABKH W4105 Box 8 30 January 10.
13 *Dominion* 19 August 1984.
14 Ibid. See also Baysting, A. *et al.*, pp. 78–9 (as Anne Collins).
15 *Dominion* 22 September 1984.
16 *Dominion* 8 October 1984.
17 *Dominion* 7 September 1984.
18 *Dominion* 8 October 1984. The speaker was Mere Solomon.
19 *Dominion* 7 June 1984.
20 NZ Ministry of Women's Affairs. *First term report,* Wellington, 1987. Also original reports are held at Archives NZ, ABKH W4105 Box 62 1984 Women's Forums.
21 Pryor, Marilyn, *A funny thing happened on the way to the forum.* Her estimates are from media reports.
22 Information from Pryor, M, pp. 3, 7, 10 and 21, MWA reports of the forums held at Archives and copies at the National Library.
23 For full list of priorities see NZ Ministry of Women's Affairs publications *The 1984 women's forums: policy priorities* and *The 1984 women's forums: what women want of the Ministry* (both 1985).
24 *Evening Post* 3 November 1984; *Dominion* 21 November 1984 reported that Hikurangi Nihoniho, 49, driver, was remanded on bail until February.
25 *Dominion* 5 November 1984.
26 Preddey, Elspeth, *The WEL herstory* (Wellington, WEL, 2003), pp. 116–20.
27 *Evening Post* 5 November 1984.
28 *Evening Post* 7 November 1984.
29 *Evening Post* 27 November 1984.
30 Undated, unattributed newspaper clipping from Archives New Zealand, Ministry of Women's Affairs, ABKH, W4105, Box 8, 30/1/10/07.
31 *Dominion* 22 November 1984.
32 Else, Anne, p. 391.
33 *Dominion* 23 November 1984.
34 *Evening Post* 5 November 1984.
35 Unattributed newspaper clipping 19 November 1984 in Archives NZ, MWA, ABKH, W4105, Box 8, 30/1/10/07.
36 Ibid.
37 See Else, A. for references. Her mother was Miriam Soljak see http://www.dnzb.govt.nz.
38 *Dominion* 20 November 1984.
39 Unattributed newspaper clipping 19 November 1984 Archives NZ, MWA, ABKH, W4105, Box 8, 30/1/10/07,
40 Ibid. Also report of the forum ABKH W4105 Box 62.
41 Ibid.
42 *Dominion* 28 November 1984.
43 *Dominion* 20 November 1984; the full list also includes advising the Minister of suitable nominees to statutory bodies and other quasi-government bodies, see NZ Ministry of Women's Affairs, *First term report,* p. 1.
44 *Dominion* 27 November 1984.
45 *Dominion* 26 November 1984.
46 *Evening Post* 24 November 1984.
47 *Dominion* 27 November 1984.
48 See article by Suzanne Pollard in *Dominion* 24 November 1984. NZ finally fully ratified in

2002 after introduction of paid parental leave. http://www.mwa.govt.nz/women/status.
49 NZ Ministry of Women's Affairs, *First term report*, p. 2.
50 NZ Ministry of Women's Affairs *First term report*, p. 1.
51 Pryor, Marilyn, p. 20.
52 NZ Ministry of Women's Affairs. *First term report*.
53 *Broadsheet* January/February 1985 p. 12.
54 Ibid., p. 14.
55 Ibid., p. 15.
56 NZ Royal Commission on Social Policy. *The April report* (Wellington, 1988).
57 Baysting, A. *et al.*, p. 84.
58 Ibid., p. 89.
59 Ibid., p. 86.

JOHN HENDERSON ~ *The warrior peacenik*
1 *NBR*, 8 August 2003.
2 *Dominion*, 17 May 1992.
3 *Canberra Times*, 29 September 1989.
4 *New Zealand Herald*, 19 May and 27 July 1982.
5 *New Zealand Herald*, 10 April 1992.
6 Press Conference, 18 May 1987.
7 *Dominion*, 20 May 1992.
8 *Dominion*, 19 May 1992.

Reference
David Lange, *Nuclear Free – The New Zealand Way*. Auckland: Penguin Books, 1990.

BRUCE BROWN ~ *The great debate at the Oxford Union*
1 David Lange, *Nuclear Free – The New Zealand Way*, p. 115.
2 Lange, *Nuclear Free*, p. 106.
3 In the course of my Foreign Affairs career I had had responsibility for disarmament and nuclear testing and nuclear proliferation issues, both in the Ministry in Wellington and in the NZ Delegation to the United Nations, New York.
4 Incidentally, I chaired the debate between that team and an Australian representative team at the Australian National University in Canberra, on 17 July 1974, when I was Deputy High Commissioner in Canberra. No doubt Walker retained some standing with the Oxford Union.
5 Lange, *Nuclear Free*, p. 106.
6 Mr Lange also remarks on Bill Young's call in *Nuclear-Free* pp. 107–8, and comments that he had no doubt that the High Commission's telegram reporting it was accurate. I hope so—I wrote it from Mr Young's agitated account, although I was not present at the call.
7 Lange, *Nuclear Free*, pp. 109–10.
8 Later Sir David and later again, Lord Wilson, after he had become Governor of Hong Kong.
9 I recollect that Mike Moore, then Opposition spokesman on trade, called on me at the High Commission in London in 1983, shortly after the EC Commission had recommended a five-year agreement but before the Council of Ministers had cut the approval of quantities from five years to three years. He was delighted to learn of the five-year proposal and, confident of election victory in 1984, said that would mean he would not have to worry about the matter in Labour's first term. In fact he did have to. He also made it clear to me—with considerable prescience about the likely repercussions of New Zealand Labour's foreign policy notions—that he expected to be Minister of Overseas Trade but did not

10 Lange, *Nuclear Free,* p. 111.
11 New Zealand's access to Britain and the EC for *lamb* was on a different basis from that for *butter*. First, unlike butter for which preferred access was then confined to Britain only, access for lamb—negotiated in the GATT "Dillon Round" of 1961—was Community-wide and further was subject to a GATT binding which meant that the access could not be reduced without New Zealand being compensated. There followed, however, several negotiations in which New Zealand accepted restrictions on the tonnage of lamb exports to the EC ("Voluntary Restraint Agreements", or VRAs) in return for reductions in the rate of duty—eventually to a zero rate. There was also a "sensitive market agreement" on lamb and an informal understanding on restraint with Ireland, which involved tonnage restrictions, especially for chilled cf frozen lamb, for it was the chilled product which competed directly with EC fresh lamb with France and most worried EC farmers and their governments. Because of this EC concern and the 1961 GATT access agreement New Zealand's bargaining power with the EC over lamb was much stronger than that for butter. In fact it was the threat by Prime Minister Muldoon (on officials' advice) not to renew the sensitive lamb market agreement with France that finally brought the French to accept the butter agreement in 1984. The Irish held out alone for longer.
12 Mr Lange touches only briefly on his call on Mrs Thatcher on the morning of the debate, Friday 1 March, in *Nuclear Free,* p. 108.
13 NZHC London to MFA Wellington, No 1753 of 5 March 1985. One point of distinction between USN and RN warships was that the RN ships by this time made only occasional goodwill visits to our region and did not have a security role there (whereas US warships did) and might therefore be judged less likely to be carrying nuclear weapons. Nor did the RN have any nuclear-propelled surface ships and their nuclear-powered submarines did not make port visits.
14 Yuri M Sokolov, "Moscow Faces the World: Restoring Common-Sense", in the *New Zealand International Review,* Vol XIV No 5, NZIIA Wellington, September–October 1989, pp. 19–22.
15 Lange, *Nuclear Free* pp. 106–12.
16 Lange, *Nuclear Free* p. 112.

IAN GRANT ~ *Lange takes the high ground while Douglas burrows deep into the economy*

1 Michael Cummings, 'What other cartoonists say', *Daily Mail,* 19 February 1980.
2 Murray Ball, NZ Cartoon Archive interview, Gisborne, 1999.
3 David English, 'Only dictators gag', *Daily Mail,* 19 February 1980.
4 Thomas Griffith, 'Finding a face for Fritz', *Time,* 8 October 1984.
5 Stephen Pile, 'For joke see marriage, dogs, fashion or goldfish', *Times Higher Education Supplement,* 14 November 1975.
6 Sir Robert Muldoon, 'Fact, fiction and faction', *Listener,* 29 June 1985.
7 Griffith, *Time,* 8 October 1984.
8 'Min's brush with history', *NZ Herald,* 20 February 1992.
9 Chris Fogarty, 'After the fallout Tom is still his father's son', *Sunday Star Times,* 14 August 1994.
10 Tom Scott, 'Life in the fast lane', *Auckland Star,* 11 November 1984.

NOTES 251

JON JOHANSSON ~ *The Falstaffian wit of David Lange: rhetorical brilliance in the Beehive*

1. Thurston Clarke, *Ask Not: The Inauguration of John F. Kennedy and the Speech that Changed America*, New York, Henry Holt, 2004, p. 114. Clarke, citing Theodore White, argued that John Kennedy's Inauguration Address represented such a passing, from the staid 1950s to the promise of a new decade and new American leadership.
2. Harold Bloom, *Shakespeare: The Invention of the Human*. London, Fourth Estate, 1999, p. 279. See also Jon Johansson, *Two Titans: Muldoon, Lange and Leadership*, Wellington, Dunmore Publishing, 2005, p. 174.
3. Tom Scott, in the *Evening Post*. Friday, 20 July 1984, p. 9.
4. See Lianne Fridriksson. 'The Prime Ministerial news conference in New Zealand's Fourth Labour Government', in *Legislative Studies*. Vol. 9, No. 1 (Spring 1994), p. 29.
5. TVNZ. 1996. Revolution. Auckland: TVNZ, November 12.
6. Vernon Wright, *David Lange: Prime Minister*, Wellington, Unwin, 1984, p. 113.
7. David Lange, *Cuttings*, Wellington, Jonathan Hudson & Associates, 1994, p. 97.
8. David Barber, *Gliding on the Lino: The Wit of David Lange*, Auckland, Benton Ross, 1987, p. 19.
9. Neale McMillan, *Top of the Greasy Pole: New Zealand Prime Ministers of Recent Times*. Dunedin, McIndoe, 1993, p. 69.
10. Barber, *Gliding on the Lino*, p. 2.
11. David Lange, 'Nuclear Weapons are Morally Indefensible', in Russell Brown (ed.) *Great New Zealand Argument: Ideas About Ourselves*. Auckland, Activity Press, 2005, p. 123.
12. Ibid., p. 124.
13. Ibid., p. 129.
14. Ibid., pp. 128–129.
15. Ibid., p. 132.
16. Ibid., pp. 125–126.
17. See Jon Johansson, 'Orewa and the Rhetoric of Illusion', in Special Edition of *Political Science* on Political Leadership in New Zealand, Vol. 56. No. 2. (December 2004).

STEPHEN LEVINE AND NIGEL S. ROBERTS ~ *Not quite Camelot*

1. Linda Clark interview with Roger Douglas, Radio New Zealand, 29 April 2004.
2. *New Zealand Parliamentary Debates* (*Hansard*), vol. 557, p. 14305, 22 August 1996.
3. The advice to beware of 'entangling alliances', which had an enormous influence in American culture and over American foreign policy, was associated with its first president, George Washington, whose farewell address was first published on 19 September 1796, near the end of his second term. It was the association with Washington, and the concept of a farewell embodying some final words of wisdom, that gave the admonition much of its force. In fact, however, Washington never used the phrase, advising his countrymen, "'Tis our true policy to steer clear of permanent alliances with any portion of the foreign world". Ironically, the phrase about "entangling alliances" actually came from Thomas Jefferson's first Inaugural Address, delivered on 4 March 1801, in which he stated that "the essential principles of our government" were "peace, commerce, and honest friendship with all nations—entangling alliances with none …". See Douglas Southall Freeman, *George Washington: Volume 7, First in Peace* (New York, Charles Scribner's Sons, 1957), p. 406; and Saul K. Padover (ed.), *The Complete Jefferson: Containing His Major Writings, Published and Unpublished, Except His Letters* (New York, Duell, Sloan and Pearce, 1943), p. 386.
4. The idea that it was 'morning in America'—that the country was experiencing a time bright with hope and promise (allegedly in contrast with the malaise associated with his one-term predecessor, Jimmy Carter)—was the theme of Reagan's successful re-election campaign in

1984. See Gil Troy, *Morning in America: How Ronald Reagan Invented the 1980s* (Princeton, Princeton University Press, 2005).
5   The resignation speech was given to White House staff on 9 August 1974. See Stephen E. Ambrose, *Nixon: Volume Three, Ruin and Recovery 1973–1990* (New York, Simon and Schuster, 1991), p. 444.
6   *NZPD*, vol. 557, p. 14305.
7   *NZPD*, vol. 557, p. 14305.
8   At the 20th anniversary party in Auckland celebrating the coming to power of the fourth Labour Government Clark struck a discordant note amid the bonhomie, recalling it as having been a "pretty miserable" time for her: "It was character-building". See Tracy Watkins, 'Lange centre-stage just like old times', *Dominion Post*, 16 July 2004, p. A3.
9   See, for example, *Reluctant Revolutionary*—a documentary about David Lange and the fourth Labour Government, written, directed and presented by Tom Scott, and produced by Danny Mulheron and Tom Scott (Direct Hit Productions, 2004); and *Someone Else's Country*—a documentary highly critical of the fourth Labour Government's economic policies, researched and directed by Alister Barry, narrated by Ian Johnstone, and produced by Community Media Trust in association with Vanguard Films (1996, but not broadcast on New Zealand network television until 2004).
10 See T. H. White, *The Once and Future King* (London, Collins, 1958), for a retelling of the saga of King Arthur, Guinevere, Lancelot and the Knights of the Round Table. The idea of 'Camelot' became associated in the US in the 1960s with the presidency of John F. Kennedy, as a symbol of grace, courage and youthful idealism. The election of John F. Kennedy took place on 8 November 1960. Three-and-a-half weeks later, on 3 December, in New York, a new musical opened on Broadway, *Camelot*—written by Alan Jay Lerner, an urbane and sophisticated lyricist (his other shows included *Gigi* and *My Fair Lady*), with music by Frederick Loewe—the right show at the right time, with hopes, dreams and a romantic outlook that became intertwined with the Kennedy presidency. Camelot closed on Broadway on 5 January 1963; the other 'Camelot'—with all that it represented—was brought to an end ten-and-a-half months later.
11 Linda Clark's interview with Margaret Pope, Radio New Zealand, 28 April 2004 described her as "the woman who began as Lange's assistant and speech-writer and ended as his wife"; the interview itself was described as "the first time she's ever spoken ... in public" about the fourth Labour Government—victory, the falling-out between Lange and Douglas, and the end of the Lange prime-ministership. David Lange refers to 'Margaret' in his parliamentary sayonara speech, describing her as "the intellect behind a lot the writing, the editor behind a lot of my lines ... the person who has kept me stable and able to keep in touch with my mates". *NZPD*, vol. 557, p. 14306.
12 Political scientist Keith Jackson also noted the 'myths' surrounding the gaining by the fourth Labour Government of a second term: see Keith Jackson, 'The 1987 General Election: Some Myths' in Margaret Clark (ed.), *The 1987 General Election: What Happened?* (Wellington, Social Science Research Fund Committee, 1987), pp. 64–70.
13 The Timaru seat had been lost by Labour in a by-election in 1985; in 1987, the new Timaru seat with different boundaries was won by National.
14 The additional seat registered by National, and the one-seat increase for Labour, were the result of the boundary changes which enlarged the House by two seats.
15 For a discussion of the concept, see Alan McRobie and Nigel S. Roberts, *Election '78: The 1977 Electoral Redistribution and the 1978 General Election in New Zealand* (Dunedin, John McIndoe, 1978), pp. 156–161.
16 Because of the boundary changes that took place between the 1984 and 1987 elections and the increase in the number of electorates from 95 to 97, it was necessary for the 1984 results to be redistributed into the electorate boundaries that were used for the 1987 election.

These figures were published in Colin James, Alan McRobie and Hugh Morton, *The Election Book* (Wellington, Allen & Unwin / Port Nicholson Press, 1987), Chapter 8. The aggregate results of the 1987 general election are contained in *The General Election 1987* (Wellington, Government Printer, 1987), E9. Appreciation is expressed to our research assistant, Tina Barton, who computer-coded the data for both elections and assisted with the initial analysis.

17 The overall swing is calculated on the basis of the total votes won throughout the country as a whole by the Labour and National parties in both 1984 and 1987. The average swing is obtained by adding up all the swings in the 97 separate electorates and dividing the total by 97. The median swing is determined by ranking the 97 electorates in order of swing—from the greatest swing to Labour through to the greatest swing to National. The East Cape electorate (north of Gisborne), where there was a swing of 1.8 percent to National, had 48 seats with swings more favourable to Labour above it and 48 seats less favourable to Labour below it. Anne Collins won East Cape for Labour in both 1984 and 1987, but after her marriage to Dr Michael Cullen she decided not to recontest the seat in 1990.

18 *The General Election 1984* (Wellington, Government Printer, 1984), E9, p. 127.

19 *The General Election 1987*, p. 139.

20 Stephen Levine and Nigel S. Roberts, 'Aspects of Electoral Behaviour in New Zealand in 1987', in Clark (ed.), *The 1987 General Election*, p. 28.

21 Details about the timing and methodology of the 1987 pre-election surveys are contained in item 27 in Clive S. Bean, Stephen Levine, and Nigel S. Roberts, 'An Inventory of New Zealand Voting Surveys, 1987–90', *Political Science*, vol. 43, no. 2, 1991, pp. 79–80. The data referred to in this chapter are drawn primarily from the mid-campaign survey carried out from 3 to 9 August 1987. The data for this chapter have been weighted in respect of the actual voting results for the country as a whole.

22 Stephen Levine and Nigel S. Roberts, 'Parties, Leaders, and Issues in the 1987 Election', in Hyam Gold (ed.), *New Zealand Politics in Perspective*, second edition (Auckland, Longman Paul, 1989), p. 443.

23 Kennedy had succeeded Eisenhower, a change celebrated by Kennedy himself, in his Inaugural Address, with rhetoric about 'a new generation'. The transition from Muldoon to Lange was equally stark. The average age of National's front bench in 1984 was 61.1 years, whereas the average age of the Labour front bench elected in 1984 was 41.9 years. "The oldest member of National's front bench was 71 years of age in 1984 and only one member was under the age of 50. By contrast, the oldest member of Labour's front bench was 49 years of age and the youngest was 35." See Stephen Levine and Alan McRobie, 'Introduction', in Stephen Levine and Alan McRobie, *From Muldoon to Lange: New Zealand Elections in the 1980s* (Rangiora, MC Enterprises, 2002), pp. x, 191.

24 That exhilaration—that sense of freedom—was reflected in an election-night column typed out in a Wellington newsroom, the analysis concluding: "… the mood in some quarters now is of jubilation, so that I find myself reminded, as I look around me, of Martin Luther King's words from his most famous speech: 'Free at Last! Great God Almighty, I'm free at last'." And, with Muldoon gone from power and Lange about to take charge, that summing up provided the headline placed on the story by the editors. See Stephen Levine, 'I'm free at last', *New Zealand Times*, 15 July 1984.

25 See Colin James, *The Quiet Revolution: Turbulence and Transition in Contemporary New Zealand* (Wellington, Port Nicholson Press, 1986).

26 The words come from a Robert Frost poem, 'Stopping by Woods on a Snowy Evening'—see *Collected Poems of Robert Frost* (New York, Longmans, Green, 1930), p. 275—and, along with the poet himself, they became associated with the Kennedy administration. Frost composed a special dedication poem for Kennedy's Inauguration and recited (from memory) another of his poems at the ceremony when the wind and bright sunlight made

it impossible for him to read it. Kennedy's friend and biographer, Ted Sorensen, described President Kennedy's affinity with the line: "He had, in the words of his favourite Frost poem, 'promises to keep and miles to go before I sleep'." See Theodore C. Sorensen, *Kennedy* (New York, Harper and Row, 1965), p. 752. The power of these words to evoke the theme of a progressive government, of an energetic leader with unfinished business remaining to be accomplished, is reflected in the title of one account of the Kennedy presidency: see Irving Bernstein, *Promises Kept: John F. Kennedy's New Frontier* (New York, Oxford University Press, 1991).

27 See Stephen Levine, '1987: A Return to Two-party Politics?', in Stephen Levine and Alan McRobie, *From Muldoon to Lange*, pp. 165–71, for more detailed commentary on Lange's behaviour during and immediately after the 1987 campaign.

28 The description comes from Helen Clark, speaking in Parliament as Labour's Leader at the end of the parliamentary session, only five days after Lange's valedictory: *NZPD*, vol. 557, 27 August 1996, p. 14373.

29 *NZPD*, vol. 410, 26 May 1977, p. 145.

30 This is foreshadowed in his Maiden Speech: "it was not the criminal law which stopped me from knocking off my trust account; it was because I was David Lange. It is not the criminal law which stops me behaving offensively in public; it is because there is immersed in me the need to account to a host of people who were involved in my upbringing, who have a part of me. If I let them down it is a condemnation of me. They will show it and I will feel it." *NZPD*, vol. 410, p. 145.

31 There is this account of 'Lange the prankster', in his early days as Prime Minister, already a gleeful trial to his colleagues and officials. Lange had complained about leaks of confidential discussions taking place in his Beehive office. "Some time later a senior public servant arrives at Lange's office to discuss policy. An excited PM greets him at the door. 'Come in,' he says. 'We've found the leak.' Walking across the room, past the inevitable tray of biscuits conveniently situated near the prime-ministerial chair, the twosome stride over to a corner. 'Here it is,' says Lange, pointing to a bucket. Above it a tiny drop of water clings to the ceiling." For a discussion of Lange's perhaps excessively convivial relationship with the New Zealand media, written nine months into his first term, see Stephen Levine, 'Laughing with our Leader', *Wellington City*, vol. 1, May 1985, pp. 68–9.

32 The words come from the end of the 1980 speech given to the Democratic National Convention by Senator Edward ('Teddy') Kennedy, President Kennedy's youngest brother, as he brought his last campaign for the presidency—for the Democratic presidential nomination—to a close. See http://www.jfklibrary.org/e081280.htm.

33 These words are very nearly the last in the song, 'Camelot', when sung in the show for the second time. Two weeks after President Kennedy's death, his wife Jacqueline told the author Theodore White that sometimes at night they would play some records and that "the song he loved the most came at the end of this record. The lines he loved to hear were: 'Don't let it be forgot, that once there was a spot, for one brief shining moment that was known as Camelot'." Her reminiscences were published in *Life* magazine on 6 December 1963. Twenty years later the words formed the title of an affectionate memoir of the late President's life, character and personality: see William Manchester, *One Brief Shining Moment: Remembering Kennedy* (New York, Little, Brown, 1983).

Notes on Contributors

Michael Bassett was an historian at the University of Auckland before becoming a Member of Parliament in 1972. He held several portfolios in the period 1984–90, including Health, Local Government, and Arts and Culture. He has published widely on New Zealand politics and history, and writes a regular syndicated newspaper column.

Jim Bolger entered Parliament in 1972 and served in Cabinet holding various posts, including Minister of Labour from 1975–84. He was Prime Minister 1990–97.

Bruce Brown served in the Ministry of Foreign Affairs (under its various name changes) from 1959–92 and had seven overseas postings, three as head of mission. He has written extensively on New Zealand politics and foreign policy.

Kerry Burke was Minister of Employment, Immigration and Regional Development, 1984–87, and speaker of Parliament, 1987–90.

David Caygill served as associate Minister of Finance and Minister of Health in the first term of the fourth Labour Government. During its second term he became Minister of Finance.

Michael Cullen was an historian at the University of Otago before entering politics. He became Minister of Social Welfare in 1987, and is currently Minister of Finance and Deputy Prime Minister.

Ken Douglas had a distinguished career in the trade union movement, becoming President of the New Zealand Council of Trade Unions. He is currently active in local body politics.

Roger Douglas entered Parliament in 1969. He was Minister of Broadcasting and Postmaster General in the third Government, 1972–75 and Minister of Finance in the fourth, 1984–88.

Ian Grant is the Executive Chairman of the New Zealand Cartoon Archive, and the author of *Public Lives: New Zealand Premiers and Prime Ministers 1856–2003*.

Gary Hawke is Professor of Economics and Head of the School of Government, Victoria University. During the term of the fourth Labour Government he chaired the NZ Planning Council, and wrote what came to be known as the *Hawke Report* on reorganising the tertiary sector.

John Henderson is Associate Professor of Political Science at the University of Canterbury. He was Director of Prime Minister Lange's Advisory Group 1985–89, and Director of the Prime Minister's Department 1987-89.

Gerald Hensley held diplomatic posts in Samoa, London, Washington and Singapore before becoming Head of the Prime Minister's Department under both Muldoon and Lange.

Colin James is a noted political commentator and journalist. He wrote two books on the fourth Labour Government, *The Quiet Revolution* (1986) and *New Territory* (1992).

Jon Johansson teaches American and New Zealand politics at Victoria University. He is the author of *Two Titans: Muldoon, Lange and Leadership*, Dunmore Press, 2005.

Peter Lange, brother of David Lange, is a notable potter.

Stephen Levine is Professor of Political Science at Victoria University of Wellington. He has written widely on New Zealand, Pacific and American politics, and Jewish History.

Denis McLean was Secretary of Defence, 1979–88, and New Zealand Ambassador to the United States, 1991–94. His most recent book is *The Prickly Pair; Making Nationalism in Australia and New Zealand*, Otago University Press, 2003.

Merwyn Norrish held diplomatic posts in Paris, New York, Brussels, London and Washington before becoming Secretary of Foreign Affairs in Wellington.

Geoffrey Palmer served as Attorney General, Minister of Justice and Deputy Prime Minister in the first term of the fourth Labour Government, and became Prime Minister for 13 months in its second term.

Margaret Pope worked for David Lange and became his second wife.

Richard Prebble was Associate Minister of Finance and Minister for State Owned Enterprises in the fourth Labour Government. He subsequently was a Member of Parliament representing the Act Party until 2005.

Nigel Roberts is Associated Professor of Political Science at Victoria University. He is an expert on electoral systems and has written widely on Scandinavian as well as New Zealand politics.

Graham Scott joined the Advisory Group in the Prime Minister's Department 1976–79 then the Treasury in 1980. He became Secretary to the Treasury in 1986, and is now a private economic consultant.

Hilary Stace has worked at the Alexander Turnbull Library, and served as an editorial officer at the *Dictionary of New Zealand Biography*. She is currently a private researcher.

Ross Vintiner worked with David Lange from 1981 to 1988, principally as his press secretary when Lange became Leader of the Opposition in 1983, and then as Chief Press Secretary to Prime Minister Lange between 1984 and 1988.

Margaret Wilson was an academic lawyer at Auckland University before becoming President of the Labour Party 1984–87. She returned to academia as Dean of Law, University of Waikato, and entered both Parliament and Cabinet in 1999.

Ted Woodfield served as Assistant Trade Commissioner in London, as Trade Commissioner in Washington, and as High Commissioner in Canberra.

Index

Abortion 87, 120, 126-7
Act Party 11-2, 28, 222
Adams-Schneider, Lance 46
Advisory Committee on Women's Affairs 120
Alliance Party 12, 219
Anderton, Jim 11, 25, 28, 39-42, 55-7, 80, 177-8, 182, 219, 224
Andrews, Doug 80
Anti nuclear movement *see* Nuclear issues
ANZUS 22, 32, 48, 62, 129-32, 136-41, 144-57, 159, 164, 171, 180, 187, 190-3, 197-8 *see also* Nuclear issues
Apple and Pear Board 78
Asher, George 98
Austin, Margaret 123, 125
Austin, Rex 32, 94
Australia 11, 14-5, 69-73, 90-1, 130, 137, 155, 161, 181-3 *see also* ANZUS, CER, Hawke, Bob
Ball, Murray 190
Ballin, Ann 107
Banks, John 202
Bassett, Michael 41, 45, 59, 113, 136-41, 153, 177, 180-1, 186, 213, 232, 239
Batchelor, Mary 122-3
Beattie, David 46
Beresford, Joanna 119
BERL 68
Bevan, Gary 80
Bill of Rights 88, 95
Birch, William 61
Bolger, Jim 42, 58, 64, 137, 141, 183, 186, 211, 214-5

Boorman, Reg 211
Bowen, Lionel 69
Brash, Don 100, 137, 139, 203, 207
Bridgeman, Doreen 124
Brock, Bill 171-2
Brockie, Bob 190, 193
Bromhead, Peter 192-3, 196
Brown, Bill 163
Browne, H. Munroe 202
Bruce, Marion 107-8
Buchanan 36, 47-9, 130-1, 139, 148, 153-4, 160, 166, 171, 181-3, 187-8
Budgets 48, 57-60, 69, 73, 231, 240
Bureau of Importers and Exporters 73
Burgess, Bevan 57
Burke, Kerry 41, 153
Business Roundtable 10, 36, 56, 73, 88
Butcher, David 41-2, 57
Button, John 70, 77
Campbell, Rob 88
Cartoons 190-8
Caygill, David 9, 41-5, 50, 56, 86, 90, 110, 113, 140, 170, 176, 180, 195, 231, 233, 241
CEDAW 120-2, 124-6
CER 61, 67-8, 70-1, 76-7, 168, 170, 174
Chick, John 161, 166
Clark, Helen 33, 40-2, 46, 48, 58, 119, 123, 128, 138, 182, 199-200, 209
Clark, Linda 218-242
Coates, Gordon 194
Coleman, Fraser 32, 41, 45, 176
Commerce Act 72-3
Commerce Commission 75
Coney, Sandra 127

Connelly, Mick 41
Contract of Employment Act 89
Cook, Len 108-9
Cooper, Warren 150-1
Couch, Ben 94
Creech, Wyatt 211
Crooks, David 136, 141-3
Crothers, Charles 86
Crowe, Admiral 152
Cullen, Michael 41
Dalziel, Lianne 128
Dasent, W.E. 108
Davey, Judith 90
Davies, Gordon 114
Davies, Sonja 120
Dawkins, John 169
De Cleene, Trevor 42, 57, 233
De Cuellar, Perez 47
Deane, Roderick 18, 43, 57, 97, 239
Delamare, Ann 89
Democrats 211
Dewe, Colleen 120
DFC 78
Douglas, Ian 90
Douglas, Ken 63, 88, 106, 131
Douglas, Roger
   economic policy 11, 18, 28, 31-2, 35, 41-4, 48, 55, 80-2, 86, 93-4, 101, 114-5, 119, 128, 131, 170, 180-1, 184-8, 191, 194-200, 204, 214-5, 218-42
   relationship with Labour Party 26, 94
   relationship with Lange 18, 42, 48, 55, 81, 59, 115, 177-81, 185-8, 200, 210, 221-5, 230-42
   Rogernomics 80, 114, 128, 196
Duffy, Michael 169
Dunne, Peter 55
Durie, Eddie 98-9
Durie, Mason 107
Easton, Brian 18
Economic Development Commission 106

Economic policy 18-29, 31-2, 55-77, 81, 85, 89-94, 128, 131-2, 196 see also Douglas, Roger; Economic summit; Flat tax; Foreign exchange crisis; GST; Sharemarket crash
Economic Stabilisation Act 76, 80
Economic summit 26, 34, 57, 62, 75, 119, 180-1, 188, 195, 204, 240
Edwards, Brian 177, 179, 185
Ellison, Anthony 193
European Community 158, 161-2, 164, 168-70, 172
Export Performance Taxation Incentive 69
Fair Trading Act 73
Falwell, Jerry 34, 158-9, 165, 204
Federated Farmers 56, 73
Federation of Labour 63-4, 79, 82-3
Fernyhough, John 132
Fiji coup 97, 129, 134, 136, 141-3, 145-6, 188 see also Rabuka, Sitiveni
Flat tax 18, 28, 74, 82, 109, 115-6, 186-8, 200, 222-5, 231, 233, 239 see also Economic policy
Fletcher, Hugh 236
Foreign exchange crisis 32, 39, 43, 69, 82, 131, 194, 219, 239
Foreign policy see ANZUS; Fiji coup; Nuclear issues
Francis, Tim 163
Fraser, Anne 121, 123, 125
Fraser, Ian 185
Fraser, Peter 9
Freedom of Information Act 37
Gair, George 31, 213
Galvin, Bernie 43
Ganilau, Epili 143
Ganilau, Penaia 142-3
Gates, Rod 142-3
GATT 78, 168-70
Gaynor, Brian 186
General elections
   1981 174-5

1984 9, 22, 26, 34, 39, 41, 76, 79-80, 85, 87, 94, 120, 128-9, 144-5, 150, 156-7, 173, 176-80, 184, 188, 192, 197, 199-202, 209, 211, 213, 216, 220-1
1987 9-11, 23, 28, 45, 48, 87, 114-7, 185, 188, 199, 209-16, 221, 223, 234-5, 237
1990 10, 23, 31, 137, 216
Gibbs, Alan 58, 113-4
Goff, Phil 9, 41, 43, 45
Goodman Fielder 71
Green, Trish 158, 163, 185
Grey Power 89
GST 22, 27, 36, 47, 57-9, 67, 82, 87, 108, 222-3, 231, 236 see also Economic policy
Hall, Roger 101
Harman, Richard 136, 180, 195
Harris, Peter 81
Hawke, Bob 137, 140, 151, 161, 181-3, 191 see also Australia
Hayden, Bill 150
Heath, Eric 192-3
Henare, Denise 96
Henderson, John 133, 177
Hercus, Ann 9, 41, 43, 45, 120-1, 123, 125-6, 128, 134, 200
Higher Salaries Commission 64
Hill, Kim 227
Hodgson, Trace 193, 197
Holmes, Frank 86, 90
Holyoake, Keith 115
Homosexual law reform 22, 87, 127
Hubbard, Anthony 201
Hunt, Jonathan 41, 43-4
Identity and culture 12, 19, 29, 199-207
IMF 131-2
Industrial Conciliation and Arbitration Act 79-80
Industries Development Commission 67, 69, 74
Industry Safeguards Bill 78
Isbey, Eddie 41-2
Iwi Transition Authority 96

James, Colin 47, 101
Jamieson, Ewan 130, 145, 148, 152
Jeffries, Bill 41-2
Jesson, Bruce 219-20, 224, 239
Johnstone, Ian 179
Joint Council of Labour 26, 52, 80, 82
Jones, Bob 89
Jones, Shane 98
Keall, Judy 123
Keating, Paul 70, 131
Kerin, John 77
King, Annette 123
Kirk, Alf 80
Kirk, John 203
Kirk, Norman 32, 36, 42, 129, 143, 174, 179
Knox, Jim 26, 52, 63, 80-1, 106
Labour Party 11, 18, 25-30, 32, 34, 36-7, 40, 44-5, 49, 52, 56, 63, 79-84, 94, 101, 105, 107, 120, 125-8, 130-1, 137-8, 150, 159, 173-88, 202, 211-13, 220, 224, 235, 237, 240-1
Labour Relations Act 27, 87-8
Labour Women's Council 120, 127
Laidlaw, Chris 159
Lang, Henry 86, 90, 97, 109, 117
Lange, David
  family 13-7
  Fiji coup 141-3 145-6, 188
  health 7, 55, 176, 225
  leader of Labour Party 18, 25, 37, 40-57, 79-80-1, 177-9, 202
  nuclear issues 33-4, 130-1, 136-41, 145-67, 204 see also Nuclear issue; Oxford Union
  oratory/rhetoric 13, 31, 51, 199, 201-7
  Prime Minister 9, 35-9, 56, 78, 81-6, 88, 90, 107-9, 112-4, 125-6, 133, 136-7, 150-3, 181-9, 191, 194-5, 199-208, 213-42
  relationship with Labour Party 28-9, 174-6
  relationship with Roger Douglas 59, 81, 186-8, 200, 210, 221-4, 230-42
  valedictory speech 208-9

Lange, Naomi 55, 175, 186
Lattimore, Ralph 68-9
Laws, Michael 112
Leask, Derek 158, 161, 164
Leitch, Peter 202
Lodge, Nevile 193, 195
Love, Ngatata 96-7
Lubbers, Ruud 47
McCaffley, Stuart 40
McLay, Jim 34, 43-4, 120, 183, 194
Mackie, Bert 96
Mahuta, Robert 95, 97, 99
Manufacturers Federation 68, 73-4
Maori 21, 22, 94-100, 102, 112, 122, 125-6
Maori Council 94, 98-9
Maori loans affair 44, 97, 184
Maori Women's Welfare League 96, 99
Mara, Kamisese 141-3
Margarine Act 76
Marshall, Russell 41, 43, 87, 112-3, 167, 186, 213
Mete-Kingi, Rangi 90
Milk Board 71
Millen, Patrick 42
Minhinnick, Gordon 193-4
Ministry of Women's Affairs 22, 119-128
MMP 12, 23, 30, 55, 211
Moore, Mike 22, 41, 43, 45-6, 129, 168-9, 171, 177-8, 180-1, 183, 187, 227, 239
Motor Vehicle Plan 70
Moyle, Colin 41, 70, 213
Muldoon, Robert 9, 32, 38-9, 41-4, 46, 55-6, 60-1, 63-4, 73, 75, 79, 82, 84-5, 105, 120-1, 127-8, 131, 144-7, 167, 173-84, 192-4, 199-202, 206-7, 209-11, 214-6, 218, 227, 236, 240 *see also* National Party
Myers, Virginia 120
Nash, Walter 91
National Party 11, 23, 31-2, 44, 48, 60, 79, 88, 94, 115, 176, 183, 211-13, 216 *see also* Muldoon, Robert
Neilson, Peter 42, 57

Neville, Pat 160
New Zealand Party 211
New Zealand Steel 75
Nisbet, Al 193
Noonan, Ros 107
Norrish, Merwyn 159, 161-3, 180
Nuclear issues 11, 18, 22, 27-8, 31-6, 47-8, 57, 128-32, 136-43, 147, 150-67, 172, 177, 181-3, 187-8, 192, 196, 200, 204-6, 216, 224 *see also* ANZUS; *Buchanan*; Oxford Union; *Rainbow Warrior*; *Truxton*
OECD 64, 168, 237
Official Information Act 103
O'Flynn, Frank 9, 41, 45, 47, 54, 133, 146-7
O'Leary, Terence 160, 163
O'Regan, Mary 126
Oxford Union 15, 18, 34, 53, 155, 158-67, 183, 185, 188, 200-1, 204-6 *see also* Nuclear issues
Palmer, Geoffrey
    Acting Prime Minster 27, 36, 136, 139-40, 153, 182
    Deputy Prime Minister 9, 23, 37, 40-6, 57, 81, 83, 88, 90, 110, 136, 177, 180, 184-5, 196, 202, 231
    nuclear issues 36, 139-40, 153
    Prime Minister 133, 187
    relationship with Labour Party 40, 175
    Treaty of Waitangi 29, 94, 98
Parker, Harvey 58
Paske, Helen 46-7
Paynter, Bill 193
Perigo, Lindsay 225
Peters, Winston 207
Petersen, Joh Bjelke 116
Picot, Brian 98-9, 109-115
Planning Council 67, 85-6, 88, 90-2, 96, 99, 106, 108-10, 114, 116
Pope, Jeremy 159
Pope, Margaret 43, 51, 55, 158, 163-4, 180-1, 205, 210, 218-231, 235-40
Poultry Board 71

Powell, Charles 163
Prebble, Richard 9, 18, 26, 33, 41-5, 55-6, 83, 177, 180, 183, 186, 196, 221, 225-6, 231, 233
Prime Minister's Department 133, 225
Pryor, Marilyn 127
PSA 102, 119
Public Finance Act 11, 87
Puketapu, Kara 97
Purdue, Connie 125
Rabuka, Sitiveni 76, 136, 143 see also Fiji coup
Rainbow Warrior 34, 42, 44, 47-8, 129, 134, 154, 170, 172, 183-4, 188, 197-8 see also Nuclear issues
Ramphal, Sonny 159
Rann, Mike 180
Reedy, Tamati 96-8
Reeves, Paul 43, 46-7, 86
Reid, Sam 15
Renwick, Bill 110
Reserve Bank 18, 39, 43, 56, 62, 72, 89, 103, 105, 219
Retailers Federation 73
Richardson, Earl 67-8, 74
Richardson, Ivor 107-8
Richardson, Ken 136, 158, 163
Richardson, Ruth 49, 64, 112, 120
Rickard, Eva 98
Rodger, Stan 9, 41, 43-4, 81, 83, 88, 102
Rogernomics *see* Douglas, Roger
Rose, Denis 92, 96, 106
Rowlands, Don 67
Rowling, Bill 33, 36, 40-1, 45-6, 50, 71, 80, 130, 138, 140, 174-5, 187
Royal Commission on Electoral Law 23, 215
Royal Commission on Social Policy 106-10, 115-7, 127, 185, 222
Rudd, Ronald 165
Rugby tours 33, 87-8, 174
Rugby Union 88-9

Russell, Spencer 43
Rutter, Frank 113
Savage, Michael Joseph 9
Scales, Sid 193
Schultz, George 47, 130, 138-41, 147-51, 154, 171, 180, 196-7
Scott, Tom 193-5, 198, 201
Seddon, Richard John 193
Sharemarket crash 10, 32, 49, 115, 214, 223
Shields, Margaret 41, 45-6, 123, 200
Shipley, Jenny 200
Shirley, Ken 55
Skinner, Tom 63
Slane, Chris 193
SMPs 70, 82
Social Credit 23, 211
Social policy 29, 85-116 *see also* Royal Commission on Social Policy
SPARTECA Agreement 78
Stalin, Joseph 82-3, 201
State Owned Enterprises 22, 37, 57, 94, 98, 100-6, 132
State Sector Act 64, 87
Stevens, Laurence 74
Street, Maryan 125, 127
Superannuation 31, 34, 61, 87, 89, 91, 110
Syntec Report 68
Tapsell, Peter 41
Tarrant, Ted 74-5
Tarriff Review Board 67
Telecom 236
Thatcher, Margaret 159-63, 166, 183, 205
Thomas, Ted 107
Thomson, David 145
Timaru by-election 40, 42, 44, 87
Tirakatene-Sullivan, Whetu 123, 125
Tizard, Bob 41, 45, 101
Todd, Hugh 193
Treasury 11, 39, 43, 56, 61, 64-5, 72, 82, 85, 91, 101, 103, 105, 107-8, 110, 112, 119, 131, 186, 218-9, 221-2, 233

Treaty of Waitangi 21, 29, 89, 94-100, 102, 110
Treaty of Waitangi Tribunal Amendment Act 21-2
Trotter, Ron 73
Truxton 147
United Nations 15, 47, 89, 120, 124, 126, 156
Vintiner, Ross 159
Wage price freeze 79-82, 179 *see also* Muldoon, Robert
Waitangi Tribunal 93-100
Walding, Joe 158, 160, 163-5, 179
Walker, Malcolm 193
Walker, Simon 159, 179
Waring, Marilyn 9, 33, 121
Wednesday Club 57
Weinberger, Casper 140
Wellington, Merv 49, 110
West, Andy 91
Wetere, Koro 29, 41, 44, 94, 97-8, 184
Wevers, Lydia 7

Wheat Board 71
Whitlam, Gough 36
Wilde, Fran 41, 123, 126
Williams, Joe 98
Wilson, David 161, 163
Wilson, Jeya 159
Wilson, Margaret 40, 45, 80-1, 120, 182, 184
Winiata, Whatarangi 96
Wolfowitz, Paul 47, 139, 148-9, 151
Women 29, 92, 112, 119, 128, 237 *see also* Ministry of Women's Affairs
Women's Forums 119-128
Women's Summit 119, 121
Wood, John 46
Woollaston, Philip 41-2
Working Women's Charter 120
Wrathall, Bill 193
Wybrow, John 41
Young, Bill 160-1
Young, Elizabeth 163